MULTIPLE EXPOSURE

MULTIPLE EXPOSURE

*An American Ambassador's Unique
Perspective on East-West Issues*

JACOB D. BEAM

W· W· NORTON & COMPANY · INC·
New York

Copyright © 1978 by W. W. Norton & Company, Inc.

Published simultaneously in Canada by George J. McLeod Limited, Toronto.
Printed in the United States of America.

All Rights Reserved

FIRST EDITION

Library of Congress Cataloging in Publication Data

Beam, Jacob D., 1908–
  Multiple exposure.

  Bibliography: p.
  Includes index.
  1. Beam, Jacob D., 1908– 2. Ambassadors—United States—Biography. 3. United States—Foreign relations—Russia. 4. Russia—Foreign relations—Europe, Eastern. 6. Europe, Eastern—Foreign relations—United States. I. Title.
E748.B333A34 1978   327.73′047   78–4123

Designer: Dennis J. Grastorf
Text type: Garamond (CRT)
Display type: Garamond Italic (typositor)
Manufacturer: Hadden Craftsmen, Inc.

ISBN 0 393 07519 2
1 2 3 4 5 6 7 8 9 0

To Margaret

CONTENTS

[7]

CONTENTS

CONTENTS

CONTENTS

CONTENTS

Preface

IF I were simply writing my memoires I would have to begin with Geneva where I started serving in 1931 as a vice-consul and emergency code clerk equipped to handle the consulate's cable traffic generated by the 1932 World Disarmament Conference and League of Nations discussion of the Japanese invasion of Manchuria. Those were indeed distant days, as I was reminded by a recent meeting with some graduate students—many of whom did not recall the significance of 5–5–3 as the ratio of capital ships which we and the British sought to impose on the Japanese.

In 1935 I was promoted to the post of third secretary of our embassy in Berlin. Looking at Western Europe as it is today, I find it hard to recollect the full horror of the next five years I spent there, but I can quickly recapture the scene by turning to my friend Bill Shirer's *Rise and Fall of the Third Reich*. [1] As the most junior member of a

---

[1]William L. Shirer, *The Rise and Fall of the Third Reich* (New York: Simon & Schuster, 1960).

rather senior staff, I was given some curious chores. Ambassador William E. Dodd, a well-known historian, ordered me to drive out to Dahlem to report on the anti-Nazi sermon which the well-known dissenter, Pastor Niemoeller, usually gave each Sunday at 7:00 A.M. This became inconvenient until I was able to arrange delivery of a transcript from my cook's Gestapo cousin who was always in attendance at the church.

After a brief spell on the German desk in the State Department, I was sent to London in 1941 and eventually became private secretary to Ambassador John G. Winant, who was admired by the British as a brave and sympathetic advocate. I have no readable memories to compete with the written histories of those times, but I did come away with a speaking acquaintance (mostly by telephone) with prime ministers and kings (including those in exile), as well as with the ranking generals and admirals of the day.

In late 1944 I joined the staff which Ambassador Robert D. Murphy was forming to take with him into occupied Germany where he was to act as the top State Department representative and political advisor to General Eisenhower. I was privileged to be among the first to see him started on this phase of a distinguished career which was to lead to his appointment as ambassador to Japan and undersecretary of state.

After service with Ambassador Murphy in Germany, I was named to head the State Department's Central European Division in 1947. Thus began my involvement first with German affairs with an emphasis on their Soviet relationship. Through this route I became involuntarily captive to Soviet and related Communist problems. The period I deal with covers the years 1947 to 1973. My aim will be to introduce personal reminiscences to illustrate and heighten the significance of historical events, without too much disruption of the narrative sequence. I hope new insights and knowledge will emerge which even the sophisticated will find of interest.

My thanks are due to the State Department for giving me access to my papers, and I am grateful to Mr. William Sparrow and his associates for their assistance in locating the needed files. Branches of the department's Research Division have offered helpful suggestions. I am greatly indebted to Miss Sandra Pectol, a veteran State Department secretary. This work would not have been possible without the speed, accuracy, and patient intelligence she has contributed to its accomplishment. Finally, it has been a pleasure to work under the guidance and with the encouraging support of Evan Thomas, vice-president of W. W. Norton & Company, and his assistant, Miss Rose Franco.

MULTIPLE EXPOSURE

Chapter I

Détente—A Fighting Word?

IN my forty years in the United States Foreign Service
I experienced the depths and the heights of American–Soviet relations. I retired from service during one of
the latter phases—in early 1973—which could be called
the era of high détente.

A slogan of this kind has broad appeal among those
who seek to use it for their own ends; it served Brezhnev
and Nixon—and Senator Jackson and Ronald Reagan—
equally well. By another paradox, it brought about a
strange shift of bedfellows in this country: bankers and
big business stalwartly supported good relations with the
Soviet Union, taking over the role of leftists and intellectuals who became that nation's severest critics.

Although a foreign word, *détente* defines a respectable
objective which perhaps is best translated polysyllabically
in Russian to mean a "relaxation of tension." Like the
"appeasement" policy of the Chamberlin–Hitler period,
it got itself a bad name by being identified with favoring
a repugnant regime. As applied to the Soviet Union,
détente was a reaction to the long and intense preceding

Cold War. To this extent it is soundly based and is irreversible as a repudiation of an unprofitable past. On the other hand, it can not disavow antecedents reflecting deep-seated historical differences and fundamental incompatibilities which continue to bear on the outlook and conduct of the American and Russian nations respectively.

Going back to the mostly forgotten past, before World War I we had little direct involvement with the Russians. We were inclined to regard them as remote and somewhat quaint, but our relations with the tsarist regime were good—except when we protested its mistreatment of Jews, a concern which even now plagues present relations.

When President Teddy Roosevelt leaned toward the Russians at the Portsmouth Conference ending the Russo-Japanese War of 1904–1905, it was probably less out of sentiment than out of fear of permitting the Japanese to become too strong. That same fear in part motivated our intervention in Russia—incidentally, alongside the Japanese—when the tsar fell during the First World War. This is a thought worth bringing occasionally to the attention of the present rulers in Moscow.

Nevertheless, Western intervention and Churchill's declared intent "to strangle the baby in its cradle" have never been forgotten and still color Soviet attitudes toward the West. In our case, between the wars the Bolsheviks became a nuisance, and not much more, in pursuing their policy of domestic subversion and sabotage. On the international plane they withdrew within themselves, or at any rate were mostly a European problem.

Curiously enough, U.S.–Russian contacts generally prospered before the establishment of official government relations in the early 1930s. As is the case today, the country was overrun by American businessmen, some doing exceedingly well. It seemed fated, however, that with the greater exposure of the two governments to each other, the greater the tension was to grow.

This was true even in our association in the last war, in which we were fortuitously thrown together. Our contribution was deliberately belittled by the Soviets, perhaps understandably so from their viewpoint, given the tremendous losses they suffered. In any event, cooperation was frequently beclouded by recrimination and deep suspicion. The story is told in *The Strange Alliance,* [1] written by Major General John Deane who was head of the U.S. military wartime missions in Moscow.

The Cold War is now a subject which invites dispute and revisionist interpretation. Essentially, it began with the struggle over the future of postwar Germany and then became global as the effectiveness of monolithic communism waxed and waned. Overall, the Cold War has so far been considerably hotter for us than it was for the Soviets.

Virtually without the loss of a single soldier in acknowledged combat, they instigated or supported military actions against United States troops helping its allies to resist communism.

They fomented costly confrontations in Korea, the Middle East, Africa, and Latin America.

They frustrated U.N. pacification efforts.

They held Eastern Europe in bondage with little cost to themselves except the sacrifice of some moral credit.

---

[1] John R. Deane, *The Strange Alliance* (New York: The Viking Press, 1947).

As mentioned before, many of the doubts and reservations that are being voiced about détente derive from the experience of closer exposure to the Soviets. First of all, we do not like the Russian autocratic tradition, which reaches back into the past and is only occasionally relieved by glorious outbursts of mysticism and appeals for freedom. Russian racism is, of course, a factor in domestic and international politics even today. Rightly or wrongly, the Russian reputation for telling the truth has never been particularly strong and has been condemned by their own writers, such as Dostoevski and others. It has been devalued even more by the Communist ethic of making the ends justify the means.

The Soviet leaders, of course, mistrust us for reasons of their own. Besides the Allied intervention in 1918–1921, they resent our actions in the Cold War as a denial of their ideological right and destiny to promote revolution.

A bit of balance is required in evaluating the present relationship. We are still profiting from some of the initial accomplishments of détente. For the time being, we have been relieved of the nightmare of another Berlin blockade. There is no foreseeable direct Soviet military threat against Europe proper. We have an overwhelmingly favorable balance of trade with the USSR, mostly redeemable in hard currency, on short to medium credit terms. If still only at an early stage, our negotiations on armaments at least provide a means of promoting reasonable understanding of the dangers threatening both sides.

Yet the USSR continues to confront us as a declared and deadly rival. While outright military conflict between us may be inhibited by the strategic balance, the

Soviets can be counted upon to spot, incite, and exploit "subcrises" in outlying reaches of the world.

At a time when the United States is withdrawing from military involvements, the USSR is developing a capacity to bring its power to bear on distant targets. It will doubtless strive to translate parity into superiority in certain fields and perhaps be tempted to make greater use of compliant proxy forces, as it has been doing in Angola. In brief, the intentions behind the buildup of Soviet military might are disguised and ominous.

I have concentrated on the Soviet Union, by way of introduction, because it has been the Communist powerhouse and the main force with which the United States has had to interact and contend throughout the world. Although its pretensions to world leadership are being challenged with increasing frequency outside its orbit, vast areas remain under oppressive Soviet control. In dealing with conditions there against the background of my service in Poland and Czechoslovakia, I feel that the fate of Eastern Europe represents World War II's most monstrous legacy and invites speculation on whether or not the Soviet yoke will endure as long as the Tatar and Turkish conquests, which for centuries laid a dead hand over the civilizations of Asia and the Mediterranean.

I sense some grounds for optimism when I contrast the access we now have to the Chinese Communists with their bitter hostility at the time I negotiated with them in Warsaw in 1958 over the Taiwan Straits crisis. Given recent changes in the Far East, our ability to deal with China directly reinforces our status as a Pacific power. Détente or whatever it is that facilitates communication may enable us to become a distinct factor which individual Communist countries must take into account in shaping their strategems and relations, even between themselves. I think there are quite a few Communist leaders who now feel this way about us: "Please drop dead, but until then, we find you useful to have around."

Chapter II

Close of the Stalin Era

BRIEF PERSONAL EXPOSURE

IN the postwar Stalinist period, the occasions for relaxation of tension between the United States and the USSR were few and scattered. With the collapse of its German and Japanese enemies, the Soviet Union made use of its overwhelming strength on land to occupy and absorb as much territory as was politically feasible, notably in Eastern Europe and certain Japanese possessions in the Far East. In other instances it probed to the point of confrontation, as happened when it occupied and tried to detach Iran's northern province of Azerbaijan to make it another Communist satellite.

Germany was the postwar prize, and the Soviet Union constantly sought to undermine the position of the Western countries by leverage on their militarily vulnerable hold on Berlin. With some justification, the Soviets feared that their vital interest in Germany would be threatened by the introduction in the spring of 1948 of a stable currency in West Berlin tied to West Germany's financial system. The 1948–1949 blockade of the Western sectors seemed to the Soviets worth a try as a measure of reprisal and pressure.

In both Iran and Berlin, the Soviets backed down. Doubtless the United States monopoly of the atom bomb was a reason, but there seem to have been contributory factors, including a policy decision to avoid an irreparable break with the United States.

It is interesting that in the case of Berlin the Soviets justified the blockade by claiming that the Western nations had lost their rights in the city by taking unilateral steps which disrupted local four-power government. The Soviets as well as ourselves were careful not to denounce the August 1945 Potsdam Agreement which established four-power control "over Germany as a whole, including Berlin." They were unwilling to part company in this regard with the occupying powers; both sides recognized the utility of retaining a legal basis for possible later agreements on Germany.

The same pattern governed the course of the meetings of the four-power Council of Foreign Ministers which were held periodically during the Stalin period. Soviet challenges intensified and broadened in scope. Communist subversion in Greece and Turkey at the end of 1946 produced the Truman Doctrine, which indirectly led to the breakdown of the foreign ministers' Moscow meeting on Germany in February–March 1947 (probably in turn contributing to the imposition of the 1948 Berlin blockade). Most seriously of all, and most costly to ourselves, was the Soviet Union's involvement and support of the North Korean attack on the South. Fears grew that the strength of the Moscow–Peking axis (actually then on the point of decline) would lead to worldwide adventures and most immediately, in the summer of 1948, to a Soviet invasion to suppress Yugoslavia's defiance.

A potential turning point in United States–Soviet relations occurred with Stalin's death on March 5, 1953. I was fortunate enough to witness the attendant events. George Kennan had been declared *persona non grata* as United States ambassador in Moscow because of his remarks while in transit through Berlin, describing Soviet practices as similar to those of Nazi Germany. (Since Kennan and I had both served in Berlin just before the war, I can appreciate the temptation to which he yielded.) Following this incident I was named to take his place as head of the embassy in the capacity of chargé d'affaires *ad interim.*

In retrospect, Kennan's experiences during his brief tenure in Moscow from the spring of 1952 to September of that year were quite revealing. His knowledge, mastery of Russian, and deep interest in the Soviet Union were well known and even antedated his first assignment to Moscow to help Ambassador Bullitt open up our embassy in 1933. Kennan seemed to be the ideal choice as ambassador at the time, and furthermore he had authority from President Truman and Secretary Acheson to engage the Soviets in frank and fundamental discussions. Members of his staff then in Moscow have told me they had the feeling that Kennan, as the leading United States expert on the Soviet Union, fully expected an early call from Stalin shortly after arriving.

Nothing of the sort happened. Instead, Kennan's talks were largely confined to Vyshinsky, the voluble and tricky Soviet foreign minister. The new ambassador was harassed by one or more apparently provocatory approaches by NKVD agents trying to draw him into secret discussions. Furthermore, he was humiliated by having his private dictation to his secretary broadcast by a listening device remotely controlled by a radio concealed in a wooden shield presented to the embassy as a gift.

While Kennan enthralled his diplomatic colleagues with learned conversation, he was ignored by the top Soviets who, one can well believe, were the losers by refusing at least to listen to his message. Frustration apparently led Kennan to play the dangerous game of drawing historical parallels, as Ambassador William E. Dodd did in his first speech in Berlin in 1933 when he made a veiled comparison between Hitler and Attila the Hun. Dodd was ostracized on the spot.

I arrived in Moscow with my wife in mid-December 1952 to take up the post as chargé under circumstances which, to say the least, had produced coolness on both sides. By virtually expelling Kennan by forbidding his return to Moscow, the Soviets had to forfeit their own ambassador in Washington and faced a suspension of diplomatic activity of their own making which, under then foreseeable conditions, was likely to continue well into the beginning of the Eisenhower presidency.

Because of the Truman administration's inability to make any new commitments in the last few weeks of its term of office, I was instructed simply to observe, report, and, above all, to avoid incidents. I was treated coldly but on the whole correctly by Soviet officials, and it was quite apparent that they did not wish to push the break further. I was informed that I could not be received by Foreign Minister Vyshinsky and that no calls were necessary beyond a small circle in the Foreign Office which included Jakob Malik, the durable but much unloved Soviet ambassador who served at the United Nations until the end of 1976. Malik enjoyed inflicting minor harassments, such as summoning me to inconsequential midnight calls at the Foreign Office. The head of the American desk, however, was businesslike and helpful.

I was able to enjoy a modicum of revenge on Vyshinsky a few weeks after my arrival. Coming to make a call at the Foreign Office, John McSweeney, our counselor, and I entered an elevator which we found occupied by the foreign minister and an aide, both of whom recognized us in silent discomfiture. The elevator happened to get stuck between floors—and for quite some time. As the minutes passed, McSweeney and I exchanged remarks in English and Russian about the inconvenience of visiting the Foreign Office in its ramshackle state. We took occasion to express our opinion that if only Vyshinsky himself knew about these conditions, he certainly would exercise his talent to put things right with the same efficiency he had displayed as public prosecutor at the purge trials. Growing redder, Vyshinsky took hold of the emergency telephone in the elevator to importune his immediate release. It was fortunate for me that when we were again talking business with the Soviets after Stalin's death, Vyshinsky had been replaced by Molotov, his preferable if not exactly congenial successor.

At the end of 1952 there were practically no American tourists or visitors in the Soviet Union. Embassy contacts with Soviets outside the restricted official circle were virtually nonexistent. The resident Americans who had the best sense of what was happening were those with Russian wives. They included Henry Shapiro of the UP; Thomas Whitney of the AP (later a leading translator of Solzhenitsyn); Edmund Stevens, then with the *Christian*

Science Monitor; and Robert C. Tucker, who was head of the Joint Press Reading Service run by the American and British Embassies in Moscow. (Tucker is now a Princeton professor and the author of a biography of Stalin.)

Harrison Salisbury of the *New York Times* was one of the best informed Americans, and seemed to be on better terms with the Soviet authorities than his colleagues. I recall a dinner he gave us which included a few Soviet guests, judiciously balanced by the presence of the Indian ambassador. A highly intelligent academic couple, a well-known Soviet chemistry professor and his wife, were among those invited. At first it came as something of a shock to hear them declare their utter conviction that the United States was waging germ warfare in Korea. They bore us no rancor, however, and took a detached view of their own country's involvement, perhaps the more readily because it had not required any sacrifice of Soviet manpower.

As an introduction to the climactic event of Stalin's death, I check back to the date of January 13, 1953, at the end of my 8:00 A.M. Russian lesson with Sofie, the embassy librarian. Sofie, who was a Soviet citizen, pointed to an item on an inside page of *Pravda* which she thought I might find of interest. It was a very brief report of the arrest of nine doctors, all with ostensibly Jewish names, on charges of murder and conspiracy. The embassy staff had already been alerted to the news when I reached my office downstairs. The sensitive information system within the local Jewish community had already become hyperactive and transmitted a shock wave, triggering in turn the mechanisms of some of the other underground networks which were available to foreign observers. The report was thought at least to portend a new drive of anti-Jewish repression, but more significantly perhaps, to reflect the existence of political trouble within the Kremlin, which had been rumored since the beginning of the year.

The first announcement of Stalin's stroke was made on the Soviet radio at 7:00 A.M. on March 3. The ensuing medical bulletins, broadcast in great detail, were diagnosed by the American and British embassy doctors as foreshadowing Stalin's early death. Incidentally, little doubt is now held about the authenticity of the official account of Stalin's fatal illness because, as Ambassador Bohlen points out in his later analysis in his book,[1] the attendant Soviet doctors were permitted to travel abroad, a privilege unlikely to be bestowed by the secret police had there been a conspiracy.

A TROUBLED FUNERAL

As described at great length by the contemporary foreign press, an uneasy calm prevailed during the days before Stalin's death on March 5. Tension was high, not only because of uncertainty over the succession but also because some people openly expressed fear that the United States might seize the opportunity to launch a surprise attack on the USSR. When Henry Shapiro of the UP went to the censor to file his report on Stalin's death, which he had just heard over the Soviet radio, the duty officer crumpled up the paper and threw it in Shapiro's face, calling him an imperialist liar.

During the five days before the funeral, the streets in the center of Moscow were filled day and night with

---

[1]Charles E. Bohlen, *Witness to History* (New York: W. W. Norton & Co., 1973).

silent, slowly walking citizens of all ages. The foreign press reported some clashes between civilian crowds and the police and army, but our embassy people who covered the city very thoroughly were never able to confirm these rumors or to talk to an actual witness of any serious disturbance. Meanwhile, the diplomatic corps spent considerable time marching to various places where Stalin's body was put on view. At the start of one such parade, the special Chinese delegation of some sixty members went to the head of the line. This infuriated the Swedish ambassador, dean of the corps, who protested successfully that if the Chinese did not assume the place assigned them by protocol rank, he would walk out.

The new Eisenhower administration was not overgenerous in its expression of sympathy. I was made special ambassador to attend the funeral, but was instructed not to fly the embassy flag in mourning which, according to our regulations, could only be done in the case of the death of an American president or of the local head of state (which Stalin was not). Looking out on the sea of flags at half staff in the square through which the cortege would pass, I decided to ignore the instructions as the better part of valor.

Together with other chiefs of mission I made a request to call on Molotov, the new foreign minister and member of the ruling triumvirate, to extend the usual message of sympathy. Twenty minutes before the appointment a flash telegram was received from the State Department ordering a change in the text. The new version stated starkly, "The United States Government presents its official condolences on the death of Josef V. Stalin."

Rather than take the risk of Molotov's opening such a harsh missive in my presence, I delivered it to him in a sealed envelope at the end of our interview. In presenting my "personal and official condolences" orally, I mentioned that Stalin would be remembered in our country as an ally and great wartime leader. With tears in his eyes Molotov rose from his chair to shake my hand, leaving little doubt that his affection for Stalin was genuine.

Although exasperating and an exponent of Stalinism in his most intransigent form, Molotov usually treated Americans courteously and with caution. Secretary Dulles enjoyed debating with him and was pleased when he (Dulles) frequently got the better of the argument. General Marshall, on the other hand, considered Molotov a shyster but gained a certain respect for him in what proved to be their last meeting in London at the December 1947 Council of Foreign Ministers. Hard put to find a pleasant topic of social conversation at a luncheon, Marshall, at Bohlen's suggestion, asked Molotov about his experiences in tsarist prison camps. Molotov's eyes lit up and he treated us to a fascinating hour-long account of a time which was obviously to him, as an old revolutionary, the happiest in his life.

New Administrations, Continuing Stalemate

The nearly coincidental changes of administration in both the United States and the USSR—Eisenhower's inauguration in January and Stalin's death in March—seemed to offer the brightest hope in years for a breakthrough to better understanding. Since Stalin had been identified with policies of threats and belligerence, a first move was generally expected from the Soviet side. The successor triumvirate of Malenkov, Molotov, and Beria, got off to a good start in the first speeches at Stalin's funeral: no mention was made of the United States which had been under bitter propaganda attack only a week before; the three speakers emphasized the need for pacification and world trade, albeit only in general terms. The occasion was also of interest to foreign Kremlinologists, many of whom, however, failed to note the significance of Khrushchev's exploitation as his position as head of the Moscow Soviet to assume a takeover role as master of ceremonies.

Minor incidents conveyed a sense of spectacular change in atmosphere. Almost literally with the disappearance of Stalin's coffin into Lenin's tomb, Soviet officials turned genial on the spot and declared their willingness to be accessible. Harassment of foreigners abated. We and the British were offered back our chanceries, from which we were about to be expelled because their proximity to the Kremlin was supposed to have angered Stalin (we declined the offer because of our need for more space). More important, there were intimations that the Soviet government was willing to help with the signature of an armistice in Korea (such proved to be the case, as related by Ambassador Bohlen in his book).[2]

President Eisenhower's speech of April 16, 1953, before the American Newspaper Publishers and Editors Association was awaited as a sign in the Western sky. The speech, when made, was promptly criticized editorially in some sections of the American press as an inadequate response to ostensible Soviet overtures and as lacking the boldness of Churchill's proposal for an East–West summit. (We gave an advance copy to the Soviet Foreign

---

[2]Bohlen, *Witness to History.*

Office, which in turn arranged to have the complete text published in *Pravda.*)

For his part, Eisenhower asked for "signs" from the Soviets: agreement on Austria, release of German prisoners still in Soviet hands, and help in making peace in Korea. He called for an end to the division of Europe and made a dramatic appeal for arms reduction and atom controls.

Each side, however, had reasons for proceeding with caution. The first was that neither of the new regimes was an entirely free agent in the matter of dealing with the other. The Republican administration was inhibited by the reaction to its previously having accused the Democrats of being soft on communism, and also by the influence of the powerful anti-Soviet bloc in the Senate.

On its side, the Moscow regime was inexperienced and was being undermined by incipient rivalries and differences over policy. These first of all produced the arrest of Security Chief Beria for treason in July 1953 and Khrushchev's relentless advance to the post of first secretary of the party, which he captured in September. Connected with these developments, rioting broke out in East Berlin and East Germany on June 17. The charges subsequently made against Beria—that he had contemplated releasing the Eastern Zone in February in favor of all-German neutralization—indicated that Germany was one of the points in dispute in the Politburo. In any event, the June 1953 uprisings discouraged the Soviets from engaging in international negotiations in which Germany would be the key factor.

Chapter III

German Reunification Is Buried by Negotiation

STATE DEPARTMENT PLANNING

MUCH against my will I was transferred to Washington in June 1953 to become deputy director of the State Department's Policy Planning Staff. It was clear that after Stalin's death I would be promptly replaced by an ambassador and I had been looking forward, for personal and professional reasons, to serving as second in command under Ambassador Charles Bohlen.

In Moscow I was thus destined to serve between George Kennan, who had been declared *persona non grata* in December 1952, and Charles Bohlen, the new appointee, both of them senior to me but old friends and colleagues. Bohlen and Kennan were to dominate Soviet affairs in the State Department from the late thirties to the late fifties. Although their opinions sometimes differed, they had the highest respect for each other, and in large degree were the architects of U.S. postwar policy toward the Soviet Union. They also had considerable influence at high levels in other Western countries. Bohlen served as ambassador in France from 1962 to

1968, but even before that time General de Gaulle frequently sought his views on Russian affairs.

Contrasting between Bohlen and Kennan, the former was the better negotiator, more patient, and more practical. As the sometime adviser and interpreter for Presidents Roosevelt and Truman and their secretaries of state, he often saved them from falling into serious error. Kennan is, of course, well known as a historian, an elegant foreign affairs commentator, and the author of the famed "Mr. X" policy of "containing" the Soviet Union enunciated in the April 1947 issue of *Foreign Affairs*. The fact that he later half-disowned this policy is typical of his role as a brilliant conceptual thinker who quickly passes from one idea to another. Kennan opposed NATO, and almost wrecked it in a series of lectures he gave on the BBC in 1958; as one friend put it, he probably disliked NATO because he had neglected to invent it.

Besides their invaluable and truly historical contributions to American foreign policy, there was another thing that Bohlen and Kennan held in common, and that was a certain intolerance of views differing from their own. In particular they seemed to have resented the interest in Soviet affairs taken by John Foster Dulles and Chancellor Adenauer. In the case of Dulles, this attitude had important consequences. Upon becoming secretary of state, Dulles failed to appoint Kennan to another diplomatic assignment, making a gift of him to the academic world. Bohlen's assignment to Moscow was opposed by thirteen Senate votes, largely because of his identification with the Yalta agreements, but also because of lack of enthusiastic support from Mr. Dulles.

Aside from the Bohlen and Kennan cases, relations

between the new secretary and the Foreign Service had their ups and downs. Dulles had served as Republican party observer on many conferences. In 1948, when it was thought he would be Dewey's secretary of state he was royally treated, but was cast into outer darkness during the years he subsequently continued to represent the Republicans on our delegations before becoming secretary of state in 1953.

At the 1949 Paris foreign ministers' meeting I had to pass Dulles's office door, which he ostentatiously left open to exhibit himself sitting behind a clean desk, reading a newspaper. Prompted by Princeton solidarity I frequently stopped in to chat with him, an experience which proved intellectually and professionally productive in that, while he did not choose me for promotions, he did not oppose my advancement. As a matter of fact, after being badly burned by his dismissal of the department's China expert, John Paton Davis, on grounds of lack of judgment, Dulles disinterested himself in the Foreign Service and left its operation to the two deputy undersecretaries, Robert Murphy and Loy Henderson.

I was unprepared for the state of affairs prevailing within the Planning Staff, which were pleasantly casual but confusing. The mixed group included Charlton Ogburn, a well-known war writer, naturalist, and protagonist of the view that the earl of Oxford was the true author of Shakespeare's works; Henry Owen, now with the Brookings Institute; John Campbell, of the Council on Foreign Relations; Louis Halle, later a lecturer at Geneva University; Burt Marshall, later with the Johns Hopkins School of Advanced Studies; as well as an assortment of Foreign Service area specialists.

The director was Robert Bowie, a brilliant Princeton

and Harvard Law School graduate and at one time a rival of Henry Kissinger's for dominance of the Cambridge community of political scientists; in 1977 he was put in charge of CIA political analysis. Since it was Dulles's habit in his early days in office to work with a very small group of trusted officials, which included Bowie, we saw very little of our director, who was constantly engaged in missions assigned to him by Dulles. During my eighteen months on the staff, we never once met as a unit with the secretary.

Upon my arrival in Washington I was asked what I would like to do. Since nobody seemed especially eager to preempt the wisdom I had brought back from Moscow I felt I should volunteer it, and so assigned myself the task of compiling a study of accommodations that might conceivably be possible between us and the Soviets, especially as regards Germany.

I recalled that several colleagues and myself from Ambassador Murphy's office in Berlin in 1946 had devised a theoretical exercise of trying to put together the then already disparate parts of Germany into a viable government unit. Even at that time it would have proved impossible to reconcile the differences that had developed between East and West Germany in matters of law, education, inheritance, business practices, etc. The problem we in the Planning Staff faced in 1953 was even more intractable. Almost any compromise we considered would have weakened by dilution the structure the Western powers were committing themselves to build. With respect to rapprochement between the two Germanys, much less unification, no departure could be made, without fatal results, from the position we had taken on the need for sound currency, elections, and freedom of economic association. Our policy planning paper suggested only that the formation of the European Defense Community might be delayed in order to facilitate discussions with the Soviets. In the end result, the EDC was rejected a few months later by the French parliament.

I was never able to learn what use Secretary Dulles may have made of our paper. At least we seemed to be thinking alike since his broadcast report on February 24, 1954, on the results of the Council of Foreign Ministers meeting in Berlin in January and February of that year confirmed in almost every detail the conclusions we had reached some months earlier in 1953. Incidentally, that conference was the first to generate respect for Dulles as an articulate, forceful, and shrewd advocate who was later to dominate the international scene.

WESTERN AND EASTERN POSITIONS

It would be well to take a look at where we stood at this point with respect to plans which had already been developed for Western European integration and which at the same time provided for West German rearmament. These plans had neither been changed nor much delayed in the interval following Stalin's death in March 1953 when both sides were feeling each other out. In fact, in early 1954 they were reaching a point of no return. It would be unfair to charge the Republican leadership with lack of imagination in dealing with the Soviets since it is unlikely that under the same circumstances the Democrats, had they continued in power, would have been diverted from their original design for Western European integration.

The stakes both sides had invested in their respective holdings in a divided Germany, and the losses each risked from setting up a unified Germany under unstable conditions, were regarded by each party as far too high to permit viable compromises. The Soviets can be blamed with holding out too long against reasonable concession, a delay which in turn produced cohesion if not absolute unity among the Western nations. On the other hand these countries were far from innocent in the matter of adhering to nonnegotiable positions. Among the obviously unpromising proposals put forward by the United States, the U.K., and France was one insisting on free elections in Germany. As Western policy took shape in the series of foreign ministers' meetings then being held, this requirement was expanded to stipulate that a Germany reunified by free elections should be at liberty to join any European economic system of its choice, that is, either the then-projected Schumann Plan, or, as a somewhat fanciful alternative, the Soviet Comecon bloc. Even though a united Germany would have been forbidden to belong to any military alliance, the proposal had small appeal for the Soviets in view of the direction West German policies were taking under Adenauer.

The Soviet plan, as presented in numerous East–West meetings, was perhaps more subtle but equally impracticable and unacceptable. In short, it envisaged popular representation through the participation of mass and Communist-front organizations rather than strictly party groups. Germany was then to be reunified by negotiation between the Western and Eastern regimes on the basis of setting up a demilitarized, neutral state over which there would be some form of four-power control or right of intervention.

The Soviet design was, of course, to prevent or slow down the creation of a West German military force and its incorporation in NATO. The Soviet efforts had only minimal effect even despite French rejection of the European Defense Community, due more to the operation of French domestic politics than Soviet threats.

It became fairly obvious after the breakdown of the crucial Moscow meeting of the Council of Foreign Ministers in February-March 1947 that the division of Germany was beyond repair. Each bloc thereafter hastened to build up its own system on either side of the line. Although the Western nations held on somewhat longer to their public advocacy of German reunification, the true state of international interest seemed to be reflected in the remark attributed to a Frenchman: "We like Germany so much that we want two of them." However, a new set of negotiations seemed called for, not necessarily in the hope of reuniting Germany but for the purpose of enabling each side to draw its own conclusions and make the necessary adjustments. This was what the 1955 summit meeting in Geneva was mainly about.

As to Austria, that country in the end became a beneficiary of the impasse over Germany and of the movement in favor of a summit meeting. A point of established doctrine among the State Department's Soviet experts had been that the restoration of Austria as a sovereign state (it had a national government but was under U.S., U.K., French, and Soviet occupation) would have to wait upon an East–West solution of the German problem. Secretary Dulles disagreed. A stumbling block in the settlement of the Austrian problem had been a Soviet claim to assets in its zone (which proved eventually to be of diminishing value). At the Berlin Council of Foreign Ministers conference in early 1954 Dulles had informed Molotov of his willingness to concede entirely to Soviet economic claims in return for abandonment of the Soviet demand that the great powers have the treaty right to reintroduce their troops into Austria under emergency conditions. Molotov only got around to closing this deal in April 1955, thus clearing the way for the signature of the state treaty on Austria in Vienna in May 1955.

BEFORE THE EISENHOWER SUMMIT

Soviet agreement to the Austrian treaty gave impetus to the campaign for a summit conference, promoted chiefly by Sir Anthony Eden who had just been named British prime minister in 1955 and who needed public exposure. French Premier Edmond Faure was under left-wing pressure to be conciliatory to the East. (When in recent times we have been accused of seeking a monopoly on détente, it is interesting to recall the end runs some of our allies frequently pulled off to solicit Soviet favor.)

Although Dulles and Chancellor Adenauer saw some risk that a summit with the Soviets might slow down the creation of a West German army, President Eisenhower agreed that such a meeting should be held later in the year. A preparatory group was set up in the State Department in April 1955 headed by the department's counselor, Douglas MacArthur II, with myself as his deputy. MacArthur handled liaison with Congress and the other U.S. government agencies, whereas I became the point of contact with our Western allies.

Corresponding to the expected Soviet agenda, three groups were set up, the first dealing with political and international security affairs, the second with disarmament, and the third with economic and cultural exchanges between East and West. The White House, and in particular Nelson Rockefeller, then a presidential assistant, took a special interest in the latter area over which, however, Undersecretary Herbert Hoover, Jr., and the department's security chief Scott McCleod, who held more conservative views, cast a somewhat jaundiced eye. When Undersecretary Hoover learned for the first time that one of my officers was working closely with Rockefeller, he forbade my assistant to attend a meeting at the White House scheduled for that same afternoon. When informed of this decision, Rockefeller just laughed, saying he knew who was behind it, but that everything would turn out all right because the president himself keenly favored East–West exchanges. Generally, the preparatory group worked well together, although Dulles was careful to keep Secretary of Defense Wilson out of earshot of our allies, in view of his occasional impromptu statements that he envisaged an early withdrawal of U.S. forces from Europe.

Dulles's peers occasionally vented their resentment on his subordinates. Once during the 1956 Hungarian crisis, when Dulles was on the run to answer a call to the White House, he ordered me to telephone some new instructions to our U.N. representative in New York, Ambassador Cabot Lodge. Lodge's understandable reply was "Who the hell are you? I don't like these instructions anyway and I'll have them changed when I come down to Washington tomorrow" (which proved not to be the case). The State Department spokesmen had a rough time on the National Security Council Planning Board, which was headed by Robert Cutler, a fearless and sprightly Boston attorney who delighted in cutting admirals, generals, and especially air force colonels down to size. Enjoying the president's full trust, as is evident from the Eisenhower memoirs, Dulles almost invariably won all the top decisions, with the notable exception of our refusal, apparently attributable to the president's good sense, to intervene militarily in Vietnam in 1954.

As to his associates, Dulles never seemed to be completely at ease with the three undersecretaries who served him in turn, General Bedell Smith, Herbert Hoover, Jr., and then Christian Herter who succeeded Dulles as secretary of state. His closest friend and counselor was his legal adviser, Herman Phleger, a distinguished San Francisco attorney. An unabashed conservative, Phleger had great gifts of persuasion and common sense. Although he was Dulles's most influential associate, he rarely preempted the secretary's power on his own.

Dulles was an erratic reader of the daily telegraphic file, concentrating his attention on only a few matters of particular interest. I never saw him get beyond the first page of any staff study, and he regularly leafed quickly through texts of speeches written for him and then usually hammered out his own final product after many drafts. He made decisions after discussion, without necessarily revealing his chain of thought. He was open to outright disagreement provided it was well presented, but would not stand for having a case reopened.

Once mutual adjustment had been reached, a certain imperial distinction attached to working for, or within range of, Dulles which was unmatched by the jobs in the White House. More approachable than General Marshall, he acted as good-mannered host at the cocktail hour on trips on his special plane, although like Marshall he did not relish others' telling stories funnier than his own.

In preparation for the summit, several informal meetings were held between the foreign ministers of NATO, mostly in Paris. Dulles also met frequently with Chancellor Adenauer, and although they spoke no common language, an unbreakable bond of mutual admiration developed between the two which ruled over Western policy and kept the weak-hearted in line. I recall that just before the summit, one of Adenauer's ministers made a speech which could be interpreted as slightly critical of the United States. At their meeting the next day, Adenauer told Dulles that he intended to dismiss the minister and would do so within forty-eight hours, but asked whether Dulles would permit him a week's delay so that he could find a replacement. Taken aback somewhat, Dulles said he had no thought of taking offense and he prevailed upon the chancellor to keep the errant minister in his cabinet.

FAILURE IS CONFIRMED IN A MEETING OF FOREIGN MINISTERS

The summit was held in Geneva on July 2–23, 1955. The inability of the conference to produce concrete results is a subject of voluminous historical record. The breakdown occurred mainly over three issues. Up until the day before the end, it appeared that agreement had been reached on a formula that German "reunification through free elections must be achieved in accordance with the national interests of the German people and in the interest of European security." At the last minute the Soviets revived their requirement that reunification be negotiated between East and West Germany, which the West, as in the past, rejected on grounds of the nonrepresentative character of the East German regime. The Soviets furthermore insisted that their security plan for joint action in the face of threats of war in Europe should have priority over a German settlement, whereas the West demanded that the two questions be linked together. Finally, disarmament was blocked by a Soviet proposal that the use of nuclear weapons be prohibited by a declaratory statement, without enforcement by inspection.

President Eisenhower's proposal for mutual "open skies" inspection of military installations through unrestricted flights and exchanges of blueprints was introduced on the next-to-last day, to the dramatic accompaniment of a violent evening thunderstorm. While our proposal was offered as a serious and practicable plan, its last-minute presentation put the Soviets off and inhibited further discussion, even of implementation by stages.

The summit was not officially proclaimed a failure but was represented as finishing on a note of sufficiently hopeful ambiguity to justify a later meeting of the foreign ministers who would attempt to clarify and carry forward the business the summit was unable to accomplish. That session met in Geneva in November and was distinguished by lively debates mostly between Dulles and Molotov. The discussion, which involved an exhaustive review of basic East and West positions, made clearer than ever before the basic obstacles to agreement on Germany. I cannot recall whether it was at this meeting or at the summit that the CIA initiated its project of trying to obtain secret insights by reading the lips of the Soviet delegation. In any event, the messages we received by conventional means were unmistakably negative.

Two consequences flowed from tacit acceptance of the inevitability of the split of Germany. One of them was

Soviet official recognition of the German Federal Republic, which was arranged during Adenauer's visit to Moscow between the 1955 summit and the November foreign ministers' meeting. This concession signified Soviet acquiescence to West German militarization as the price the Soviets were willing to pay for the division of Germany and consolidation of their Eastern European empire.

A second consequence was Soviet agreement given, as previously related, just before the summit, to Austria's neutralization and independence. The question is still asked why in Austria's case they "gave up" territory under thier control. To my mind, the only plausible explanation is that they feared the likelihood of a total or partial union of Austria with Western Germany. The Soviets were doing poorly economically in their zone and not much better politically throughout Austria, where the Communist party suffered complete failure. The Federal German Republic, already established and off to a good start, was beginning to exercise considerable drawing power. The Soviets may have thought there was a danger that the three Western zones of Austria might move spontaneously to join the new German state. Soviet intervention and confrontation with the Western occupying powers would have been almost inevitable under these conditions. Furthermore, there was not a Communist government in Austria to which the Soviets would have been irretrievably committed, as they already were in Eastern Germany and the European satellites. Thus they could afford to accept Austrian neutralization and a relaxation of their control in return for limiting the risks of confrontation within the divided Europe which they had planned for and created.

American administrations of the 1945–1955 decade have been severely criticized by present-day "revisionist" historians for placing a higher price on building up Western Europe than on reaching overall settlements with the Soviets. Our past policies must be judged by today's results, which in all likelihood would be less satisfactory if we had made some of the concessions now urged upon us by the revisionists. The half-accommodations and types of *modus vivendi* developed then were validated in the 1970 Soviet–Federal Republic settlements (to be discussed) and in the inter-European agreements of the 1975 Helsinki Conference, which seem to have brought territorial differences under better control.

On the other hand, a basic and hauntingly ominous flaw persists—the division of Germany. Over the years it has offered Europe a sort of artificial stability, but its final cost is uncertain. To an even greater degree than the subjugation of the Eastern European countries, whose national identities are at least assured, it flies in the face of history and affronts the cause of freedom, as the Berlin Wall grimly reminds us.

Chapter IV

Apprenticeship in Yugoslavia

U.S. SUPPORT OF YUGOSLAV INDEPENDENCE

SUBSEQUENT chapters will deal with ideological revolt against Soviet domination in the satellites—which was attended by violence in the case of Hungary and Czechoslovakia. Here I shall digress for a few pages to explain, out of sequence but by way of throwing light on what comes later, that I received some prior education in anti-Soviet heresy by serving as counselor of embassy in Belgrade from April 1951 to November 1952.

I was snatched from my post as counselor in Djakarta, Indonesia, because Joseph Alsop had convinced the State Department that a Soviet invasion of Yugoslavia was imminent in the spring of 1951, thus necessitating the assignment of a bachelor to Belgrade.

I had the pleasure of serving in Belgrade under George V. Allen, a shrewd and affable veteran who later was sent as ambassador to India. Allen became a great favorite of Tito on whom he called regularly with gifts of a new camera or other piece of equipment, provided from Washington official sources. George Kennan, the former U.S. ambassador to Moscow and Allen's eventual successor in Yugoslavia in 1962, was apparently less appreciated, since one of his contributions, so it is said, was to lecture Tito on how to deal with the Russians.

Three things should have induced the Tito regime to stick with the Soviets: their common stake in Communism; Yugoslav gratitude for their liberation from the Germans at Soviet hands; and a certain sympathy for the Russians deriving from traditional Serbian Pan-Slavism. The breaking point in 1948, however, was Soviet interference in Yugoslav affairs, and, having successfully repulsed this threat, Tito was not about to yield to any other outside national influence.

When I arrived in Belgrade in the spring of 1951, the Tito regime had largely overcome its fear that the Soviets would follow up their instigation of Chinese intervention in Korea with a move against Yugoslavia. Instead, Yugoslavia was basking in the munificence of American support, which started with a drought relief program in 1951 and later included the supply of American surplus military equipment. The late ambassador Allen told me that in this connection some talks of a strategic character between American and Yugoslav generals took place. I can find no record of these discussions, but our supply of arms on a grant basis certainly established an implicit interest in Yugoslavia's security on our part. The withdrawal of American forces from Austria following the conclusion of the State Treaty in 1955 vitiated our ability, however, to be of military help.

U.S.–YUGOSLAV DIFFERENCES

Relations at the top level were good during my term of service in Belgrade from 1951 to 1952, and Tito appeared genuinely grateful for the help we had given him during the war and for our current programs of assistance. Controversies, however, which were kept alive at lower levels and caused considerable annoyance, arose over such matters as American public reaction to Communist treatment of the Catholic church and over charges that the U.S. was harboring war criminals who had escaped from Yugoslavia. Moreover, the Yugoslav media were controlled by a dogmatic anti-American hard core who occasionally could be as virulent as their colleagues in the satellite states. A minor irritant was the moralistic and didactic attitudes of many of the young Yugoslav bureaucrats; some of them, who had come from the best families and had turned Communist in reaction to King Alexander's regime, were already identifying themselves with anti-Western attitudes of the emerging Third World.

By far the most serious dispute concerned Trieste. Upon Germany's defeat, American and British troops occupied the city of Trieste to prevent its seizure by victorious Yugoslav forces. At the 1946 Paris Peace Conference which drafted the peace treaties with the German satellite governments, the status of the Trieste area was taken up, that is to say, the future of the predominantly Italian city of Trieste and of the adjacent territory of Pula, which contained some Italian settlements but was dominated by a Slovene majority.

An allied commission was dispatched to the scene, headed by a Soviet general, who at that time, of course, was a staunch Yugoslav ally. The U.S. representative was the late Philip Mosely of Columbia University, who gave me the following contemporary account. A determining factor was the economic and cultural hinterland of the respective areas. One of the criteria chosen was the number of railroad lines serving each territory. It was seen that three lines connected Trieste city with Italy and only one with Yugoslavia. When the commission returned to Paris to write its report, the Soviet chairman announced that Trieste city was bound to Yugoslavia by three lines and to Italy by only one. When his colleagues protested, the Soviet general smilingly suggested a compromise of two and two; he was just as genially overruled.

The resulting provisional division of the territory into two zones—Trieste city as Zone A under American and British administration, with Yugoslavia in control of Pula in Zone B—was a constant source of trouble. In 1948 the U.S. and the U.K., in order to help Italian Premier de Gasperi win an electoral victory over the Communists, declared themselves in favor of a final settlement giving both Zone A and Zone B to Italy, thus enraging the Yugoslavs.

During my time in Belgrade there were periodic border incidents and charges of mistreatment of minorities in each zone. I remember being called to the President's Palace, when I was temporarily in charge of the embassy, for a very rough conversation with Tito. In the summer of 1952 a protest parade, which was organized to march past our office, broke in our front windows. As soon as I was able, I left for the Foreign Office to register indignation. I told the competent deputy minister that I had long admired the bravery of the Yugoslavs and had seen them stand up to the great powers with nerves of steel. I said that I regretted it all the more to see them now acting like Italians. (This gratuitous slap at our Italian friends has been on my conscience, but it did serve its purpose by putting an end to all further demonstrations.)

It was obvious that the only rational final solution

would be the assignment of Zone A to Italy and Zone B to Yugoslavia. Ambassador Allen told me that Tito had suggested this to him in early 1951, and it is known that Tito again made the same proposal to Foreign Minister Eden during the latter's visit to Belgrade in the fall of 1952. Because of American and British involvement in Italian politics and Italy's continued claim to the entire territory, a settlement was delayed until 1954. In the spring of that year Undersecretary of State Robert Murphy wound it up after delicate negotiations. The Zone A/Zone B division was approved in principle by the Italians and Yugoslavs but the latter then proved to be the more difficult party. They refused to be bribed, but a seemingly fortuitous and "separate" provision of some $60 million in additional U.S. aid had to be adumbrated to put them in a receptive mood. While we could have had an earlier settlement for nothing, the price of our disengagement was well worth paying. An immediate benefit was the opening up of normal channels of Italian–Yugoslav trade, which has continued to prosper.

A shift predictably took place in overall Yugoslav policy. The Trieste settlement removed the danger of hostilities with the Americans and the British, however remote this possibility may have been, and gave Tito a freer hand to deal with the Soviets. Taking advantage of the Soviet desire to normalize relations after Stalin's death, Tito worked out the basis of a favorable accommodation during Khrushchev's visit to Yugoslavia in 1955. (It is interesting to note, however, that Tito continued to accept the gift of American arms for almost another year.) With pressure removed from both of his diplomatic flanks, he started to look for a different world forum in which to assert and capitalize on his country's stance of independence. This, of course, led him to his association with the Third World and his pretension to a leading role within the movement. The result has been that while Tito's present policies may occasionally embarrass the Soviets, they have frequently been more detrimental to Western interests.

Speculation in Moscow over Yugoslavia's future after Tito had already gotten off to a good start by the time of my departure (as U.S. ambassador) from the Soviet Union in 1973. Soviet journalists professed to foresee, if not indeed hope for, a certain degree of disintegration. A scenario suggested by a rather sinister professor, reputed to have Central Committee connections, was winning some credibility; his hypothesis was that should Yugoslav domestic difficulties coincide with a Middle Eastern crisis involving East–West confrontation, the Soviet Union might feel "compelled to move" to protect its strategic interests. My Yugoslav colleague in Moscow, however, appeared quite content with the existing state of relations.

Chapter V

Revolt in Poland and Hungary

COLD WAR GAMES WITH THE SATELLITES

AFTER the Geneva summit and the November 1955 follow-up meeting of the foreign ministers, I was appointed the deputy assistant secretary of state in charge of Soviet and East European Affairs. Besides my Soviet experience, I was thought to qualify in the Eastern European area because of my service in Yugoslavia.

When I took over my new assignment in the department in late 1955, bitter memories and experiences colored our association with the Soviet satellites. From the beginning the consolidation of the Communist regimes in the Eastern European countries gave us nothing but trouble, the same being true with respect to Yugoslavia until its break with the Soviets in 1948. Their spy agencies and ours began to play dangerous games with each other. When we came out ahead, the incidents were sometimes amusing, for instance our ambassador's success in 1948 in smuggling the endangered Polish peasant leader Mikolajczyk out of his country under a load of coal.

Other incidents involved harassment of our aircraft,

studied mistreatment of our citizens, and sometimes their kidnapping, as was perpetrated by the Poles in the case of the family of Noel Field, a State Department official in the late 1930s who defected after the war, but whom the Poles arrested presumably because of rumors that he was acting as a double agent. Expulsions of Communist diplomats from the United States as spies occurred during the middle 1950s at the rate of about one every two months. Most of the guilty were employed as international civil servants on the staff of the U.N. (The practice of that organization has been to request convincing justification of guilt.) One of my duties was to deliver the expulsion notices in person to the ambassador concerned, in the full knowledge that one of our own staff would be forfeited in retaliation.

Except for such unpleasant forms of communication, there was little traffic between us and the satellites. At international meetings, Secretary Dulles reproved their spokesmen for wasting his time by parroting Soviet positions. By late 1955 the machinery of the Cold War was operating with added refinements. Our side countered massive Communist propaganda with ingenuity and style. Radio Free Europe, established in 1950, won large satellite audiences and Radio Liberation (now Radio Liberty) tried to penetrate the Soviet Union. It was also the era of such stunts as the CIA's release of balloons from Germany which carried "freedom messages" eastward with the prevailing winds.

Although direct political contacts with, and within, the satellites proved difficult, my office in the State Department, in cooperation with our intelligence agencies, kept close watch on the satellite countries and their relations with the USSR. We carried this out through press research and defector interrogation. While realizing that another explosion, such as occurred in the East Berlin and East German riots in June 1953, was always possible, we devoted more attention to the evolution of liberal forces which emerged after Stalin's death.

Taking Russia as a historical example, liberalism has depended for its inspiration and success upon the degree to which the intellectuals, the youth, and the workers have been able to collaborate. This combination produced the Russian Revolution and in a certain sense has served to set a pattern in the Eastern European countries which the Soviet Union took over after the last war. Except for the intellectuals, other dissident elements in the Soviet Union unfortunately have not had much of a chance to play a major role nor to work in unison in today's static Soviet society. Even though Khrushchev and his associates gave the signal and clearance for post-Stalin change, the trend developed further and faster in some of the larger Eastern satellites.

Poland and Hungary were among the first to take encouragement from the tentative signs of relaxation. As we shall see, Poland was the more fortunate in being able to make the transition in orderly fashion, whereas in Hungary the pressures of protest produced violent explosion. The Polish and Hungarian intellectuals took the lead in dissent, and to some extent they interacted with each other.

In the spring of 1956 the Polish party reformists had pushed themselves forward on the world stage and had forged a kind of alliance with the international press which proved mutually profitable. In studied disregard of party discipline, they told key foreign correspondents about what was going on within the local cells. These reports, which were played back to Poland by radio from abroad, helped disseminate the reformers' views, their aims, and the nature of their opposition.

It was not long before our country became involved, at least emotionally. The American press was strongly represented in Poland, especially by Sidney Gruson of the *New York Times,* and his wife Flora Lewis, who were sought out by influential party reformists to be their spokesmen to the Western world. Interest among the some six million Polish-Americans, particularly as organized in our larger cities, was intense, if somewhat ambivalent. They of course had great sympathy for the Polish people, but also a mistrust for the Communist regime, reformist or not. We in the State Department kept in close touch with their leaders and congressional representatives, and had their support in furnishing public encouragement to the liberal movement through official press statements and radio scripts. If the CIA had done no more than to further this cause by providing the facilities of Radio Free Europe (which it then secretly financed) it would have justified its existence.

KHRUSHCHEV'S SECRET SPEECH STRIKES FIRE IN POLAND

The Soviet Twentieth Party Congress meeting in Moscow in February 1956 gave sanction and impetus to the Polish reformers. Khrushchev's famous "secret speech" of February 25 denouncing Stalin's cult of personality and his abuse of powers set off the explosion. Although knowledge of the two-and-a-half-hour speech leaked out only gradually, the message it conveyed was spread rapidly by interested party officials. On February 29, Jozef Winiewicz of the Polish Foreign Office alerted our ambassador, Joseph Jacobs, to the "great importance" of the Soviet Congress which, he said, foreshadowed a new era of democratization within the "Communist camp."

A frantic search then ensued for the text of the Khrushchev speech. Robert Amory, former CIA deputy director of intelligence, has divulged that the U.S. moved in on the Yugoslavs, appealing to them in the light of our economic and military assistance granted to them over the years, to provide us with the full text, which we knew to be in their possession. Apparently our request was taken to Tito himself, who turned it down, however, on the advice of Rankovic, then his minister of internal security. All of a sudden several versions showed up for sale on the Polish market. When the State Department, with British help, had settled on an authentic text, the speech was issued June 4 in a departmental release, stating simply that it spoke for itself.

Its promulgation to the world in a version never directly challenged by the Soviets produced effects which Khrushchev could hardly have counted on. Its impact probably helped stimulate the riots which broke out in Poznan on June 28 in protest against harsh autocratic abuses of the kind denounced at the Soviet Twentieth Party Congress.

That day in Poznan began peacefully enough with a demonstration at eight o'clock in the morning of several thousand workers and their families from the Cegielski engineering plant who protested against salary and tax scales which almost literally made it impossible for them to live. Two officers from our embassy who reached Poznan during that night were told that the shooting was started by the security police, who killed upward of fifty people. Our officers reported that regular army units called to the scene openly sympathized with the rioters, and perhaps for this reason were not ordered to use their weapons.

As the Polish crisis evolved, I worked closely with Undersecretary Hoover and Deputy Undersecretary Robert Murphy. We had to decide whether or not to lend public support to the reformists and blast their Stalinist enemies. German government authorities favored such a course, whereas other NATO allies felt that outright Western endorsement of the new forces would create problems for them with the Soviets. We decided that our official media should encourage full and objective reporting of events and opinions which in themselves overwhelmingly favored reform; sympathetic U.S. government comment was added occasionally, stopping short of full endorsement.

During the summer of 1956 the reform elements strengthened their position considerably, calling into being a tacit alliance of intellectuals, publicists, workers, and youth, as well as older people whose memories gave them cause for protest. As a reaction to Poznan, the party itself in its search for a reform candidate had begun to look toward Wladyslaw Gomulka, who had been its first secretary in 1943, had been imprisoned by the Stalinists during 1949–1953, and had had his party rights restored in July 1956. The remaining Stalinists relied mainly on popular fear of the Soviets who, however, had a rather weak base within the country itself. It is interesting to note that by the time trouble started in Czechoslovakia in 1968, the Soviets had established a sounder base for subversion through an intensive advance infiltration of agents.

The tensions of the summer of 1956 climaxed at the

session of the Polish Central Committee set for October 19. On that morning, and in the middle of the first meeting, Khrushchev arrived in Warsaw, apparently unannounced, with a formidable Soviet delegation which included top military leaders. Rumors of an intended coup by a pro-Soviet group the night before had inspired worker contingents to stand guard over the residences of the Politburo members. In the midst of the Central Committee's session on the following morning, First Secretary Ochab informed his audience of the Soviet delegation's arrival, and adjourned the meeting. Both sides then went into secret session, the Poles making it clear that Gomulka was speaking for them as their next first secretary of the party.

The talks were attended by considerable drama, as evidenced by reports which differed mainly in their degree of sensationalism but which were later confirmed as substantially true, that Gomulka had threatened to put his case before the Polish people by radio, and that the Soviets had moved their "communications forces" permanently stationed in the country into positions nearer the cities. The Soviet delegation departed during the night, and in a long speech to the Central Committee on the morning of October 21, Gomulka outlined his understanding with the Soviets which surmounted the crisis.

The speech was a masterpiece which pleased the reformers and their Western supporters, while at the same time avoiding giving offense to the Soviets. In short, Gomulka repudiated the Stalinist "cult of the individual" and declared that there can be different roads to socialism and the best model should be chosen from the experiences of all countries "building socialism." (Here it may be noted that he was on safe ground in reflecting the language of the Soviet–Yugoslav declaration of June 1955.) As to "Polish–Soviet frictions," he said they belonged to the past and the Polish party would "rebuff anyone who tries to weaken Poland's ties with the Soviet Union."

On the matter of democratization, Gomulka was restrained and, in the light of his later deeds, fairly honest. While praising democratization, he said, "We shall not allow anyone to use the process to undermine socialism or destroy the party." Similarly, with regard to criticism, which he acknowledged was useful, "including that of the press," he said, "We have the right to demand that each criticism should be creative and just."

Understandably, the Polish story received top world attention which was diminished only slightly by rising tensions in the Middle East, soon to break out in the British, French, and Israeli invasion of Egypt. Gomulka was getting a good press, particularly in the United States through the lively and imaginative reporting of our correspondents. The skepticism aroused over the regime's harsh handling of the Poznan riots in June gave way to a feeling that the United States "ought to do something for Poland." This came through as an all-clear signal from the Polish-Americans who were placated by the regime's release of Cardinal Wyszynski and his reinstatement in October 1956. Washington officialdom, which had earlier adopted a hands-off attitude toward Gomulka, now believed that having successfully survived his confrontation with the Soviets, he merited and could benefit from U.S. official attention. Such also seemed to be the public mood during that election year.

On October 20 Deputy Undersecretary of State Murphy and I requested Polish Ambassador Spasowski to call on us to give us a report which would help us understand developments in his country. While generally endorsing what was happening, Spasowski was very cautious. The conversation turned to the emphasis Gomulka had given to the need for economic reform and the likelihood that Poland would request outside help. (Gomulka doubtless had in mind the Soviets.) At this point, Spasowski's brash young aide loudly interrupted that, of course, assistance from the United States would be appropriate and welcome.

On October 24 Undersecretary of State Hoover instructed our ambassador in Warsaw to communicate to the Polish government the American government's friendly offer of such aid as circumstances might require. Mr. Hoover mentioned that his personal interest was reinforced by memories of his father's work in Europe after World War I. The Polish reply, received from Deputy Foreign Minister Winiewicz, was not couched in the most gracious terms. While acknowledging the importance of the approach, Winiewicz said it could have no effect on Poland's commitment to socialism. He complained about American denial of "most favored nation" treatment to Poland and regretted that the word "aid" had been mentioned by Mr. Hoover. Without deviating from its intention to stand on its own feet, Poland nevertheless, he said, would appreciate being declared eligible for purchases of cotton, wheat, and "know-how" on credit terms similar to those which the United States offered other countries. Over the next few months agreements were worked out for the supply of several hundred million dollars worth of grains and cotton to Poland on generous credit terms.

In winning their game with the Soviets, the Poles had been both skillful and lucky. Several factors favored them. Khrushchev was hardly likely to repeat Stalin's mistake of breaking with the Yugoslavs, which in Poland's case was entirely unnecessary. Poland's leaders were loyal Communists who had no wish to change the social or economic system nor to repudiate the protection the Soviets afforded them against the Germans. Gomulka's nationalism was somewhat diluted by his Pan-Slavic sympathies, and the Soviets evidently felt that concessions to Polish popular aspirations for more freedom were, under Gomulka's auspices, not only worth the risk but would be expedient in preventing the issue from causing trouble elsewhere, a hope which soon sorely deceived them.

HUNGARY—IDEOLOGICAL REVOLT TURNS INTO TRAGEDY

In his book *Waging Peace,* President Eisenhower remarked that the Polish revolution "was coming to a rest on a high plateau," whereas he summed up the contemporary events in Hungary and the Middle East with a quotation from John Milton: "All hell broke loose."[1]

The spirit of revolt in Poland and Hungary owed its origin to the post-Stalin ferment which was then sweeping the Communist parties of Europe and was thriving on interaction between them. The ruling parties seeking greater freedom from the Soviets profited by the example of Yugoslav independence, although they usually

---

[1]Dwight D. Eisenhower, *Waging Peace* (New York: Doubleday, 1965), Chapter 3.

stopped short of totally embracing Yugoslav doctrinal heresies (except *in extremis,* as in the final moments of the Hungarian and Czechoslovak convulsions).

In retrospect, several differences served to set off the Hungarian experience from the Polish. It is significant that the Poles do not refer to their successful confrontation with the Soviets as a "revolution" but prefer the descriptive circumlocution "the October events." In Hungary a latent revolution had already taken place before the confrontation with the Soviets, in the sense that Stalinism was so firmly entrenched there as to exclude a change in leadership in time to direct and control the ferment and pressures that had been building up during the spring and summer of 1956. Had such a change in authority occurred, as it did in the case of Poland, the scenario for Hungary might have been far different. Although doubtless an early clash with the Soviets would have been inevitable, it need not have led to bloodshed, since an accommodation with the Soviets could possibly have been worked out before passions ran wild.

In a manner reminiscent of the tactics of the 1848 Hungarian Revolution, groups of students and intellectuals met together in "protest societies" throughout the summer of 1956. The substitution of Gero, a known hard-liner, for the only slightly more obnoxious veteran Stalinist Rakosi in the post of first secretary, left the party and government demoralized and brought the dissenters out in the streets. Imre Nagy, a former premier popular with the peasants whom Rakosi had ousted in 1955, had been a reformist candidate.

The first clash occurred in the early afternoon of October 23 when a group of student leaders headed a parade which grew to some forty thousand by the time it reached the statue of the 1848 Polish-Hungarian freedom fighter General Bem. After protest speeches, some tinged with anti-Russian outbursts, the crowd went on to Parliament Square where it attracted white-collar workers, laborers, and off-duty soldiers, growing in number to about ninety thousand and apparently it milling around aimlessly for some hours. Somebody then shouted "Down with the Stalin statue," and with this last cry the crowd overflowed into Stalin Square where it started to demolish the statue with blowtorches. (The Czechs, incidentally, were much more prudent and waited until 1961 to tear down Stalin's statue in Prague.)

At eight o'clock that evening, October 23, Gero, who had just returned from a visit to Belgrade, started a radio address. The crowd, which had moved to the Budapest radio building, hoped that he had been converted to Titoism; it became infuriated when he reverted to the old hard line which in effect rejected the people's demands. Firing broke out, reportedly started by the state security forces, and continued throughout the night. (Our chargé in the legation at Budapest, who telegraphed us a current account, informed us he was typing his report on the floor, in order to avoid local shell and rifle fire.)

After the revolt was suppressed we talked to several refugees who came to Washington, including General Bela Kiraly, who witnessed the October 23 mass meeting. He told us that the atmosphere had an eerie quality. As the crowd grew it became more determined not to disperse until something happened. With no one apparently in charge, the people had no idea what to expect, so that the firing of the first shots broke the sense of frustration.

The picture of what happened thereafter becomes ob-

scure. The old Russian saying "He lies like an eyewit-
ness," while it has mainly indigenous application, is pertinent to the Hungarian revolt. Its pace was so swift and
the personal experiences so varied as to leave room for
honest differences. The following is a plausible synopsis,
based on contemporary accounts as illuminated by recent
talks with some participants who were on the spot over
twenty years ago.

After a night of fighting in Budapest, Nagy became
prime minister on the morning of October 24 at about
the time an announcement, of uncertain origin, was
made over the radio that Soviet troops were taking part
in defending the country against "counterrevolution."
Here it should be explained that Soviet forces were still
present in Hungary despite earlier Soviet assurances to
withdraw them as no longer needed after the conclusion
of the Austrian state treaty. The timing of the announcement made it appear that Nagy had requested the intervention of these forces, which appears not to be the case.

On the afternoon of October 24 Soviet Politburo
members Mikoyan and Suslov arrived as troubleshooters
from Moscow. Reportedly on their insistence, Kadar was
named first secretary on October 25 (and was destined
thereafter to play a most ambiguous role). The new Hungarian government called for a ceasefire and Nagy announced that he would negotiate with the Soviets for a
withdrawal of their forces. A brief lull then ensued in the
crisis.

On October 27, Secretary Dulles delivered a major
speech in Dallas, Texas. Quoting scripture, he compared
dictatorships "like unto whited sepulchers which indeed
appear beautiful outward but are within full of dead

men's bones and of all uncleanliness." He went on to suggest a formula for our relations with the satellites which he set forth in the following carefully worked out terms:

> The United States has no ulterior purpose in desiring the independence of the satellite countries. Our unadulterated wish is that these peoples, from whom so much of our own national life derives, should have sovereignty restored to them and that they should have governments of their own choosing. We do not look upon these nations as political military allies. We see them as friends and as part of a new and friendly and no longer divided Europe. We are confident that their independence, if promptly accorded, will contribute immensely to stabilize peace throughout all Europe, East and West.[2]

(As Ambassador Bohlen reports in *Witness to History,*[3] on Dulles's instructions he delivered a paraphrase of this speech, to top Soviet officials in Moscow on October 29.)

On October 28 the Hungarian government had won agreement on the withdrawal of Soviet forces, and on October 30 the Soviets issued an ostensibly conciliatory official communiqué which in summary stated that the USSR and the Eastern European countries should build relations on principles of complete equality and noninterference in internal affairs. Downright mistakes had been made in the past, but the USSR was ready to discuss the future of technical advisers in these countries. The decla-

---

[2]Eisenhower, *Waging Peace,* p. 71.

[3]Charles E. Bohlen, *Witness to History* (New York: W. W. Norton & Co., 1973).

ration also stated that the USSR was prepared to examine with other Warsaw Pact members the question of the stationing of Soviet troops in Hungary.

Here again the picture becomes obscure and considerable mystery remains to this day concerning the line of authority within Hungary at the height of the crisis. Under pressure from the successful insurgents, and confronted with reports that the Soviets were adding to their troop concentrations, on November 1 Nagy as prime minister declared that there would be a multiparty system, announced Hungary's withdrawal from the Warsaw Pact, proclaimed Hungarian neutrality, and asked for inscription on the U.N. agenda of Hungary's request for neutrality and the grant of a four-power guarantee. Kadar, in a speech delivered three hours later on the same day, praised the rebels and promised that the party would "cleanse itself of the crimes of the past," but warned against the dangers of counterrevolution.

Kadar thereupon left to conspire with representatives of the Soviet Presidium at the border town of Uzhgorod. The outraged Soviet leadership sent their troops back into action early in the morning of November 4 to crush the revolt, which ended with Nagy's replacement by a new regime with Kadar in top control.

A case is being made today by some commentators and historians to vindicate Kadar's conduct of more than twenty years ago. It is claimed that he acted consistently during the crisis in that he supported Nagy up to the latter's declaration pulling Hungary out of the Warsaw Pact. Kadar's accomplishment in the later twenty years in developing a comparatively moderate regime in Hungary has, of course, won him more favorable repute than Gomulka in Poland, who became increasingly autocratic

[70]

in power despite his regime's auspicious beginning. A paradox persists, however, in Kadar's collaboration with Soviet repression in Hungary after the revolt and in his failure to save Nagy's life. After taking refuge in the Yugoslav mission in Budapest, Nagy was enticed out onto the street by a ruse involving a promise to the Yugoslavs that he was to be given safe conduct to Rumania. With what must have been Kadar's acquiescence, if not connivance, Nagy was picked up by the Soviets and, together with two other Hungarian patriots, was apparently subjected to a form of trial and executed in June 1958. Whether or not the execution took place in Hungary or in the Soviet Union has never been established. His tragedy seems to have been that he lacked the time, and probably the ability, to establish himself in responsible control during his government's brief period of tenure.

As to the Washington scene, at 10:30 on the night of November 3 (Washington time), the State Department's watch officer summoned me with the news from our legation in Budapest that the Soviet troops had launched an all-out attack. We had an open line with the legation which gave us continuous contact until cut off about ten o'clock the next (Sunday) morning. At about two in the morning (Washington time) Mr. Hoover, who was acting secretary because of Mr. Dulles's sudden illness, called me to say that he had received a clandestine message that Cardinal Mindszenty and his secretary were on their way to seek asylum in our legation. In response to his request for advice, I pointed out that in principle we opposed asylum but that it was justified in this case since it involved hot pursuit endangering human life. Hoover said that he would call me back and I subsequently learned that he checked with President Eisenhower. We then gave the legation authority to admit the two Hungarians.

My colleague, the Austrian minister in Prague Dr. Kirshchlaeger, now the president of Austria, later told me that the cardinal was headed toward the Austrian legation in Budapest but could not get across the river because of the fighting, otherwise the Austrians, instead of ourselves, might have had him as their guest for almost fifteen years. Incidentally, once he was with us, the cardinal opened a voluminous correspondence with President Eisenhower, for whom I had to write replies, presumably because of my responsibility for the cardinal's stay. My impression of him, acquired through our proxy acquaintance, was that he was a brave, patriotic priest but lacked the intelligence of his Polish counterpart, Cardinal Wyszynski.

Communication with our legation in Budapest ended on Sunday morning with the transmission of a pathetic plea for help from one of the two Hungarian state ministers who had not yet been arrested by the Soviets. It was delivered personally to our legation by Minister Bibo who addressed his appeal to President Eisenhower. Referring to the "ten-year-old liberation policy which the United States pursued with so much firmness and wisdom," the message said that abandonment of this policy would lead to "a most certain road to war." It urged the president to have the Western powers halt their attack on Egypt and have the Soviets withdraw from Hungary.

In the ensuing weeks charges were made that the United States in one way or another had incited the revolt. Such accusations were, of course, spread by the Soviets, but were also taken up in unfriendly quarters in

Western countries. It is fair to say that the concept, if not the policy of liberation, fell on willing ears in Hungary (but not only in that country). I recall a meeting at which CIA Director Allen Dulles was present when the question was asked whether it would not be wise for us to try to cool down the rioters. The almost irrefutable answer was that it did not behoove the United States to take a position of seeming to discourage protests in the name of freedom. According to a Hungarian participant in the revolution, the Hungarian public was in no way concerned with the idea of "help" from any source, since the revolt seemed to be winning. In my friend's view, U.S. intervention of any kind, whether by way of support or restraint, would have been fruitless.

Bohlen mentions that Ambassador Llewellyn Thompson in Vienna suggested that the United States press the USSR for a firm commitment to withdraw its troops in six months or a year.[4] Bohlen opposed the idea on the grounds that the Soviets would have plenty of time to consolidate their regime in the interim. He himself tentatively proposed that the U.S. offer the Soviets a high-level conference on disarmament in return for compliance with U.N. decisions, but he later agreed with our assessment in the State Department that the timing was not right.

I know of no reasonable or responsible authority who can establish a claim that Hungary's fate could have been otherwise under the circumstances. The revolt was overshadowed by the simultaneous British–French–Israeli attack on Egypt, and it is tragic that the two sets of aggres-

---

[4]Bohlen, *Witness to History,* p. 423.

sion coincided. In fact, we know that each side exploited the transgression of the other to accelerate and aggravate its own. A British, French, and Israeli cabal of ministers was held in Sèvres in late October to plan the attack on Egypt. According to Keith Kyle, formerly with the *Economist,* writing in the November 11, 1976, issue of the BBC *Listener,* it was the French who insisted on speedy action before the U.S. election on November 7; apparently they feared that Eisenhower, once elected, would go ahead with his policy of détente with the Russians at the expense of the three nations' interests in the canal.

For their part, the Soviets were fully aware of the dangers of delay respecting Hungary. As Ferenc Vali observes in *Rift and Revolt in Hungary:* "They [the Soviets] had to act swiftly and deftly before the Western world, then mesmerized by the Suez incident, could come to its senses. A *fait accompli* had to be created before the West or the world would be ready to act."[5]

Leaving aside considerations bearing on the presidential election then nearing its end, the use of American or Western forces to aid Hungary was automatically ruled out because of the certainty, inadequately appreciated even today, that military action to assist Hungary would inevitably have involved Austrian territory and the instant loss of Austria's year-old neutrality. It is true that we might have urged a more vigorous campaign against the Soviets, but here again we found it difficult to go beyond the measures we took in the U.N. against our offending allies and friends. Luck, plus planning, yielded the Soviets maximum short-term results.

---

[5]Ferenc Vali, *Rift and Revolt in Hungary* (Cambridge, Mass.: Harvard University Press, 1961), p. 363.

My association with the Hungarian revolution ended on a final note of frustration. As evidenced by frequent calls at the department by the Yugoslav ambassador, the Yugoslavs were highly alarmed by the vigorous action the Soviets were taking. This in part explains the somewhat tortured argument in Tito's November 11 speech in Pula, reportedly made after secret consultation with Krushchev. First, he said that the use of Soviet troops on October 23 had transformed a justified revolt into a national uprising, but then declared that the Soviet intervention of November 4 had been "necessary" because Nagy had failed to act against reactionary elements. In view of Yugoslavia's concern, and also because of Tito's reported indignation with the Soviets for having induced Nagy to leave the Yugoslav mission under false pretenses, some of us in the department thought it might be useful to invite Tito to visit the United States.

Accordingly, we drafted a letter which Secretary Dulles signed while in the hospital. Cardinal Spellman was belatedly consulted and mounted a drive to have the invitation cancelled, ostensibly because of Tito's continued imprisonment of Cardinal Stepinac. (Vladimir Dedijer, Tito's biographer, told me that Tito had actually suppressed a plot by Stepinac's Serbian enemies who had planned to assasinate the cardinal while in prison, in revenge for his alleged wartime atrocities.) The withdrawal of the invitation to Tito was fortunately arranged without bitterness and, indeed, with a certain amount of wry humor on the Yugoslav side. I still believe an opportunity was missed which might at least have saved Nagy's life by urging Tito to intervene more vigorously on Nagy's behalf.

The recent return of St. Stephen's crown to Hungary brings to mind an episode in its travels. Just after the Nazi surrender, an American sergeant driving an army truck sought out a representative in Frankfurt of Ambassador Robert Murphy, who was General Eisenhower's political adviser. The sergeant asked the State Department official "where he wanted the stuff delivered." Examination showed that the "stuff" included the coffin of Frederick the Great, once entombed in the Garrison Church in Potsdam; the bust of Nefertiti, which had been in the Kaiser Friedrich Museum in Berlin; and the crown of St. Stephen. These objects had been handed over by the Germans to the American forces to prevent their capture by the Soviets. Frederick was shipped off for reburial in Hohenzollern, his ancestral home, and the other items were placed temporarily in a museum vault in Wiesbaden. I was then attached to Ambassador Murphy's staff and on his behalf I visited the museum frequently. I established to my personal satisfaction that the crown was too small to fit the head of an average twentieth-century man. As is now known, the crown was held secretly for many years in the vaults of Fort Knox.

Another booty of war was about a ton of Soviet paper currency which had been captured by the Germans and stored in the vault of the Reichsbank in Frankfurt. My colleague, now deceased, Frederick Reinhardt, later to be our ambassador to Italy, had previously served in Moscow and had suffered the usual financial victimization at Soviet hands. He conspired with the U.S. Army to repack the currency and send it to our embassy, which undoubtedly could have lived off it for a number of years. Our army in Germany was inclined to be cooperative since it felt bitterly about the Russians: our soldiers had been forced literally to club defecting members of the Ukrainian Vlassov Army into boxcars to return them from our zone of occupation to the Soviet Union—and certain death—as a result of Western agreement to Soviet demands at the Yalta Conference. Reinhardt's project to dispatch the currency to our Moscow embassy fell through because the U.S. Treasury Department heard about it and returned the money directly to the Soviet authorities.

Chapter VI

Poland—A Chance for "Bridge Building"

NEW APPROACH TO COMMUNIST LEADERS

WITH Hungary lost to the West under tragic and on the whole uncontrollable circumstances, the U.S. turned its attention to Poland, not only to see what could be saved but to strengthen the reform trends which the Gomulka regime had fostered and consolidated. Our attitude was based on a combination of favorable factors: popular admiration for Polish aspirations for independence, satisfaction with the restoration of greater tolerance which included the church among its beneficiaries, and a feeling of relief mixed with a sense of obligation to help the Polish people.

Political problems, however, remained on both sides, namely, Gomulka's sworn loyalty to the Soviet alliance and our aversion to supporting a Communist regime. Since there was a strong mutual desire for agreement, a workable, albeit somewhat illusory, basis for U.S. economic assistance was worked out whereby it was recognized that Gomulka as a good Communist would be free to be demonstratively ungrateful and the Eisenhower regime would square itself with Congress by certifying that Poland was not a member of an international Communist conspiracy.

As the Poles had themselves suggested at the time of Undersecretary Hoover's offer of assistance in October, they sent a small economic delegation to Washington in the spring of 1957. It was headed by Henryk Kotlicki of the Polish Finance Ministry. Kotlicki had been ordered to treat his mission as a technical one and used to wince at well-intentioned praise from the American press of Poland's newly declared enthusiasm for independence and reform. During the war Kotlicki had served as a secret liaison officer between the beleaguered Warsaw ghetto and the Polish resistance movement in the city. (He reportedly lost his job during Gomulka's anti-Semitic campaign of the late 1960s.)

In June 1957 an agreement was signed with Poland for a credit of $95 million for the purchase of mainly U.S. surplus agricultural products. Gomulka publicly described this as a rather modest contribution "compared with our needs." Despite Polish requests for credits for a wide range of commodities, we considered the agreement a fair first attempt, taking account of the need to satisfy ourselves that the country in its state of economic disorganization could use our assistance efficiently. We dispensed with the then-standard forms of inspection which had caused irritation elsewhere. We relied on reports from the regular embassy staff, and over the years we found no grounds for complaint about Polish performance. By mid-1960 we had committed some $365 million in credits and had become a factor in Polish foreign trade.

After serving four years in the Washington offices of State Department, my turn came up for a post abroad and in March 1957 I was named, and received agreement to be ambassador to Austria. I viewed the assignment with mixed reactions, first because Austria was settling down to its enjoyment of constructive but unexciting neutrality after its survival of the Hungarian crisis; more importantly, because I knew I would become vulnerable to displacement to campaign contributors who might have their eyes on Vienna. In the meantime my friend and colleague William Lacy, who had been nominated for Poland, became ill and I was asked if I would mind taking his place. I graciously complied, being secretly delighted with a more adventurous assignment—although my wife was not—and as soon as I was confirmed by the Senate, I had myself sworn in on April 9, 1957. My next step was to make a farewell call on President Eisenhower.

I had come into contact with the president by attending various White House meetings in a subordinate capacity and was amused by his utter and profane detestation of the organization I worked for, which he frequently referred to as "that goddamned State Department" and which he, like many other presidents, entirely dissociated from his secretary of state, whom he revered. He was in a towering rage the morning I called on him, greeting me with "Do you know what your goddamned State Department has done? They won't let me trade with China. If I have a fish and they have a stone, Walter Robertson [assistant secretary of state for Far Eastern Affairs] tells me we can't exchange because they are Communist."

I assured the president I had nothing to do with China and only wished to serve him in Poland as best I could. He then expressed his admiration for the Poles, recalling that just after the war he had visited Warsaw with Marshal Zhukov to review a march past of the victorious Soviet and Polish forces.

Before leaving for Warsaw I obtained authority to make contact with any Polish citizen or official I considered appropriate, which was considered something of a concession at that time. Earlier administrations had believed that U.S. officials should have no relations with Communists who occupied solely party offices, the reasoning being that the parties, although they held power, stood for unrepresentative rule. Thus, party first secretaries were generally eliminated as unspeakable and nonspeakable. An exception, of course, was Stalin, who was considered good political value and had been sanitized by his wartime alliance with us.

Such an approach worked to our disadvantage. It cut us off from the real sources of authority and enabled party leaders to denounce the U.S. publicly more or less with impunity. In fact, government officials who also held party offices often advised us with a straight face to discount or disregard attacks by a particular first secretary or a ranking leader, on the grounds that the latter's concentration on party business deprived him of a proper awareness of foreign policy.

The latitude given me by the State Department never became operative during my Warsaw tour since, to the best of my knowledge, the only non-Communist Westerner ever to be received by Gomulka during my four years of service was Vice-President Nixon, in 1959. Gomulka was not on the list of personalities on whom the Foreign Office suggested I call. He was unapproachable at large receptions, where any Westerner moving in his direction was intercepted by a security or Foreign Office aide. By contrast, Khrushchev, when he visited Warsaw in July 1959, dove into the group of diplomatic guests, joking, baiting his audience, and stirring up trouble wherever he could, while Gomulka stood glumly in the background.

The earlier aloofness which prevailed between American officials and Communist party bosses has, of course, now been reversed with a vengeance. On becoming general secretary in 1964, Brezhnev played hard to get and was inaccessible to Westerners. One can speculate whether he feels happier with his present visible responsibility for the management of U.S.–Soviet relations than with his earlier better guarded position which guaranteed him a behind-the-scenes authority of last resort.

As a result of varied exposure, I have come to the general conclusion that the transaction of business with a country ruled by a nonrepresentative regime is to a certain extent done "with mirrors." Frequently it offers opportunities to exploit differences between state and party institutions to gain access to rival levels of power. During my time in Poland we had a fairly wide choice of channels. Because the new American connection was both popular and remunerative, the regime acquiesced in an improvement of relations—as long as it could retain control of domestic reaction.

Within the given range there developed a tolerable balancing of mutual antagonisms. As regards foreign policy, the Polish Foreign Office claimed that it was not a slave to Soviet example but I was rarely able to discern how the presumed differences benefited the U.S.; in fact, Polish action on the Far Eastern international control commissions was highly damaging to us. Still, the handling of bilateral business eased considerably under the Gomulka regime, with a successful expansion of business and cultural contacts. Despite occasional downdrafts, our relations with Poland in recent years have been consistently better than with any other Communist country, perhaps not even excepting Yugoslavia.

My arrival as ambassador in early August 1957 unfortunately coincided with the beginning of a cooling-off period. A few weeks of friendly introductory talks with the principal officials with whom I would be dealing were, however, vouchsafed. These included Jozef Winiewicz, deputy foreign minister in charge of American affairs, who had served six years as ambassador in Washington. A witty and sometimes mischievous man, he worked hard to ease the path of U.S.–Polish relations, warning us in advance of Gomulka's moods and his periodic outbursts of temper. This same service was provided by Witold Trampczynski, then minister of foreign trade. The contributions of these two men, both Polish patriots, benefited the interests of our respective countries.

Adam Rapacki, the son of the well-known founder of the International Cooperative Movement before the war, was a former socialist whom the regime coopted to lend it respectability. Although courteous and agreeable, he was not particularly friendly to the U.S., which he blamed for being subservient to Adenauer. He won renown by giving his name to the Rapacki Plan of 1957, proposing the denuclearization of central Europe.

An intriguing figure in every sense was Prime Minister Cyrankiewicz. Cynical and glamorous, he was mistrusted by Western politicians because he had absorbed the Polish Social Democratic party within the Communist regime. At home his moral reputation was not much better since he ostentatiously enjoyed nightlife and high living. He was respected, however, for having stood up to the

[83]

Germans and for having helped many Jews in the concentration camps where he was confined for over four years. He was grateful for the treatment he received from the Americans who liberated him, and at our first meeting we cleared up some long-standing details that had troubled our relations.

GOMULKA'S RETREAT FROM LIBERALISM

Even before I left Washington in August 1957, reports were coming through the Western press that the new dispensation in Poland was turning sour. The changes had brought about no improvement in living standards. A vivid account of the sordid poverty of the city dwellers was provided in the novel *The Eighth Day of the Week,* written by Marek Hlasko,[1] a young author who might have become as famous as Graham Greene had he not drunk himself to death at an early age. More threatening to the regime was the fact that the freedom of expression which had served it so well in its hours of crisis was being turned against it in protests voicing disillusionment and demands for a further easing of restrictions.

In short, the fate of reform in Poland was taking the predictable course it had followed elsewhere in the Soviet Eastern European empire. The contagion of freedom was spreading and heretical ideas were being entertained about the attractions of social democracy. Even though he was not Moscow-trained, Gomulka reacted to these anathematized trends as an orthodox Communist might be expected to do. Furthermore, he had his Soviet problem. After his triumph in brinkmanship in October 1956

---

[1]Marek Hlasko, *The Eighth Day of the Week* (New York: E. P. Dutton, 1958).

when he faced the Soviets down, he had deemed it wise to consolidate his gains by a visit to Moscow in November in which he strengthened his alliance with the Soviets only a few days after they had crushed Hungary.

By far the most outspoken organ of protest was the so-called student paper *Po Prostu,* written by young political activists with a large university following. In December 1956 it suggested that it might be better to dissolve the previously tainted Stalinist Communist party and start a new one. A new union of socialist and rural youth declared in April 1957 that they would not be the "passive executors of party and government policy" but would struggle to restore socialist practice in its "humanistic essence." Even the official party organ *Trybuna Ludu* criticized the government, while urging greater freedom of discussion. Since the paper was under Gomulka's direct control, he replaced the entire staff in early 1957.

In January 1957 elections for a new parliament, the Sejm, were held with significant results. The candidates receiving the highest percentage of votes in their precincts were in this order: Gomulka, 99.4 percent; Lasota, the editor of *Po Prostu,* 98.4 percent; and Zawieyski, the Catholic leader in Cracow, 98.3 percent. The non-Communist population had given Gomulka their mandate but with a mixed bag of associates more or less representative of the country's political trends.

Although Gomulka had won a plebiscite victory, his party was in a chaotic state. Dangerous thoughts, such as suggestions for humanistic reform and disbandment of the party (proposals which brought down disaster upon the Czechs when they pursued them further), risked bringing his leadership into disrepute with the Soviets and hard-liners like Ulbricht in East Germany. My wife

[85]

and I, who had served in Yugoslavia and the Soviet Union, could not believe that such heresies would be long tolerated in a Communist country, and apparently Gomulka came to the same conclusion.

The confrontation was precipitated by his banning *Po Prostu* in early October 1957. Rioting, which was met by shooting by the police, continued for three nights close to the American embassy. Besides students, the action included other malcontents, and I recall our maid's asking for time off to search for her husband who, she explained, was just another crazy Pole looking for trouble. Some dozens were injured but no deaths were reported. Tension was so great that Cardinal Wyszynski used his pulpit to urge the students to show moderation to preserve the gains they had won.

Gomulka's resort to force, which together with a bit of luck saw him through a serious crisis, alienated many of his Western admirers and provoked criticism, causing a rift between him and the American press. Perhaps some of this criticism was unduly severe because he had acted in the only way he believed possible to save his regime and its achievements which still enjoyed substantial popular support. Gomulka must have been an interesting man to know at this time. In his public appearances, he was modest, fairly genial, and revered by his audiences. He was recognized for his courage, a given instance of which was related to me by a Polish journalist who shared a cell with him during the Stalinist period. After a particularly brutal interrogation, Gomulka lowered his pants and, exposing his rear end, invited his tormenters to "kick it or kiss it." Later events, which seemed to have accentuated less admirable traits, revealed him to be suspicious, narrow-minded, and dictatorial.

[86]

SPUTNIK—A SPECTACULAR COMEBACK

Coincidental with these happenings in Poland, there occurred an event which had a deep effect on the country's political orientation—the launching of the Soviet Sputnik on October 4, 1957. It seems as if everything conspired to exaggerate its effects to the detriment of American prestige—the somewhat frightening science-fiction setting, the skillful play of Soviet propaganda, and, most effectively of all, the angry accusations of stupidity and incompetence which were raised against the Eisenhower administration by its domestic critics and which were purveyed by the international press. U.S. international standing had already suffered from the frustrations of Hungary and Suez.

The administration's mostly plausible but belated explanations made little headway against such criticism. A world meeting of scientists held in Rome in 1954 had urged the construction of an orbiting satellite for launching during the International Geophysical Year set for 1957. The U.S. announced in 1955 its willingness to undertake the project as a gift to the scientific community. Its development was assigned to the U.S. Navy under the title of Project Vanguard, and was to be kept separate from the missile program. Vanguard languished, however, because of budget cuts. It was known in scientific circles that the U.S. had the capability of putting a satellite in orbit in 1956 but did not do so because there was no obvious need for a crash program.

In the meantime the Soviets made no secret of their own plans to construct a satellite, and in September 1957 made public an estimate of its weight. Theodore Streibert, then head of the USIA, told me that the Soviet program was discussed at that time in a talk he had with Nelson Rockefeller, then White House consultant, and CIA Director Allen Dulles. Dulles even mentioned that the satellite would be the size of a basketball. The likelihood that the Soviets would be the first to succeed was viewed with equanimity since "demonstrability" on our part did not seem to be called for.

The Polish official press seized upon the event as a cheap way of affirming loyalty to the USSR, and took upon itself the mission of advertising and praising the Soviet success. The press strongly indicated, using confirmatory citations from American commentaries, that the Soviets had at last attained technological and military superiority over the United States. My Soviet colleague condescendingly expressed the hope that we would soon join his country in space. Poles who feared a reinforcement of Soviet influence showed considerable distress, and this included a member of the Central Committee and his wife whom we met at the house of an American journalist. The lady in particular queried my wife emotionally as to why the U.S. had failed the Western world by letting the Russians get so far ahead.

There is evidence that Sputnik had a more important long-term result. In the middle of January 1958 rumors began to circulate in Warsaw about an important three-day meeting between Gomulka and Khrushchev. On January 17 the press carried a brief announcement that a meeting had been held between Polish and Soviet leaders January 10–13 at a hunting lodge on the Polish–Soviet frontier. Information later spread around Warsaw that the gathering had included Khrushchev and Gomulka, with their top military and economic advisers.

Under the cloak of mystery, authoritative Polish

sources passed the word that important decisions had indeed been reached which might not be known for some time but which had provided a "definitive basis" for Polish–Soviet solidarity. It was hinted this was appropriate in view of the "new correlation of forces" and the need to discuss problems of Germany, U.S. relations, and European security in this context. A Polish journalist who was a member of the Central Committee told me privately that Khrushchev had persuaded Gomulka that the Soviet Union represented the "wave of the future" and that Poland had better capitalize on its opportunities as quickly as possible. He predicted that U.S.–Polish relations would take a rocky course. What actually seemed to be in the making was the working out of a balance between the various forces bearing down on Poland.

Gomulka's ostensible strengthening of his ties with the USSR at the beginning of 1958 accentuated certain irritants in U.S.–Polish relations. One of these was the question of the Polish broadcasts of Radio Free Europe (formerly secretly financed by CIA but since 1968 openly funded by Congress and operated under U.S. government supervision). These had been helpful to Gomulka in his struggle for reform but soon began to reflect the bitterness and disappointment which the revisionists felt and communicated to the American press. The first intimation I had of official displeasure was an inquiry put to me by Prime Minister Cyrankiewicz at a Norwegian Embassy reception, asking if I was aware what RFE was saying about himself and his wife. An examination of the scripts indeed showed some broadcasts to be quite scurrilous, although amusing.

RFE was immensely popular and it was estimated

about 80 percent of the adult population listened to it. However, a change seemed necessary which would involve moderation of a style which threatened to cut off official communication between us and the Poles. In the end a set of guidelines was drawn up which reconciled the interested American parties, including the Polish-Americans who had favored a hard stand. These regulations are still in effect.

"Games" with Police Controls

Wiretapping was an annoyance which had to be endured, by both sides. In early 1958 we moved the embassy offices in Warsaw temporarily into what had been the headquarters of the Polish state radio. Naturally, one of our first steps was to set about debugging the edifice. Without revealing any secrets, I can say that we were lucky enough to find the power supply cable which, when activated by us in reverse, caused the instruments to "sing" and be easily removed. I immediately protested to the Foreign Ministry and received an "official and personal apology," with the explanation that the previous occupants had "probably forgotten to take away their technical equipment."

Two years later we were called upon to make another temporary move into a former palace in Warsaw's old city. Our security operatives went into action again with commendable but perhaps excessive enthusiasm, since the demolitions at one point took them into the bedroom of a well-known Polish artist living next door. Their efforts, however, yielded results and again a protest was made to the Foreign Ministry, with a specification of the number of microphones found. This time there was a waiting period of several weeks before an officer was summoned to the ministry to be informed that our protest could not be accepted. The ministry stated that the Poles had recently moved into their new consulate in Chicago and had found microphones "placed there by the FBI." The number mentioned corresponded exactly to the number we had notified to the ministry in our own case.

Surveillance was something of which every Pole was conscious, and some lived with it blithely. On a certain New Year's Day I was invited, with our American correspondents, to a champagne breakfast by the editors of *Trybuna Ludu.* We had several good friends on the staff, despite the fact the paper was the hard-line mouthpiece for the Central Committee. On this occasion our host gave us a graceful toast, and then, tapping on the wall, repeated, "And a Happy New Year to you, too."

The secret police was active and obviously proud of its antecedents which could be traced back to the Polish Count Dzierzynski who was coopted by the Bolsheviks to be the first head of the postrevolution Cheka. His statue adorns Djerjinski Square, the site of the dreaded Lubyanka Prison in Moscow. The former count is credited with inventing the institution of prepackaged confessions at treason trials. It is said that as prosecutor he worked hard to make these confessions genuinely voluntary, getting down on his knees and, with tears streaming down his cheeks, imploring the culprit to confess for the sake of the Communist party. The poor suspect later received his death sentence with some surprise.

After the October 1956 changes and, it is understood, even today, Polish police methods are generally more lenient than those prevailing in other Communist countries. One reason undoubtedly stems from Gomulka's own experience of long imprisonment during the Stalin-ist years 1948–1954. "Administrative arrests" of politi-cal opponents became the exception rather than the rule, and punishment usually took the form of loss of jobs. Despite some warnings, many Poles fearlessly and mostly with impunity continued seeing their foreign friends. Cardinal Wyszynski, for instance, pointed out to an American visitor in 1960 his fully packed suitcase stand-ing by the door, explaining he was ready to return to jail at a moment's notice. What remained of the Polish nobil-ity was treated with a certain indulgence. A Count Po-tocki was a hunting companion of Gomulka's; a "red" Prince Radziwill lived comfortably in the gate house of his former estate; and a Poniatowski descendant of the last of the Polish kings worked in the Ministry of Agricul-ture boosting Poland's chief exports to France, horse-meat and snails.

The international press was, of course, one of the sus-pect categories. During my term, four American corre-spondents were either expelled or denied return, some on charges by the secret police which we protested. The most spectacular expulsion was that of Abe Rosenthal of the *New York Times* who in 1960, somewhat prematurely (the Poles thought), wrote about the obsessions border-ing on insanity which some ten years later led to Go-mulka's downfall in 1971. Unfortunately we failed to invoke the right of retaliation which the West Germans so successfully applied. My friend on *Trybuna Ludu* told me that Adenauer had called in the first Polish corre-spondents admitted to Germany, pointing out that there were four of them in Bonn whereas there was only one German in Warsaw. He said that the Poles were wel-come in Germany, but, should the Polish authorities as much as frown at the one German journalist in Warsaw, all four Poles would be immediately expelled.

CATHOLICISM—COMMUNISM'S STRONGEST COMPETITOR

Among those constantly under suspicion, a small group of Catholic leaders enjoyed a charmed life for a brief period. They numbered about a dozen Catholic publicists and scholars, highly respected for their intelligence, courage, and eloquence. Taking the name of *Znak* from the Polish title of their monthly publication, their political philosophy was based on the belief that despite differences in world outlook between Catholics and Marxists, they wished to "cooperate within the framework of the socialist system in everything which is good, moral, and creative for the individual and the community." They further explained that "whereas the Polish Marxist alliance with the Soviet Union is an ideological one, Znak accepts this alliance on grounds of political necessity, *in spite* of its ideology."

Znak was too useful a force to be ignored. Toward the end of October 1956 Gomulka met with its leaders and invited them to propose five candidates for the January parliamentary elections. Znak candidates did extremely well and, joined by four other Catholics, had a total membership of nine. With the shift toward greater orthodoxy, the importance of the Sejm, which was Znak's best sounding board, declined and in the next elections they were cut down to five seats.

While Znak was supported by Cardinal Wyszynski, the cardinal had his own ideas, and under his leadership the church preserved more of its gains from the October 1956 reforms than any other group, including the intelli-

[93]

gentsia. Enjoying the backing of some 80 percent of the population who are Catholics, he could be said to have been his country's single most influential figure. Gomulka respected him and is known to have met with him at least once in a session which lasted some nine hours. The results were reportedly meager. Gomulka spoke at great length about his plans for modernizing Polish life, including the need for birth control and Marxist educational reform, whereas the cardinal refused to yield on Church dogma.

THE RAPACKI PLAN

In professing their loyalty to Polish–Soviet solidarity, the Poles nevertheless strove mightily to convince Westerners that there were real differences in emphasis in the way alliance policy was carried out. These were expressed largely in matters of style, for instance, when Gomulka, doubtless considering himself a cut above the other satellite leaders, refused Khrushchev's invitation to join that unholy crew on the Soviet ship engaged to take them to New York for the 1960 U.N. General Assembly. The Polish attitude is worth examining in relation to the so-called Rapacki Plan to bring about nuclear disengagement in central Europe. The Plan was significant as a touted Polish initiative and also because of the fact that it was one of the few cases, if not the only one, where the U.S. and other individual Western states discussed separately with a secondary member of the Soviet bloc political and military questions of larger than purely bilateral interest.

The plan was submitted to the U.N. General Assembly in 1957 in the name of Polish Foreign Minister Adam Rapacki. It provided that no nuclear weapons should be produced or stationed within the territories of West and East Germany, Poland, and Czechoslovakia. The prohibition would apply to armaments of NATO and Warsaw Pact forces in the respective areas. The supporting arguments adduced by the sponsors were: the presence of nuclear arms in these areas of tension increases the dangers of confrontation and works against the unification of the two Germanys. The Poles claimed that the plan would actually favor the West, which would have to withdraw its nuclear forces only some 200 kilometers, whereas the Eastern forces would have to withdraw their nuclear weapons some 750 kilometers.

The purpose of the plan seemed to be, and certainly its adoption would have led to, a delay in building up NATO and its military potential. The Polish proposals therefore met with NATO's adamant opposition and especially that of Chancellor Adenauer, who as a policy matter rejected the thought of any restraints on West Germany in which Communist countries would participate.

In early 1958, and probably as a result of their January meeting with the Soviets on the Polish border, the Poles launched an intensive selling campaign. In order to meet Western criticisms voiced in the U.N., they circulated a revision in February 1958 which linked provisions for the control and reduction of conventional forces with the nuclear prohibitions. It also spoke in general terms of the need for inspection systems for enforcement. I was invited to several personal conferences with Rapacki and his adroit legal adviser Manfred Lachs (later Poland's judge on the International Court of Justice) who hinted that the Soviets were offering some of the same objections as the Western countries and, as regards inspection, had only agreed most unwillingly. I tried to test these assertions with my Soviet colleague, Abrasimov, who merely observed that the Rapacki Plan was a Polish initiative which the Soviets supported.

I myself was half-persuaded that we might gain something by showing interest and probing possibilities for reducing conventional forces and instituting inspection and controls. For my pains I incurred the wrath of my colleagues in Bonn and Paris. On May 3, 1958, the State Department gave its final answer in a note to the Polish Foreign Office. Presented in polite terms which acknowledged Poland's good intentions, it stated that the plan was too limited in scope; it failed to recognize the inadequacy of detection techniques; nuclear weapons were necessary for the West to counter Soviet troop masses and the plan made no provision for balanced limitations; and finally, it would perpetuate the division of Germany for which the Soviets were to blame by excluding their area from the Marshall Plan.

Given our strong rejection, I was apprehensive that Deputy Foreign Minister Winiewicz, to whom I read the note, would deliver a blast, to which I would be obliged to reply. Instead, he was in high good humor and asked me to transmit his thanks to Washington for its careful consideration of the plan. I can only surmise that the Poles felt they had acquitted themselves of their duty to the Soviet bloc and had enhanced their international standing in carrying out their mission.

ECONOMIC NEGOTIATIONS WITH A BLOC COUNTRY

The only other important set of negotiations which we carried on with Poland were in the economic and financial field. In fact, Poland was the first Communist country with which we had such postwar dealings on any extensive scale. Our role of creditor conferred upon us the dual status of limited partner in and interested observer of a Communist system.

It is axiomatic that under communism, economics is politics. In the Soviet Union, for instance, more political empires, even lives, have been won or lost over decisions of whether category A (heavy industry) shall have precedence over category B (the consumer sector) than over questions of human rights. In Poland the issue was complicated by abnormally low labor productivity. I was treated to a visible example when I paid a visit to the Zeran automobile works in Warsaw to hear Gomulka deliver a speech. When I arrived I saw a worker stretched out on a steel girder overhead drinking a bottle of beer. One of his comrades shouted from below to ask what he was up to. He replied, "I'm building socialism." I noted that he scuttled down in a hurry when Gomulka appeared on the scene.

One of the main reasons for Polish low labor productivity is that the tighter margins in Poland's less mature economy (as compared with the Soviet) have prevented the "second contract" dispensation from working successfully. The "first contract," it should be explained, is that whereby the citizen tacitly engages to refrain from subversive political activity. The "second contract," which helps keep peace within Communist societies, is the system which permits the worker to bridge the gap between low wages and rising prices by taking a second job, possibly in the services sector, or by engaging in the black market or by stealing from the state (with reasonable immunity from prosecution).

[97]

The failure to provide such relief caused periodic labor unrest which on the whole has been handled with understanding by the Polish government. The workers in the Poznan riot of 1956 were in the end treated leniently, and in late 1970 labor demonstrated its power by a series of strikes in the Baltic seacoast towns which, as is well known, finally brought about Gomulka's downfall and his replacement as first secretary by Gierek, the party boss from Silesia. In the summer of 1976 the regime felt compelled to rescind price increases which the workers protested by strike threats.

On the positive side, today's Poland has a balanced economy and natural resources which should be adequate for its size. It has productive farming and grazing lands in its eastern and central areas, and the western part possesses a ready-made industrial base in Silesia, which Poland took over from the Germans. Weakened in the past by incompatible minorities, the country now enjoys a closer ethnic unity, by virtue of its compression into predominantly Polish territories, than it has for centuries, although there are some natural regional antagonisms between the eastern and western parts of the country.

While Poland's economic troubles stem mostly from its position in the Soviet bloc, it faces some indigenous difficulties as well. Although private ownership of 83 percent of the farming land doubtless yields higher productivity than can be obtained under extensive collectivization, the older farming methods are obsolete in many ways and have perpetuated irrational fragmentation of the land through diverse inheritance. There is a woeful lack of artificial fertilizer for the farms and feed grain for cattle, but this is due, of course, to the state of the overall economy. Restraints on the private sector, which in particular hamper the development of much-needed secondary services, limit initiative and an expansion of domestic commerce.

Poland's economic dependence on the Soviet Union has been the latter's penultimate sanction, the last sanction, of course, being the threat of military intervention. In practice such dependence has been both a bane and a boon. Before October 1956 the Soviets bought Polish coal at below-cost prices. Today Poland suffers from the straitjacket planning of Comecon, the overall bloc economic organization. On the other hand the Soviets have periodically bailed out Poland by large credits when a combination of its troubles have faced it with disaster. Furthermore, even as an unwilling protégé, Poland enjoys some benefits such as access to raw materials, including oil, at lower than world prices.

American assistance became substantial after first being proffered in 1956–1957. While it has not been of a size to make us a dominant factor in the Polish economy, or to enable us to influence Polish policies significantly, our aid has eased some of the government's problems and given it a slightly wider freedom of action, especially in matters of international trade. Given our large agricultural surpluses of the time, very little sacrifice was involved on our part, making it possible through Public Law 480 to offer interest-free long-repayment terms, extending up to twenty years. The grain, tallow, and modest quantities of cotton we provided were of immediate help in relieving shortages. More difficult problems arose in meeting Polish requests for industrial equipment, first of all in the matter of licensing items which might be of military use, and second, because of the difficulty of finding large credits at higher interest rates for exports of intrinsically greater value than surplus produce.

A breakthrough which enabled the Poles to accumulate dollar reserves came in 1960 with our granting of most favored nation treatment in return for the settlement of claims by U.S. citizens for the sequestration and nationalization of their properties in Poland. Polish exports to the U.S. for the year 1958 came to $29.7 million, and their imports from the U.S., to $105.2 million, mostly in the form of surplus agricultural products. The initial estimate of the value of the American properties at the time of nationalization added up to about $300 million, but was later scaled down to $125 million in sustainable cases. In the bargaining process the Poles maintained that most favored nation treatment was unlikely to generate any substantial increase in exports. We contended the opposite and were proven right, since ten years later, in 1968, after the granting of most favored nation treatment, Polish exports amounted to $96.9 million, against imports from the U.S. amounting to $82.4 million. In the long run, our supplies of feed grains created a favorable cycle which has increased the amounts of meat and other foodstuffs for export. As to our claims, we settled for $40 million payable at 2 percent interest over twenty years, yielding us compensation of about 45¢ on the dollar, which is about average for cases of this kind and which was something more than we expected to get from the Poles.

Over the years, the U.S. has been very generous in adjusting repayment terms. We have liquidated portions of the debt by having the Poles assume local currency payments to the numerous American pensioners who have returned to Poland as their country of origin. We have also used balances to finance joint research projects, particularly in the field of agriculture, and we made a gift of $2.17 million to a children's hospital in Cracow. Greatly expanded U.S.–Polish trade, which for the period January-August 1976 ran at a rate of $421.66 million in U.S. exports, against $212.2 million in U.S. imports from Poland, is being financed by a combination of Export-Import (Exim) Bank and commercial credits.

A DRAMATIC VISIT

Vice-President Nixon visited Warsaw on August 2–5, 1959, after his Soviet trip. His visit presented in an encapsulated form a visual and written record of the state of U.S.–Polish relations as they then were.

A few days before Nixon's arrival, I was summoned personally by Foreign Minister Rapacki to receive a protest, and a request to furnish an explanation, regarding a presidential proclamation which had just been issued in Washington deploring the state of the European "captive nations" living under Communist rule. Rapacki told me that he and his colleagues felt that the proclamation would render Nixon's visit useless. In the absence of advance notice and instructions, I merely replied that the proclamation reflected the views strongly held by certain members of our Congress and that the president had been enjoined to issue it by congressional resolution, as he had done in past years. Rapacki then said the Polish government held to its previously expressed view, but the Soviets had urged it to go forward with the visit.

I sent Frank Siscoe, the embassy's extremely able counselor, to Moscow to brief Nixon on the plane trip to Warsaw. At the airport disembarkment in Warsaw, I had a few words with Siscoe who reported that Nixon was tired and despondent, since he felt he had not done well in Moscow. What happened next was so unanticipated as almost to pass for a miracle.

August 2 was a Sunday, and in announcing Nixon's arrival the local papers failed to mention the airport where he would land. We ourselves were only informed in the morning that it would be the military airport at Babice instead of the commercial one nearer town. I thought it would be a good idea to flash news of the place and time to the Voice of America and to RFE, who were standing by for the visit. When my wife and I left for the airport about an hour and a half before arrival time, the militia were beginning to line the streets, thus publicly revealing the route of passage through the city.

The cortege that was arranged for the trip into town was a modest one. Mr. Nixon was placed in the first open car with Oskar Lange, a former economics professor at the University of Chicago who had the rank of vice-president as a member of the Polish Council of State. Mrs. Nixon and my wife followed in the second car with Mrs. Lange, while I was placed in the third car with Deputy Foreign Minister Winiewicz.

Outside the security gates we found that a new world had come to life. Although the airport was some ten miles from Warsaw there were clusters of cheering people by the roadside. The groups became crowds as we entered the city. The cheering was not boisterous but of a friendly, welcoming kind, obviously meant to honor the United States. So many flowers were thrown into Mrs. Nixon's car that it had to be stopped to remove them as an encumbrance. As the demonstration, orderly though it was, took on a mass character which involved some three to four hundred thousand people, the looks of the accompanying Polish officials became grimmer and grimmer. Abe Rosenthal wrote a vivid and moving account of the welcome for the *New York Times* which should then have won him the Pulitzer Prize, to be bestowed on him a year later when he was expelled for psychoanalyzing Gomulka as a candidate for an asylum.

That evening I had the Nixon delegation to dinner to brief them on the next day's talk with Gomulka. They included Dr. Milton Eisenhower, Admiral Hyman G. Rickover (who had been born near Warsaw), Professor William Y. Elliott of Harvard, USIA Director George Allen, who had formerly been my chief as ambassador in Belgrade, and Assistant Secretary Foy Kohler from the Department of State. All of them stars in their own right, some of them undertook to advise the vice-president to be tough and to stand up to Gomulka. Mr. Nixon, by then greatly restored by his public welcome, told them brusquely to shut up and, turning to me, asked what I had. I said that the Foreign Ministry had not been very communicative but I thought we were in luck, because that morning the party paper *Trybuna Ludu* had carried a long commentary on the visit. I explained to him how Communist decisions are made and promulgated, surmising that the policies outlined in some detail in the article had been carefully considered and approved by the Polish Politburo. Summing them up briefly, I gave Mr. Nixon some notes which I asked him to read that evening, since I was sure the commentary set forth the Polish case, as proved to be exactly so the following morning.

The meeting of August 3 took place in the Mysliwiecki Palace where I periodically held my talks with the Communist Chinese ambassador, and where the vice-presi-

dent and Mrs. Nixon had been lodged (with full knowledge of some of the palace's security shortcomings). On
the U.S. side were the vice-president, Dr. Eisenhower,
Ambassador Allen, Mr. Kohler, and myself, with our
interpreter. Gomulka headed the Polish group which
included Prime Minister Cyrankiewicz, Foreign Minister
Rapacki, and Deputy Foreign Minister Winiewicz. Later
a veil of secrecy was contrived to impart mystery to the
meeting, the main results of which were in fact to give
us a reading on Gomulka, and for each side to confirm
the usefulness of strengthening relations for their separate purposes, in spite of deep ideological and political
differences. The meeting also illustrated the debating
skills of the two principals who at that time were at the
height of their powers.

Gomulka opened the session with a sharp attack on the
congressional resolution commemorating Captive Nations Week which President Eisenhower had proclaimed
a few days before. He asked whether Nixon considered
the Polish leaders on the other side of the table as representatives of an enslaved nation or of the Polish people.
He said he recognized that the proclamation stemmed
from domestic politics and the views of minority elements. Nixon answered that Congress was reflecting the
opinions of substantial groups of U.S. citizens that the
governments of their countries of origin did not represent the expressed will of the peoples. He said that the
president had not sought the resolution and he (Nixon)
disclaimed any attempt on the part of the U.S. to interfere in Poland's affairs.

Gomulka complained bitterly about U.S. official support of RFE, whose crude and insulting propaganda ema-
nating from West Germany was, he said, symptomatic of

Adenauer's opinions. Nixon parried with a reference to Communist incitement of mob attacks on himself and his wife during their visit to Venezuela. When Nixon thanked the Poles for the welcome he had received on his arrival, Gomulka denounced the *New York Times* (viz., Abe Rosenthal's article) for reporting that the popular reception constituted a demonstration against the Polish government.

Differences over Germany were next discussed. Gomulka deplored NATO rearmament of West Germany and the U.S. and British refusal to recognize de facto Poland's western boundaries, as General De Gaulle had done. There could be no change of existing boundaries except by war. Since Adenauer envisaged German reunification by the absorption of East Germany, two Germanys must continue to exist and, according to Gomulka, even the British and the French acknowledged this openly.

Nixon replied that the reason for West German rearmament was that West Germany had become an integral part of Europe and thus came under the control of the European community. As to German aggression against Poland, the U.S. would oppose it in the same way it had countered the British and French aggression against a power (Egypt) which had been fairly unfriendly to the U.S. Nixon pled for peaceful German reunification in order to avoid a later explosion in the heart of Europe.

Nixon asked me to state our position on the nationalization negotiations. Gomulka said that our claims were unrealistically high and he denounced our withholding of further credits, pending a settlement, as "interfering in Poland's internal affairs" by making it impossible for the government to draw up plans for economic development. Nixon thereupon delivered a stern lecture on congressional insistence on the protection of U.S. interests.

In discussing the general problem of allied consultation, Nixon discretely invited Gomulka to say something about his personal experience in dealing with Khrushchev. As expected, Gomulka praised his Soviet counterpart as a generous and understanding man. When Nixon asked whether Khrushchev might be disturbed by the improvement in U.S.–Polish relations, Gomulka replied, "No, surely not," adding, "It is none of his business."

As the talk was drawing to a close, Gomulka apparently felt the need to vent his personal feelings about the Germans, which he did with a vehemence that became embarrassing. Nixon adroitly turned him aside by asking whether he had ever met President Eisenhower. When Gomulka said he hoped he would have the opportunity some day, Nixon said he was sure Gomulka would find it a privilege, since President Eisenhower was a general devoted to peace who had formed a great admiration for the Poles on his visit to Warsaw just after the last war.

A STOLEN GLIMPSE

The success we achieved with the Nixon visit produced some negative results as well, since the demonstration celebrating Nixon's arrival scared the living daylights out of the Polish Communist leaders. For one thing it taught them that they could not rely on the Polish people under all conditions and it provoked an immediate conscious effort to limit Western, and especially American, influence. At about that time we had been discussing cultural exchange programs and an arrangement whereby the U.S. would subsidize the importation of American books and periodicals. Now the authorities who had been previously cooperative suddenly froze up. The official Polish reaction seemed to have been adopted for the protection of the Communist regime, whether or not the Soviets had helped instigate it.

By way of illustrating how all-pervasive Russian influence can be, I fall back on an account of what it was like to live in Poland under the partition which ended only after the First World War. Antoni Slonimski, Poland's foremost poet and wit who died in his eighties in the summer of 1976, used to relate that the Poles in Austria had it best, since they provided the empire with its finance ministers; conditions were at their worst in Germany, which was determined to stamp out Polish culture; whereas in the Duchy of Warsaw, the Poles shared the fate of the Russians, which in turn depended upon whether a good or a bad tsar was on the throne.

In 1960, pressures began to intensify in the Soviet Union and be felt in Poland. The aborted Eisenhower–Khrushchev–De Gaulle–Macmillan summit of May 1960 produced a cooling off in our official contacts, although the Poles had the good manners to stand aloof from Soviet attacks on the president. The Sino-Soviet controversy was brewing and came to a head at the November-December 1960 world Communist party meeting in Moscow. The dispute finally forced the Poles to come down on the Soviet side despite reports, which the Poles did not discourage at the time, that the Chinese had given them moral backing in their 1956 confrontation with the Soviets. The regime accordingly had less leeway to develop ties with the U.S., although it found it to its advantage to settle the American nationalizatin claims in the summer of 1960.

The year 1961 brought even greater strains, starting

with the U.S. expedition against Cuba. For the first time we were subjected to organized local demonstrations, which, however, were kept under reasonable control. Emanations from President Kennedy's ill-fated meeting with Khrushchev in Vienna in June filtered back to Poland in the form of Soviet-inspired reports drawing discreditable comparisons. Tensions arriving from the mass movement of escapees from East Germany through Berlin caused great uneasiness in Warsaw. On July 6 I reported to Washington the information given me by a Polish editor, in whom we had confidence, that the East Germans would surprise the world shortly by imposing physical restraints and obstacles to prevent further escapes. A later official enquiry established this to be the first and only advance notice we had of the erection of the Berlin Wall. On August 11, two days before the wall went up, Foreign Minister Rapacki, who was absent from the city, passed me a personal message asking that we refrain from "faits accomplis" which might complicate the Berlin situation.

Since 1956 Poland had sought to win recognition as a Soviet ally and commonwealth member which enjoyed a fair amount of independence. The sophistication of Polish actions, in contrast with the heavy-handed allegiance paid to the Soviet Union by its other satellites, made this appear to be so. A certain amount of sophistry was needed on the part of all concerned—the Poles, the Soviets, and the West—to make appearances conform with reality. During the tense years of 1961 and 1962 the illusion was put under a strain by the Poles' more obvious subservience to Soviet world policy and by a retreat from the liberal domestic practices introduced in 1956. This view of things was brought to the attention of both the

U.S. and Polish governments in a way that I would have preferred to have happened otherwise.

As of possible use to the new Kennedy administration, in January 1961 I submitted in writing "An Examination of U.S. Policy Toward Poland During the Past Four Years." It is a matter of history that later in the year a copy of this report was furnished to the Polish authorities by a second secretary of our embassy who had been entrapped by the secret police. (Because the dispatch was marked "SECRET" the culprit was sentenced in federal court to thirty years' imprisonment, a term which seemed excessive to myself and to the district attorney who later helped to have it reduced to ten years, leading to the convicted man's eventual release on probation after four years.) In Warsaw, in the meantime, before I became aware of the theft, I noticed receiving quizzical glances, not wholly unfriendly, from high Polish officials at diplomatic receptions. In my dispatch I had written (in standard departmentalese) as follows:

> U.S. and Western policy as a whole has not led to the more liberal evolution in Poland which could have been expected in late 1956 and early 1957. On the other hand it has probably retarded and restricted the retrogressions which have occurred. The beneficial interest of the West has been appreciated by the regime as an asset to be utilized; it is recognized that its continuance depends on adherence to certain standards of comportment. . . .
>
> Viewing the scene from Warsaw as dispassionately as possible, we feel that the U.S. is frequently being charged slightly more than the traffic should bear. Although Poland is a small country and not the chief transgressor, we should continue to exercise vigilance in disbursing generosity. It is probably beyond our immediate capability to

halt the envelopment of the Polish nation by subtler communist forms and pressures than those employed in the early post-war years. Taken as a whole, however, Poland's proven identity, its sympathy and respect for the United States can be kept amenable to American influence by realistic and adaptable courses of action.

Chapter VII

Warsaw—The Chinese Talks

A New Mission

SINCE August 1, 1955, the United States had carried on talks with Communist China through ambassadors of the two countries who met periodically in Geneva. The talks were broken off in 1957 and, when they were resumed in 1958, the task was assigned to the U.S. and Chinese ambassadors serving in Warsaw. Thus, from September 1958 until November 1961 when I left Warsaw, I took on the additional function of negotiating with the Chinese Communists.

However difficult discussions with the Russians may be, they are usually perceived by both sides as having specific ends in view which allow for some possibility for agreement. I found this not to be the case with the Chinese, who committed themselves to dogmatic and fixed positions which were nonnegotiable. They rarely, if ever, changed these positions, letting them stand until they were obsolete, at which time they would substitute others equally nonnegotiable.

I limit these observations solely to my Warsaw experience with the Chinese. Their attitude may have changed since the deaths of Mao Tse-tung and Chou En-lai. I nevertheless consider them fully capable of reverting to their earlier style.

My involvement began with the outbreak of the 1958 crisis over the Taiwan Straits. With its threat of Soviet intervention, for a few weeks in September of that year that crisis produced tensions as serious as any which had come to a head up to that time, including those generated by Berlin.

The 1958 confrontation was provoked by the Chinese, apparently in reaction to the impasse that had been reached in the series of talks which by then had been going on between us and the Chinese for some years. Historians have described in great detail these different sets of discussions which started as far back as the 1946 Marshall mission to China, and which covered the Panmunjom Korean truce discussions and ended with the 1954 Geneva political conference on the Far East. At that conference the pattern was set for the United States–Chinese ambassadorial talks which formally opened in the summer of 1955. Certain residual trends from that period helped shape the situation we faced in 1958.

The Chinese Communists deeply resented our attitude toward them after their takeover of the mainland in 1949. Indeed, fairly good personal relations developed between officials of both sides during the 1946 Marshall mission. Our common cause against the Japanese was taken for granted and our military contributions to victory in World War II were perhaps acknowledged less grudgingly by the Chinese than by the Soviets. The Chinese Communists expected their rout of Chiang Kai-shek to be accepted simply as an objective fact; there is evidence that after their capture of Shanghai they even hoped, and were prepared, to establish formal relations with the United States. What turned their leaders against us was the violence of U.S. official reaction to our "loss of China," and the stern measures of retaliation and discrimination which we imposed on the new Chinese regime.

The motives of the respective sides impelling each toward contact with the other have varied at different times. The conservative Republican leadership of the first Eisenhower administration would have liked, ideally, to quarantine the new China from the non-Communist world, but realities could not be ignored. There was the matter of winding down the Korean War, which was linked with the ever-sensitive issue of the return of American prisoners. The Chinese were naturally looking for any kind of forum in which they could press their claim to widen international acceptance.

Despite United States opposition, such acceptance was bound to come with the growing need of many states to protect their interests. The British stake in Hong Kong and the Leased Territories led them to agree to a less than satisfactory form of mutual recognition. The lesser Asian countries understandably sought early accommodation with their giant neighbor, while the Soviet Union actually sponsored Chinese membership in world organizations. Curiously enough, it was Soviet insistence that the Chinese be included in the 1955 United States–Soviet Union summit meeting in Geneva that made the idea of bilateral United States–Chinese talks a more attractive alternative in our eyes.

THE FIRST PHASE

United States–Chinese preparatory talks were held more or less parallel with the summit during August 1955, with each side revealing in public statements the subjects it proposed for negotiation. The United States originally suggested only two topics: the repatriation of citizens of the respective parties and declarations on the renunciation of the use of force in the Taiwan Straits. The Chinese list was more ambitious: the withdrawal of United States forces from Taiwan, the development of trade and cultural relations, a meeting of the United States and Chinese foreign ministers, U.N. membership for the Chinese People's Republic, as well as the eventual establishment of diplomatic relations with the United States. Keeping in mind its formal ties with Nationalist China, the United States backed away from agreements which would call for or imply recognition of Communist China. The latter's purpose was naturally the reverse, namely, to use the talks to seek equal standing with the United States in world affairs.

Lengthy dispute over an agenda was avoided in an early understanding that the talks would first address themselves to the repatriation of particular citizens in each country and then "to certain other practical matters now at issue between both sides."

The return of citizens, which in the case of the United States meant Americans held captive by the Chinese, was the subject of most immediate importance to us when the ambassadorial talks opened in Geneva on August 1, 1955. The Chinese, like the Russians at the end of World War II, did not scruple to use prisoners as political pawns and they deliberately rationed their releases of our citizens as a way of keeping our interest in negotiation alive. In fact, on the day before the opening of the talks, the Chinese gained credit with the announcement that they were freeing eleven American airmen who had been imprisoned in November 1954.

So critical was the repatriation issue to the launching of the talks that both sides hastened to reach accord on it at an early stage. On September 6, 1955, the Chinese released another installment of twelve Americans. On September 10 the two sides concluded and promulgated an "Agreed Announcement," the first and only one to be produced during the long history of the talks.

The Agreed Announcement contained parallel declarations reading as follows:

> The United States [the People's Republic of China] recognizes that Chinese in the United States who desire to return to the People's Republic of China [Americans in the People's Republic of China who desire to return to the United States] are entitled to do so and declares that it has adopted and will further adopt appropriate measures so that they can expeditiously exercise their right to return.

It may be asked why the Chinese were able to evade the agreement shortly after its announcement by claiming that it did not apply to Americans in jail who had been convicted of crimes against the Chinese state. The reason was not negligence on our side but the necessity for us to find a formula which would preclude the Chinese Communists from exercising jurisdiction over all Chinese in the United States, and especially those who were citizens of the National Republic of China.

The agreement broke down over the refusal of the

Communists to release so-called American criminals. While bad faith was at the bottom of the Chinese decision, the United States tried in 1955 to establish a kind of equivalence of treatment which might benefit our prisoners in Chinese hands. At the risk of offending the Nationalists we offered to free all Chinese serving sentences in the United States for any type of crime, provided they declared their intention to depart for the Chinese People's Republic. It appears that one convicted murderer applied, hardly sufficient incentive to the Communists, who cared too little about their people as individuals to order a general release of Americans in China.

The breakdown of this first and only agreement undermined the whole fabric of this, the opening set of negotiations. Originally we had stated that we would not pass on to the discussion of other subjects until work on the first agenda item, repatriation, had been successfully completed. Because the Chinese vaguely indicated they might review or reduce sentences, we did not wish to assume the onus of breaking off the talks and so we proposed taking up the renunciation of the use of force in the Taiwan Straits, the only other matter of real interest to us.

As the two parties went down the list of subjects mooted for discussion, the Chinese emphasized those which would win them a degree of implied recognition, such as the relaxation of trade restrictions, reciprocal visits of newsmen, a meeting of foreign ministers, etc. The respective positions taken on all these subjects were so diametrically opposed that a virtual standstill had been reached in December 1957, the time when the "United States representative," Ambassador U. Alexis Johnson, had to leave for his new post as ambassador to Thailand.

In a certain sense the United States welcomed this chance to deemphasize the so-far futile series of negotiations. We accordingly proposed that the talks be continued at a lower level of representation and that Ambassador Johnson be succeeded by his principal assistant, Edwin Martin, who held the rank of first secretary. The Chinese angrily rejected this suggestion, with the result that the talks remained in abeyance for nine months until September 1958.

Summing up this first phase, the United States, except for its inability to free all prisoners, had cause to be relatively satisfied with the way it had protected and even enhanced its standing in the talks to date. As a result, the United States had won credit for conciliation through its willingness to negotiate with the Chinese Communists: in the battle of press statements and leaks which reflected more or less accurately the arguments of the respective sides, the United States had come through as the more patient and reasonable party; our claim that the Chinese had reneged on the repatriation agreement seemed plausible on humanitarian and legal grounds; the military situation in the straits had been kept under control; and finally, the Eisenhower administration had successfully defended Nationalist Chinese interests and its own ties with the so-called China lobby at home. In short, the pressures from which the talks originated had temporarily relaxed.

SUSPENSION OF TALKS—AND CHINESE THREATS

The Chinese Communists on the other hand seemed to be far from happy with the course of events. They had failed to win any practical concessions from the United

States or advance their campaign for greater recognition. They angrily denounced the United States suggestion to continue the talks at a lower level as an act of sabotage. Having had no reply to a letter which they had addressed to the United States government in March 1958, Peking issued a long statement on the following June 30, with an ultimatum that they would consider that the United States had decided to break off the talks if within fifteen days it had not resumed them with a designated ambassadorial representative.

In a press conference on July 1, Secretary Dulles replied that the United States intended to continue the talks by every available means and indicated that a memorandum was being sent to the Chinese proposing a shift to Warsaw. While denouncing the United States again, the Chinese replied publicly that a few days' delay would not be objectionable. After the date of the ultimatum had expired, the State Department instructed Edwin Martin, who was serving in London as first secretary of the embassy, to address a letter to Ambassador Wang Ping-nan in Warsaw informing him that the United States ambassador in Warsaw, namely myself, had been appointed to continue the talks in the capacity of "U.S. representative."

Since no acknowledgement of the letter was received from either Peking or Wang, I was directed to approach the Chinese Embassy in Warsaw on August 4 to arrange a meeting for August 7. Our embassy was informed that the matter had been referred to Peking.

From this point onward, and for the next few weeks, the drama shifted to the world scene. The state of play became considerably rougher, with the Chinese laying down a blockade of the offshore islands and threatening to take them over by military means as a possible prelude to attacking Taiwan. At this juncture a resumption of the talks with the United States did not figure prominently in the Chinese Communists' plans.

So as not to perpetuate any illusions which may be held on the subject, it is just as well to state here that the talks, when they were eventually resumed with my appointment to serve as "U.S. representative," played a largely peripheral and incidental role in this particular crisis. The late Kenneth Young in his book *Negotiating with the Chinese Communists,*[1] professes not to have revealed any secret information in violation of the agreement between the Chinese and ourselves to preserve the confidential nature of the talks. (In fact, the Chinese sometimes, albeit rarely, flagrantly disregarded this rule.) As a high official in the Far Eastern Bureau of the Department of State, Kenneth Young was undoubtedly privy to the whole series of talks. His assertion that his detailed account observes the injunction of secrecy is nevertheless substantially correct. The paradox, if any, can be explained by the fact that many of the important statements of position put forth by each side during the 1958 summer crisis were contained in public declarations issued outside, and usually in advance, of each meeting.

During the month of August the Chinese certainly pursued their ends by means other than negotiation, failing even to mention the desirability of resuming the talks. They chose instead to mount a strident military-psychological campaign against the United States which was reinforced by aggressive military operations against

---

[1]Kenneth T. Young, *Negotiating with the Chinese Communists* (New York: McGraw-Hill Book Company, 1968).

the offshore islands, and, more menacingly, by hints, doubtless orchestrated with Moscow, of possible Soviet support.

Here I shall step back to recapitulate briefly the events that led to my direct involvement. Perspective depends to some extent upon personal interpretation.

On August 23 the Chinese Communists commenced a blockade of the offshore islands by artillery and air bombardment. The United States added two carriers to its Pacific fleet. On September 4 the Chinese imposed a twelve-mile interdiction zone around the islands. The United States announced that it would convoy supply ships up to the three-mile territorial limit.

In a press conference on September 4, Secretary Dulles referred to past United States efforts to achieve a negotiated settlement but stated that the United States would not avoid the use of force if driven to it in this instance.

On September 5 Moscow indicated that retaliatory blockades against United States aggression might not be confined to the straits, stating that the USSR would not remain inactive nor simply quietly watch events.

On September 6 the State Department informed me urgently that a Chinese broadcast proposed a resumption of the talks, thus breaking a month of silence on this subject. The White House took due note, expressing the hope that the Chinese were responding to Dulles's statements of September 4.

On September 7 Khrushchev, in a long letter addressed to President Eisenhower, declared that the USSR would regard an attack on an ally as an attack on itself. He did not specifically support, however, the current Chinese military actions in the straits. President Eisenhower replied publicly that he would welcome it if the USSR would concern itself with the current threat to peace.

The State Department telegraphed me that on September 8 Chairman Mao took the unusual step of intervening personally in the crisis with a statement that he was hopeful the talks would soon be held in Warsaw.

AMERICAN INITIATIVES ARE DECISIVE

The crisis buildup put a greater strain on the United States than on the Communists, as the latter had doubtless planned. Although the Nationalists still enjoyed recognition from more U.N. members than the People's Republic, the widely based anti-Chiang Kai-shek publicity campaign gained strength by being linked in this instance with Dulles's presumed predilection for diplomatic brinkmanship. Furthermore, there was uncertainty, even in professional military circles, about the Nationalists' ability to resist a Communist assault in the straits. Pressures on the United States to make concessions were intense and bore in upon the administration from our allies, from congressional quarters, and especially from the influential American Eastern press.

Although the president and Secretary Dulles faced up to such criticism with calm and firmness, they saw obvious advantage in seizing an opening which seemed to assure them at least a partial victory in getting negotiations started. For their part, the Communists doubtless felt the heat in risking a direct challenge to American air and sea power and they apparently concluded that the crisis pressures had cleared the way for their preferred tactic of both talking and fighting.

Secretary Dulles, in a press conference on September 9, expressed optimism that there should be "quite a lot to negotiate," and even suggested that the scope of the talks be broadened to achieve constructive results. He said he hoped at least for a *modus vivendi* in the straits, or a cease fire. In a TV broadcast on September 11 the president reported to the nation on the steps the United States had taken to avert the grave danger to peace. He ended with the thought that if the talks failed, the U.N. might be able to exert its influence.

Both the president and Secretary Dulles included an announcement that I, as the United States ambassador in Warsaw, had been instructed on September 9 to inform the Chinese ambassador that we were ready to open talks in that city at the ambassadorial level. Having failed to communicate with me for over a month, Wang, doubtless with the aim of embarrassing us, replied on September 12 that he was ready to meet with me at his embassy on the next day.

THE "U.S. REPRESENTATIVE" ARRANGES A MEETING SITE

Wang's maneuver coincided with a debate then in progress in Washington about the location of the talks. I had suggested that they be held alternately in the respective embassies. The Department of State rejected this on the ground that it would imply an unsuitable form of recognition. In the meantime the Swiss, in a gesture reflecting their sincere concern with the gravity of the crisis, offered their embassy premises. When I suggested to Wang that we jointly approach the Swiss, he proposed instead that we meet in our respective embassies by rotation and that, failing this, we request accommodations from the Polish Foreign Office.

The Poles, who had not been unaware of what was going on, then came forward with the offer of a small palace in the main city park. We and the Chinese accepted this as a last alternative, both of us thereby paying a price which affected the secret character of the talks.

It was obvious that once we had arranged to hold the talks outside of our respective embassies, over which we had nominal security control, we were inviting participation by third (Polish) and presumably fourth (Soviet) parties. Soon after the talks began, we had reports that our conversations were being picked up by local radio listeners, as had happened in 1952 when Ambassador Kennan's dictation to his secretary in Moscow was broadcast by the transmitter concealed in his sitting room. In any event, at one of our sessions in the palace the electronic system became confused with an audible playback which caused the American delegation mild amusement, whereas the Chinese chose to listen in imperturbable silence.

Since Soviet—Chinese relations were comparatively good in 1958, the Chinese perhaps initially acceded to this form of leakage as a way of passing information to the Soviets in order to allay suspicion. The United States derived no corresponding benefit from this practice, since it inhibited confidential communication. On exceptional occasions we arranged private meetings with the Chinese in our respective embassies, but the fact that the Warsaw talks continued to be held in the insecure building furnished by the Poles helped reduce them to secondary and mainly routine importance.

After all was said and done, the first meeting of the ambassadors was set for September 15. The world press, which wished to treat the event as a sensation, descended on Warsaw in full force a couple of days in advance and started badgering the United States and Chinese delegations, as well as the Polish Foreign Office, for news. I was in the fortunate but somewhat uncertain position of being without instructions. I had not been called to Washington for consultation but was provided with the services of Ralph Clough, an exceedingly able Chinese language officer who had seen service in China before the 1949 break and was then head of the China Desk in the State Department.

Clough arrived from his post in Bern on September 14 about the same time as our telegraphic instructions. Both of us were greatly reassured by what Washington had sent us. The keynote of our presentation was to stress the need for an immediate cease fire between the Chinese and Taiwanese, and to keep hostilities from spreading. We were to counter Wang's expected accusations with a prepared statement of our position; thereafter we would follow up with a series of questions and cross-questions to try to find out what might be new or significant in the Chinese position. The State Department wished the discussion to be as nonpolemical as possible, and had no desire to overplay the theatrics of the situation.

On September 15 at 3:00 P.M. the two delegations met at the Mysliwiecki Palace, in the city park. The United States group of four arrived first and was taken by the Polish chief of protocol to an apartment in the left wing adorned with a bar provided by the Poles in order, so they informed us, to enable us to "entertain our Chinese friends." Wang's delegation was escorted to a corresponding apartment to the right of the main entrance. The protocol chief then invited the two groups to convene in the central salon. He performed the introductions which Wang and myself acknowledged by formal bows. We then took our places after thanking the protocol chief.

The arrangements offered by the Poles were practical as well as elegant. The four tables, each about twelve feet long, had been placed to form a square with the sides separating the delegations, who sat opposite each other. The two delegation heads were in the middle, flanked on either side by their adviser and interpreter. In addition, each delegation had a reporter or note taker. No agreed minutes were kept, but the interpreters and advisers frequently intervened to correct each other in a spirit of more friendly cooperation than sometimes prevailed between the principals.

The accepted role was that the opening statement would alternate at each meeting, but I soon found out that Wang was always intent on having the last word. Each session formally ended when one of the principals, after declaring he had nothing more to say, then proposed a date for the next meeting. Wang, however, indulged in an infantile habit of prolonging the discussion with trivial remarks, thus pressing his adversary, in the name of reason, to conclude his end of the dialogue. On one occasion Wang asked that the meeting end at a certain hour since he had to greet his foreign minister at the airport. I seized upon this as the one and only chance I had to have the last word. (Ambassador Johnson, my predecessor in the talks, told me that he had profited from a similar opportunity.)

As a matter of fact, the American delegates who

successively dealt with Wang found him quite tolerable. At the time of the Marshall mission to China in 1946 he had served as liaison officer between the American and Chinese groups and had made friends with several Americans of whom he spoke warmly, including the late Walter Robertson who eventually became assistant secretary of state and had charge of the Warsaw talks at the Washington end. While reciprocating his regard for Wang, Robertson gave me a firm order not to walk out of any meeting, as Ambassador Arthur Dean had done at the Panmunjom truce negotiations in 1955 (with the vain threat that he would only return when he had received an apology from the Chinese). On the contrary, I was to regard myself as authorized to employ any suitable alternative, including the use of physical violence on Wang, Robertson added jovially. In practice, the language in our Warsaw talks only rarely became indignant, and we had a tacit agreement that each of us would refrain from attacks upon the other's head of government. In debate Wang was not a man to trifle with, since he was armed with the memory and experience of all the previous negotiations.

Wang Ping-nan was an old revolutionary who in pre-Hitler days had worked with the World League Against Colonialism in Berlin where he met his first wife, reportedly a German baroness. Known in China as a Chou En-lai man, he disappeared from sight in 1964 but resurfaced in 1975 to serve as an escort for distinguished foreign guests. His future, of course, may again become clouded by Chou En-lai's death.

FIRST MEETINGS

At the first meeting on September 15, 1958, in Warsaw, Wang waived his right as senior ambassador to speak first. Accordingly, the United States led off with our call for a cease fire as an immediate first step. We declared that we recognized the existence of a long and serious dispute over Taiwan and the adjacent islands, and were not demanding that either party abandon its territorial claims at this stage. Our purpose was to reduce and eliminate acts by either side which might be regarded as provocative by the other. Otherwise peace would be threatened by an enlargement of military action. We stressed that the dangers were very real and that our common task was to reduce tensions in the Taiwan Straits.

Replying in a tone more aggrieved than belligerent, Wang insisted that Taiwan's status was a Chinese domestic affair and that the issue of a cease fire with the American and Nationalist occupying forces did not exist. It was China's sacred duty to liberate Matsu and Quemoy. Wang said that should the Nationalists, however, withdraw from the offshore islands on their "own initiative," the Chinese would not pursue them. He stated further that after the "recovery of these islands" the Chinese would strive to liberate Taiwan and the Penghus "by peaceful means, avoiding the use of force for a certain time."

The discussion of the Taiwan dispute in this and subsequent meetings never got beyond the opening statements of the respective sides. China insisted that the United States was occupying Chinese territory and interfering in its internal affairs. Almost every proposal which the Chinese put forward in the talks, whether it dealt with cultural exchanges or trade matters or anything else, was habitually introduced by a call for total withdrawal of United States forces from the area. Within this absolute limit, the Chinese made a pretense of being flexible, for instance, in their stated intention not to harass Nationalist troops evacuating the offshore islands and to suspend the use of force for a "certain time" in liberating Taiwan itself.

The United States was no less arbitrary about essentials, namely, that under its defense treaty with Taiwan it was protecting sovereign territory against Communist attacks. At this particular stage of engagement with the Chinese, the Eisenhower administration was nevertheless under heavy political and military pressures to moderate the crisis. Thus it was willing, even anxious, to negotiate changes affecting the offshore islands which would reduce their importance.

DULLES MAKES OUR LAST PROPOSAL

The USSR meanwhile had no intention of letting the Warsaw talks usurp its role in world affairs, and it weighed in heavily again, first with a denunciatory speech by Foreign Minister Gromyko at the United Nations General Assembly on September 18 and then with a letter from Khrushchev to the president dated September 19 which was so abusive that the original was returned to the Soviet Foreign Office as unacceptable.

In his answer before the General Assembly, Dulles reserved the right to place the dispute before the United Nations should the Warsaw talks fail. Khrushchev's threats were supported by declarations that neither the USSR nor Communist China was frightened by atomic blackmail, and that should the Chinese People's Republic "fall victim to such an attack, the aggressor would receive a rebuff by the same means." The letter somewhat ominously mentioned the Sino-Soviet Treaty of 1950 which obligated each party to respond automatically with all means at its command if the other were attacked.

The Communist Chinese Foreign Minister Chen Yi chimed in with a statement on September 20 that "no force on earth" could stop the Chinese from taking Quemoy and Matsu. He expressed "profound rage" at Dulles's suggestions for a cease fire and for possible submission of the conflict to the United Nations where the People's Republic of China "has been unjustifiably deprived of its rightful place."

As a result of these events, and with the intention of offering a decisive response, the State Department instructed me to put forward a carefully considered proposal at the seventy-eighth Warsaw meeting on September 30. The proposal was written personally by Secretary Dulles.

Cast in the form of a draft "Agreed Announcement," each side would *note* in parallel declarations: (1) that the People's Republic claims that Taiwan and the Penghus are Chinese territory and is determined to possess them by force, and demands that the United States withdraw; (2) that the USSR supports these claims and demands, and has stated that it will abide by its treaty of friendship, alliance, and mutual assistance with the People's Republic, and that it will fulfill its obligations in the event that the United States will not withdraw, thus leaving expulsion as the only recourse; (3) that the United States disputes these claims and is committed to Taiwan's collective defense and that the president has authorized and is prepared to use United States armed forces if appropriate for the defense of Taiwan and the Penghus; (4) thus, that an international dispute exists which threatens peace and security and which ought to be resolved by renunciation of force.

In further parallel declarations, each side would *propose:* (1) the Chinese Communists will suspend hostilities contingent on a reciprocal suspension of operations in defense of Quemoy and Matsu; (2) a solution will be sought by negotiation, mediation, conciliation, arbitration, or judicial settlement; (3) through interim provisional measures, each side will prevent harassments and provocations between the mainland and the islands; such means may include reduction of forces and armaments.

In conclusion, both sides would agree to continue conversations to implement the foregoing.

At the September 30, 1958, meeting Wang rejected the United States proposal summarily, saying it contained nothing new and was merely an effort by the United States to cloak its war preparations. Thus ended the last offer to be made by Dulles and the last specific plan to draw the Chinese into balanced negotiation. On the same day in a Washington press conference, Dulles had mentioned the possibility of some important changes in United States policy should there be some response from the Chinese. That response never came.

We were shortly to learn that the crisis probably reached its highest point of tension during the period September 19–30. Although the world Communist press intensified its campaign of pressure and threats, we found out later that tension had eased sufficiently to permit the top Chinese leaders, including Mao, to make a several-day tour of the Yangtze valley. Meanwhile military reports indicated that the Nationalists were holding their own on the offshore islands and on October 4 Dulles sent a reassuring personal message to Taipei, observing that the Communists seemed fearful of directly involving the United States, that he was optimistic, and that United States flexibility had paid off.

Incidentally, it became quite apparent about this time that Dulles had never liked nor put much faith in the Warsaw talks. He was willing to use them as a lightning rod and a means to build up a conciliatory record should he be forced to go to the United Nations. The talks embarrassed his relations with Chiang and he played them down, once he felt himself out of trouble. During his visit to Taipei late in October he declared on October 25 that perhaps the talks had been of value in establishing a direct channel to Peking, but "it is hard to see useful results." I recalled that this had not been Washington's feeling some six weeks earlier when it had telegraphed me that it was "imperative" to get the talks started by September 15. Since I shared Dulles's relief that the crisis had passed, I felt that due allowance could be made for the colossal vanity of this very complicated man.

The delegation's reporting channel had borne up well during the crisis, assuring an effective exchange with Washington. Immediately after each meeting, we would telegraph a flash summary of the high points. This was followed by the full transcript. Then, later in the evening or the next morning, we would telegraph our comments and recommendations.

We in Warsaw shared Dulles's view that indeed we had been fairly flexible, albeit under some compulsion from world opinion, and we were somewhat surprised that the Chinese had not responded in any way. Some of the piecemeal concessions we had put forward providing for a thinning out of forces and demilitarization of areas might, if accepted, have weakened our military position to some extent, or at least have had a demoralizing effect on the Nationalists.

While more subtle play might have brought the Communists some advantage, they faced two kinds of dilemma. Acceptance of our proposals would have implied recognition of our right to remain on Taiwan. A greater danger for them, however, was the growth of the idea that there should be "two Chinas" which should live in peace with each other. In October the Communists launched an intensive propaganda campaign accusing the United States of "hatching a plot to create two Chinas." These charges flowed over into our meetings where we found them easy to handle. I was able to disavow our guilt by reminding Wang that the United States recognized the Nationalists as the sole representative of China. This reply infuriated him all the more, but it soon became clear that the Chinese could live more comfortably with our position than with the belief that was gaining currency among many United Nations members that a "two-China policy" was probably the best for peace. The Communists must have been dismayed to learn that even the Indians, who had been their consistent supporters, shared this belief.

By the end of September, Nationalist transports and barges, escorted by small United States naval craft up to the three-mile limit, were getting through to the offshore islands with little difficulty with supplies and ammunition. Nationalist planes equipped with United States Sidewinder heat-homing rockets were knocking the Communists out of the skies. In our Warsaw meetings

Wang protested our violation of the twelve-mile territorial limit (which we, of course, did not recognize) and denounced the Sidewinder as a "cruel and unusual weapon" signifying an extension of United States aggression.

The unmistakable turning point and dénouement of the crisis came with a surprise broadcast address by the Chinese minister of defense on October 6 to his compatriots in Taiwan and the offshore islands. He announced that out of "humanitarian considerations" the bombardment of the islands would cease for seven days and that the Nationalists could send supplies to the islands, provided there was no United States escort. The statement said the issue between the United States and China was the United States invasion and occupation of Taiwan and the straits; this should be settled in the Warsaw negotiations. Speaking to his "compatriots" on the islands, the minister declared that China's internal problems should be negotiated "between you and us."

The purpose of the maneuver was obviously to divide the Nationalists from the United States by holding out the prospect of a cease fire while inviting them to try their luck with a separate deal. The minister emphasized that the Communists' break in the bombardment bore no relation to the American-proposed cease fire, and should not be construed as a sign of weakness. During his previously mentioned visit to Taipei in late October, Dulles made his own contribution to the de facto easing of tension by getting Chiang Kai-shek to agree to a communiqué declaring that the chief means of achieving the Nationalist "mission of representing the minds and hearts of the Chinese people is the implementation of Sun Yat-sen's three principles—nationalism, democracy, and sound well-being—*and not necessarily the use of force"* (italics added).

Again it happened that current events were reflected in, but not much influenced by, the contemporary talks in Warsaw. At our meeting on October 10 the American delegation naturally expressed gratification at the October 6 announcement of the bombing halt and we stated we were ready to elaborate mutually satisfactory guarantees to make it permanent. We announced that we were suspending our escorts to the islands (and, in fact, a few days later also withdrew a carrier). Wang angrily repudiated our declared interest, stating that the measure was a unilateral act which had nothing to do with the talks, whose main purpose was to negotiate total withdrawal of United States forces. Although the bombardments were later resumed under a somewhat erratic regimen of bombing on even-numbered days of the month, the back of the military confrontation had been broken.

AT WARSAW, WE TALK OF OTHER THINGS

In summary, the encounter over Taiwan produced a de facto stabilization which was to last some years and was probably not of a kind the Communists would have deliberately planned. Instead of reducing the United States presence in the Far East, they brought upon themselves an increase and entrenchment of United States power somewhat similar to the situation in Korea. When the Sino-Soviet dispute broke out in the open some months later, it became clear that the Chinese had strained the alliance by demanding from the Soviets a too-direct and potentially dangerous form of involvement. Thus they had alienated their most powerful associate and laid the basis for a further triangular relationship between the great powers which was to benefit chiefly the United States. In practice, however, they did profit from our own behavior to the extent that it restrained the Nationalists from adventurous aggressive actions.

As to the temper of the negotiations, it is true that long enmity and inhibitions on both sides (ours being the obsession against recognition) encouraged a pattern of diplomacy by communiqué and declarations. It is nevertheless rather surprising that during this time we never received from the Communists any hint of a private approach of a kind that might have been useful for them to make if only for the sake of obtaining clarifications and better information. It has been remarked that the Chinese have never been particularly strong in diplomatic negotiation, as shown by their experiences in modern times with the British, the Japanese, and more lately the Russians. Certainly they gained nothing from the 1958 crisis over Taiwan.

By the end of the year the Taiwan confrontation had been drained of its drama, leaving the Warsaw talks to pursue a somewhat erratic and certainly less consequential course. The United States felt free to follow a less rigid pattern. Dulles, who possessed toughness, tactical skill, and a lawyer-statesman gift of articulation, was succeeded in 1959 as secretary of state by Christian Herter, who had an easier way of doing business which seemed to conform to President Eisenhower's mood, and that of the American public.

In the new game that followed some former positions were strikingly reversed, with the United States advocating closer contacts with mainland China, while the Communists withdrew into ever-deeper obduracy in ways that appeared puzzling and contradictory.

As was seen more clearly later, China's troubles were beginning to pile up, partly as a result of its frustration over Taiwan. Its freedom of action was becoming increasingly limited by domestic problems resulting from the failure of the Great Leap Forward in industry, as well as by the widening of the split with the Soviets. By the time of Khrushchev's visit to the United States in 1959 a parting of the ways had been reached and the Soviets evoked "the spirit of Camp David" to preempt for themselves the role of peacemaker. Khrushchev spread this impression on the journey he made to Peking ostensibly to celebrate the tenth anniversary of the People's Republic. There he inferred that his hosts' total militancy against imperialism exceeded the Leninist requirement that only wars for national liberation could be justified in Communist eyes.

In Warsaw there was certainly an ample budget of disputes to keep the talks alive. For instance, the Chinese denounced in numbered "serious warnings" United States military actions. These included our supplying the Taiwanese with weapons, especially the modern Sidewinder, and our convoying Taiwanese supply ships up to the three-mile limit off the Chinese coast. Another irritant was the intermittent shelling of the offshore islands, which apparently continues to this day. An issue somewhat more embarrassing to us was President Truman's January 1950 statement ostensibly forswearing United States interest in the politics of Taiwan. We had to explain that the declaration predated the Korean War in which China had been condemned as an aggressor by the United Nations, thus necessitating our current defense of Taiwan. Exclusion from the United Nations was incidentally a grievance the Communists enjoyed exploiting,

[136]

charging the United States with a lack of reality in failing to recognize a nation of (then) six hundred million. Dulles instructed me to reply that we did in fact recognize them—as a "firebrand and disturber of the peace in Asia."

We occasionally chivvied the Chinese about their relations with the Soviets. We were well supplied by the State Department with conflicting statements, and when the Soviets seemed to be less hostile to our cause, we inquired whether the same attitude might soon be reflected in Chinese policy. Wang replied affirmatively to our query whether China subscribed to Khrushchev's disapproval of the use of force but claimed it did not apply to Taiwan since this was a Chinese domestic affair. He said sabotage was the motive of our question.

One matter which the United States pursued with great earnestness, and never failed to bring up in each meeting, was the Communist treatment of the Americans they still held in prison. Since the renewal of the talks in 1958, the number detained varied between five and four, with an occasional release of an American who had served his sentence. It was raised back to five with the arrest in March 1960 of the Roman Catholic bishop James Edward Walsh on grounds of espionage. As mentioned earlier, the United States took the stand that in the September 10, 1955, agreement on the reciprocal repatriation of citizens, we were tricked by the later refusal of the Chinese to return Americans who were held in jail on espionage and subversive charges. We recalled that Wang had volunteered the information to Ambassador Johnson in 1955 that the agreement had been read to those Americans under detention at that time, thus implying they were covered by its terms. We continually pled in the talks for a review of the American cases and possible pardons as steps which would redress injustice and produce a favorable reaction in the United States. I asked friends in the Polish Foreign Office to pass on this view to Wang. Although the Chinese seemed to have treated our prisoners correctly and permitted visits by relatives as well as the dispatch of Care packages through the Red Cross, they were adamant against their accelerated release. In fact, they only freed the last American sometime after Nixon's 1972 visit.

In the more relaxed postcrisis atmosphere, we tried to test Chinese susceptibility to change by offering several affordable gestures of goodwill. Foremost among our initiatives was a proposal to exchange newsmen. Although the subject gave us something to talk about for the better part of a year, the negotiations broke down over the insistent Chinese demand for the unconditional admission of the newsmen they would propose. This we could not accede to because of our laws excluding Communist visitors, but we did explain that a required waiver of objection would almost certainly be granted automatically, possibly on the basis of equal numbers chosen from lists submitted by each side.

It was quite clear in the summer of 1960 that the Chinese had no wish to expose their country's troubles to the view of foreign correspondents. In Warsaw we had nothing new to offer, and in rejecting our exchange proposal in a long public statement issued on September 13, the Chinese foreign minister declared that there was no need to waste time on minor questions as long as the major issue of United States withdrawal from Taiwan remained unsettled. Coming on the heels of our one hundredth meeting on September 9, at which Wang protested the five-year record of futility, we speculated that the Chinese might break off the talks. At the next meeting on October 18, however, Wang seemed only too happy to polemicize over these "minor issues" and we came to the correct conclusion that the Chinese had no intention of terminating the talks, not, at any rate, before the advent of the new United States administration.

A KENNEDY INITIATIVE

In 1961 all of us dealing with Chinese affairs, including the outgoing State Department high command, were eager to help the incoming Kennedy administration reap the benefits of expected change. Although the new administration had imagination and a fresh outlook, it was unfortunate in not being able to put together and present a China program of their own before the Bay of Pigs affair in April when Kennedy openly assumed responsibility for our abortive coup against Castro. The president's credentials to deal with Communism were also blemished by his meeting in Vienna with Khrushchev in June when through inexperience he submitted to unmerciful bullying by the Soviet premier.

Prior to these events, and at the first meeting in Warsaw in March after the president took office, Wang said that his government was waiting with "a great sense of anticipation" for the United States to unveil a new policy to replace the past one which had proved so unrealistic and sterile. As a matter of fact my chief adviser, Ralph Clough, had been recalled to Washington for consultation and returned to Warsaw for the meeting with suggestions for what, the State Department hinted, might be a new form of presentation of the familiar topics of the return of prisoners and the renunciation of the use of force.

Partly under the influence of the extraneous efforts just mentioned, it soon became clear that the same basic impasse remained. Accordingly, the State Department tried to add some new elements to enhance the attraction of our approach to the Chinese. The department developed with great care, but without success, a comprehensive proposal of our own for the exchange of newsmen. Washington also resorted to certain innovations, which seemed to us somewhat ingenuous, such as holding out the possibility of selling wheat on favorable terms and offering Care packages to the Chinese needy. Wang turned these offers aside with dignity, saying that while China was going through difficult times as a new country, it would rely on its own resources to solve its problems. The dialogue frequently became embittered by Peking's public attacks on President Kennedy which seemed intended to promote China's antiimperialist leadership role. Wang echoed these attacks routinely, but gave way when reminded of our tacit agreement to refrain from personal diatribe.

Despite the prevailing inhospitable atmosphere, the administration felt it should assume the responsibility for making an honest and well-considered effort at accommodation. An opening occurred when, after the 105th meeting on June 29, 1961, Wang invited me for coffee and a private talk about Laos. He began by saying that the Pathet Lao attacks would stop if the United States withdrew its advisers and forces. China had a 500-mile frontier with Laos, he said, and "Souvanna Phouma is the only possible head of state." Wang, who was in a cordial mood, then waxed philosophical. If the United States would also withdraw from Taiwan, he said, there could be a peaceful settlement with Chiang. He mentioned that there were already many former Nationalist generals on the mainland and Chiang would be treated honorably and be eligible for "an even higher position." As for the United States, Wang explained, his government "criticized it for its own benefit."

Although Washington thought Wang had only raised Laos in order to fish in troubled waters, it felt that his mood and initiative should be followed up. On Laos, I was instructed to reply that some Americans were being held prisoner and that guarantees, which would be enforceable through the International Control Commission, were needed to assure Laos's independence. As regards contacts between the United States and the People's Republic, I was told to discuss our current problems generally along the following lines.

A realistic and flexible approach should be taken by both sides who should seek step-by-step improvements, no matter how minor. Until now the Chinese had shown only basic hostility toward the United States, demanding total surrender in the present dispute. This attitude had aroused American suspicions and had made us more vigilant. Our newsmen had suggested that reciprocal visits and trial exchanges might be helpful. Dr. Samuel Rosen of New York, who was known for his surgical skill in correcting deafness, had been invited to China but we had been obliged to refuse permission under present conditions. We were willing to consider issuing him a passport if this would relieve the existing impasse. (Incidentally, we learned that one of the Chinese leaders was interested in treatment by Dr. Rosen.)

Finally, I was told to say that the American people were unwilling to turn Taiwan over to the Communists against the people's will. In the meantime we should try to identify common points of interest and make use of even the smallest possibilities to promote cooperation.

I put these points before Wang at a private meeting on August 15, 1961. He seemed quite receptive and said he would get in touch with me shortly. At his later invitation I met with him privately at his embassy on September 1. The atmosphere at this encounter was completely different from the previous occasion. Wang said the international situation had changed considerably and that the latest "provacative moves by the United States must affect our present meeting." He then read from a prepared text.

The dispatch of United States troops to Berlin, he said, had precipitated a new crisis. Was this intended to lead to a European conflict? The United States had increased its forces in South Korea and Okinawa. Current United States policy "went beyond Dulles and further isolated the United States." Kennedy could have changed all this, and what of his electoral professions of peace? He had shown no intention of negotiating. Taiwan remained the chief problem and Wang hoped that the United States would propose constructive steps for withdrawal. According to him, the situation was so tense that we should hold ourselves ready to meet again at short notice.

I said I was shocked by Wang's extraordinary response. He had proposed these private talks, but they would no longer be useful if conducted in this spirit. We sincerely regretted he had rejected our suggestions and our government would have to draw its own conclusions.

Strangely enough, after delivering his written statement, Wang became all smiles and invited our delegation to an elaborate Chinese dinner in the next room. To my very great regret I had to decline, since I was obliged to leave forthwith, on Washington instructions, to greet President Kennedy's sisters who were arriving at the airport on a visit to Warsaw. I departed two days later for an assignment of several years in Washington.

Chapter VIII

Czechoslovak
Reform—The Noblest Try

TO PRAGUE VIA WASHINGTON

FOLLOWING my departure from Warsaw in 1961 after completing slightly more than four years as ambassador, I took up my assignment as an assistant director in the newly created Arms Control and Disarmament Agency (ACDA).

I arrived at a time when President Kennedy interested himself very much in disarmament and I recall his asking Henry Kissinger, then a Harvard professor, to come to Washington to give him a briefing. The session did not go very well because the president became fidgety after an hour of Kissinger's lecturing, and excused himself to keep another appointment. Kissinger said with dismay that he was not even halfway through the subject. He was vaguely promised a return engagement but when he sent through a follow-up inquiry a few weeks later, the reply of the White House staff, which included several of his former associates at Harvard, was notably unenthusiastic.

Service in the Disarmament Agency proved frustrating because decision-making was concentrated in the White House staff and the Departments of State and Defense.

The agency was not represented on the "Presidential Executive Committee" (EXCOMM) which handled the 1962 Cuban missile crisis. The Disarmament Agency did, however, produce useful work in preparing for the treaty banning atmospheric and underwater nuclear tests signed in Moscow in August 1963. After that it became enmired in the question of banning underground tests. During my time, savage memoranda were exchanged between the scientists and military men, each accusing the other of lying regarding the ability to detect underground nuclear explosions. I could not dispute the conclusions of either faction.

My four-year term of service in Washington was considered to be up in 1966. When Secretary Rusk offered me the post of ambassador to Czechoslovakia, I happily accepted and arrived in Prague in August of that year.

POSTWAR TROUBLES

By going to Prague in 1966 I was returning to a setting of frustration and troubled relations in which I had been earlier involved. Even during the war, our dealings with Czechoslovakia had begun to take a rocky course due to our differences with President Beneš who headed the government in exile. Because of the Munich Agreement and Beneš's fear of Germany, disillusionment with Western Europe had induced him to play the Russian card by concluding a new wartime alliance with the Soviet Union, despite the fact that the earlier one signed in 1935 had done his country little good. In addition, Beneš reflected the Pan-Slavic sympathy of the Czechs* with the

---

*Here I am following the internal State Department practice of using the adjective "Czech" to describe the nation and peoples of

Russians (which met sudden death with the events of 1968). When Beneš returned to Czechoslovakia as president again after the war, he seemed to us to make too many political concessions to the Communists who, however, formed the largest party in the country in 1946; with 38 percent of the vote, their leader Gottwald became prime minister.

At the December 1947 meeting of the Council of Foreign Ministers in London, which I mentioned previously, the Czechs had an observer delegation with whom it was my duty to keep in touch. Since we found them to be consistently supporting Soviet policy, I was sent on a brief visit to Prague after the conference. Ambassador Steinhardt was in Washington, but Mrs. Steinhardt asked me to dinner with Jan Masaryk, then foreign minister. He was deeply despondent and when I asked him for an appointment on the following day, he said it would not be worthwhile and instead I should see Clementis, his Communist deputy minister.

The experience was surprising and profitable. A Slovak and a man of charm and intelligence, Clementis suggested that we review together the results of the London conference. He checked off the points where he thought the U.S. was wrong and the Soviets right, and others where he considered the reverse to be true. I found him remarkably objective and flexible in his approach. I was sorry when he was hanged in 1952 for involvement in the so-called Slanský conspiracy. (Slanský was an early party first secretary who was Jewish and had offended Stalin. He was arrested in 1951 with eleven other Jews,

---

Czechoslovakia, except when it is necessary to identify them separately as Czechs and Slovaks.

all of whom plus Clementis, were executed.) As is now well known, our government did its best to save Clementis by transmitting a message from his wife not to return home from his assignment as head of the Czech U.N. delegation in New York.

When I returned to Washington in December 1947, I brought back proof supplied by the Prague embassy's chief intelligence expert that the Communists were drawing up lists of persons to be arrested in a coup reportedly planned to take place within the next few weeks. The prevailing mood in our government was that a Communist takeover was probably inevitable and that our next concern was to limit the danger internationally. The State Department conveyed this view in mid-February in a telegram to the American ambassador in Paris in reply to a proposal that the U.S., the U.K., and France take joint steps, and perhaps action in the U.N., to stop Czechoslovakia's headlong slide into communism.

By that time, however, it was too late. The Communists had presented Beneš with an ultimatum that they be allotted 60 percent of the seats in the cabinet, including the ministry of defense, in addition to interior which they already had. Thinking they could force new elections, the incumbent ministers resigned on February 20, but instead, the Communists took over the vacant positions virtually by an unopposed coup. With the help of street "action committees" the Communists won the elections eventually held in May and assumed complete governmental control. The internal operation had been so well prepared, and was so swift and deft, that there was little evidence of direct Soviet intervention. It was hard to establish a connection with the presence in Prague of Soviet Deputy Foreign Minister Zorin, who came ostensibly to discuss grain shipments; the most visible giveaway was the distribution of newly minted Soviet rifles to Communist street patrols.

Stationed as I was in the department as chief of the Central European Division, for me the spring of 1948 was one of those unfortunate periods of competing crises which I again had to endure in the summer of 1956. The Palestinian question was a paramount issue at the time, and trouble with the Soviets was brewing over Berlin. Immediately after the breakdown of the December 1947 Council of Foreign Ministers meeting in London, the U.S., the U.K., and France decided that in order to put an end to economic chaos in the areas of their authority in Germany, including the western sections of Berlin, they would have to replace the inflated paper money then circulating with a stable, reformed currency. I helped work on a plan with the Treasury and Defense Departments. Foreseeing that we might provoke a Soviet reaction, the Treasury representative and I suggested that the secretary of state, General Marshall, himself sign the staff study. The answer from my bureau was that "the old man is too busy with Palestine to be bothered," with the result that my immediate supervisor and I were the ones to initial final approval for the State Department.

Because of the spreading violence in Palestine, and also because the administration was preoccupied with the Marshall Plan, it was equally difficult to get top priority for study of the question of whether we should or could take decisive steps to prevent a Communist coup in Czechoslovakia. Most probably there was little we could have done. Beneš's postwar policies of Soviet collaboration had undermined our assets in the country and both he and Masaryk were ill and broken men when the crisis

[148]

struck. Masaryk either jumped or was pushed out of a window on the night of March 9, 1948, in Prague, and Beneš yielded the presidency to Gottwald after the Communist electoral triumph in March.

Two historic results flowed from the events of this period. Soviet Marshal Sokolovsky broke up the Allied Control Council in Berlin by walking out on March 20 in protest against our projected introduction of currency reform in that city. Shortly thereafter, the Soviets started pressures which led to a traffic blockade against the Western sectors in Berlin. The Departments of State, Defense, and the Treasury, as well as the Federal Reserve Board, gave full support to our currency action in Berlin. The capture of Czechoslovakia by Communist subversion cast an especially sinister shadow because the nation had been founded in the United States by a World War I refugee government which proclaimed national independence and a state constitution, in Pittsburgh in May 1918. The loss of Czechoslovakia and the threats against the Allied position in Berlin accelerated the foundation of NATO, which came into being on April 4, 1949.

NOVOTNÝ—NO BRIDGE BUILDER

When I was assigned to Prague in August 1966, de-Stalinization had not yet caught up with Czechoslovakia, and Secretary Rusk realized there was little that could be accomplished there. He asked me, however, even at the risk of our appearing naive, to start off by trying to interest the Czechoslovak government in a reasonable and independent approach to the Vietnamese conflict. At that time, of course, dismay over the war was growing ever deeper within the Johnson administration, as illustrated in an incident described to me by the late Teddy Weintal,

Washington reporter for *Newsweek*. The president had told a small gathering of American correspondents that if he could get Prime Minister Kosygin to come to Washington and have him stop the war in Vietnam, he (Johnson) would take Kosygin down to Garfinckel's show window and publicly kiss his ass. Shameful to relate, one of the Americans present later repeated the story before another group which included a Soviet correspondent. The latter pestered his American friends with questions as to what Garfinckel's was and where it was located, apparently attributing some occult significance to mention of the downtown Washington department store.

The U.S. position on Vietnam which we were to ask the Czechs to consider was updated as follows: we were willing to engage in unconditional discussions with Hanoi; we were not seeking the destruction of the North Vietnamese government; we did not oppose reunification of Vietnam but insisted that it come about through free choice, but we could not recognize the rebel National Liberation Front as the sole spokesman for South Vietnam; we would stop the bombing of North Vietnam if we knew there would be reciprocal action from the other side. Our political objectives were limited to supporting resistance to aggression, and we were not attacking communism itself. We pointed out that small nations had a stake in our cause.

While it did credit to our intentions, the experiment met with scant success in the introductory calls I made, first upon Foreign Minister David and then upon President Novotný. At our first meeting on August 29 David spent the better part of a half hour denouncing the United States for its ruthless bombing of Vietnam, for creating great international risks as the principal disturber of world peace, and for its failure to follow the socialist example of both practicing and preaching coexistence. He also complained (with some justice, as will be explained later) about our failure to return the Czech monetary gold looted by the Nazis and then (and still) in our possession. When he paused for a moment I explained that because I understood this was meant to be a courtesy call, I had not brought along a list of our own grievances compiled by the State Department, but with his permission I would ask my counselor who was with me to fetch the list from our embassy which was nearby.

The foreign minister was somewhat taken aback, but we engaged in polite conversation while waiting for my colleague to return. When we resumed our discussion, he listened to our bill of complaints dealing mostly with the harassment of our citizens visiting and resident in Czechoslovakia; in the end he consented to consider carefully, and to pass on to President Novotny, our memorandum on Vietnam which I had been instructed to leave with him.

Two days later when I presented my credentials to President Novotný, he was notably frank if nothing else. He said there was no possibility of changing his government's position on Vietnam and he completely endorsed the stand of the Soviet Union and its associates. He said that Czechoslovakia was not a satellite and had decided independently that this was the right course. He emphatically declared that it was futile to attempt to detach his country from the Soviet Union, its greatest loyal ally. I denied that this was our intention and said our hope was that his government might come up with some new suggestions. Novotný stressed that profound differences separated us and he complained bitterly about our withholding the return of the looted gold, adding as an after-thought that if Czechoslovakia were a great power, he would be tempted to come over and get it. He seemed embarrassed when I asked the interpreter to repeat the translation of this last remark.

To ease matters a little, I asked Novotny what "as a leader" he conceived his country's chief problems to be. Claiming that Czechoslovakia was run by a collective leadership and a democratic government, he defined his main tasks as the rooting out of capitalism and the integration of ideology with overall planning. His chief concern in foreign affairs was to prevent Germany from ever again dominating Czechoslovakia's economic future.

I have furnished the foregoing details to show that by comparison with our experience with the Poles, our relations with the Novotný regime offered a dismal example. His government's attitude was confirmed in a call I made a few days later on the first deputy foreign minister who greeted me by saying that he was busy and had only fifteen minutes which he thought, however, would be enough, since we had little to discuss. He foresaw that I would not have much to do and advised me to spend my time visiting the historical sites of his country which were very beautiful.

I soon came to the conclusion that President Johnson's program of "building bridges" with Eastern Europe was neither for Novotný nor for me. Despite the official freeze, the regime left itself a way out, however, by permitting private visits and exchanges. A Time/Life tour by some fifty leading American industrialists in 1966 was well received and met freely with several ministers as well as State Planner Ota Sik (later to be exiled as a Dubček supporter) in whom the American businessmen detected already strong free-market leanings. The Ford Foundation sent a mission to arrange an exchange of some twenty graduate students each way. The program operated fairly smoothly, but as in the case of all the Communist countries which were eager to gain access to our technology, the problem was to prevent the Czechs from overloading their groups with scientists and engineers, while trying to limit our selections to language specialists and philosophers.

As a consolation during this difficult period we had access to "the brightest and the best" in the contacts we were able to make with the Czech cultural world. This diverse and lively group included writers, journalists, actors, and motion picture producers who were then approaching the peaks of fame and achievement they attained under Dubček. Most of them were registered Communists, a circumstance attributable to the fact that the Czechoslovak party was one of the largest in the world in proportion to the country's population, and thus embraced many types and strains. Superior numbers carried the party to power but its heterodoxy was soon to bring down the well-entrenched Novotný regime. This group generally had a different approach to the United States and thought little about Vietnam as an issue between us. Seeking the stimulus of contact with the West, they harbored a forbidden interest in things American and were well acquainted with the broadcasts of the Voice of America and Radio Free Europe. As a group they were self-confident, articulate, and becoming increasingly influential. Some of the more courageous survived Dubček's downfall and still speak out as dissenters against the present policies of his successor, General Secretary of the party Husak.

[153]

As regards foreign policy, 1966 and 1967, the last years of the Novotný regime, were marked by total negativism. The United States was not the only disfavored nation and several other Western European countries had running disputes with Czechoslovakia. Austria resented the brutal behavior of the Czech guards on its border, but more importantly was pressing a claim of approximately one billion shillings for Czech expropriation of Austrian property after the war. In 1967 the Turks threatened a break if the Czechs failed, within a matter of forty-eight hours, to halt an arms shipment to the Greek Cypriots.

The British, who had an able Czech-speaking scholar as ambassador, enjoyed only mediocre standing because of memories of Munich. Although the French were forgiven these memories because of their shared wartime suffering, their position was largely ornamental. The Canadians and Indians gained little credit for their public display of immunity from American influence. The West Germans won a victory of sorts in their establishment of a small economic office whose staff promptly became the best informed foreigners in Prague. The Czechs welcomed the economic tie but maintained their grievance against the German Federal Republic because of its refusal to repudiate the Munich Agreement *ab initio,* that is, as if it had never legally existed.

Czechoslovakia's outlook on the world was in every respect the Soviet view. It supported the Soviet side in the dispute with China and was the first satellite to follow the Soviets in breaking off relations with Israel over the June 1967 war. (Besides the Czech airline representative, I was the only person to see the Israeli minister off at the airport, for which I later received Mrs. Meir's personal thanks.) No matter how much we tried, it was impossible to discuss foreign affairs intelligently with Czech officials. Our embassy had the added cross to bear of dealing with an officer installed as head of the American desk who had the face of an angel and the black soul of Stalin.

The Czech scene attracted few prominent Americans. One of them was Richard Nixon, who visited several European countries as a private citizen, accompanied by former Kansas congressman Robert Ellsworth. As mentioned earlier, I admired Nixon for the success he made of his visit to Poland in 1959. On arriving in Czechoslovakia, he wanted to visit Lidiče, the town near Prague which was wiped out by the Nazis in 1942 in retaliation for Heydrich's assassination, but he had been advised that his going there would create a bad impression in Bonn, where he was to visit next. I told Mr. Nixon he had to go to Lidiče and sent him off in a car with a wreath. The press had been alerted and he was greeted by a crowd of some two thousand, whom he addressed in a graceful speech. He was annoyed, however, that we had not sent an embassy photographer.

TWO SERIOUS INCIDENTS

Besides routine unpleasantness, my first year and a half in Prague was marred by two nasty incidents. First, on October 30, 1966, a woman passenger on an Aeroflot plane from Moscow noted that her seat companion, an American, did not return to the plane after a brief emergency stop at Prague. Since she knew he was destined for Paris, she called up our embassy there on arrival to report the circumstances, the embassy in turn informing us by telephone. A first inquiry at the Foreign Office brought us no response, but a day or so later we were told that a Czech with dual American nationality had been arrested for offenses against the state. The man in question was a naturalized American named Kazan-Kamarek who had worked with French intelligence in 1948 and had taken part in a border raid from Germany in which a Communist Czech guard had been killed.

Kazan-Kamarek, a tourist agent in Cambridge, Massachusetts, had been attending a conference in Moscow where the Soviet secret police had become aware of his identity. They had asked the Czechs whether they would like Aeroflot to make an unscheduled stop in Prague, a suggestion which was readily agreed to. Collusion was later established by a witness who saw the Aeroflot porters in Moscow put the passenger's baggage in the plane last so that it could be readily off-loaded in Prague.

The State Department protested vigorously to the Soviets, who blandly claimed that the stopover was necessitated by an emergency. In our protest to the Czechs we demanded access to the prisoner. Since this was denied, the State Department at my suggestion refused all further visas to Czechs going to the United States, including an important technical delegation about to depart. I was soon called to the Foreign Office to receive representations that the United States was bullying a small nation, a fact I did not deny, recalling Novotný's remarks about the rights of great powers. I pointed out that Czechoslovakia had the body and there would be further trouble if it were not promptly delivered.

On February 1 Kazan-Kamarek was tried and sentenced to eight years' imprisonment on charges of espionage and subversion. On February 4 he was expelled, but before leaving was presented with a bill for $165 for board and lodging while in jail. Our consul advised him to pay it by personal check, and in a last conversation with him at the airport, told him the embassy would stop payment by secure telegram once the plane had taken off. A few days later I received a message from the State Department reprimanding me for advising an American citizen to default on his signature.

The second incident opened with a call on August 16, 1967, from Mrs. Jordan, the wife of Charles Jordan, the European representative of the American Jewish Joint Distribution Committee. Mrs. Jordan reported that her husband had not returned to his hotel from an after-dinner walk on the previous evening. Jordan, whom I had known from similar visits he had made to Warsaw, was respected by the Eastern European governments for his work in trying to resettle in Israel the few Jews left in these countries after the war. In a call he had made on me a few days before, he reported that he was receiving the cooperation of the Czech authorities despite the break in relations with Israel over the Five Days' War which had broken out in June 1967.

After Mrs. Jordan's report, I visited the Foreign Office daily, sometimes twice daily, only to be told that while Jordan had been seen walking to another hotel, there were no clues to his disappearance. On Sunday August 20, our duty officer heard the Czech policemen who guarded our embassy gate mention that a body had just been recovered from the river nearby.

Much later, on November 18, 1975, Josef Frolik, a Czech intelligence agent who had defected in 1969, testified substantially as follows before a meeting of the U.S. Senate Subcommittee on Internal Security: Charles Jordan, during his visit to Prague, had been kept under

Czech surveillance. The surveillance detail noted, but failed to prevent, his kidnapping by a Palestinian commando unit, which murdered him. Frolik further testified that, in reply to American inquiries, the Czech government said it had no knowledge of Jordan's whereabouts but later fell back on the statement of one of the postmortem doctors that Jordan had committed suicide. According to Frolik, the only steps taken by the Czech government were to expel a secretary of the Egyptian Embassy in Prague as well as the Palestinian unit in Czechoslovakia.

During the heyday of the Dubček regime in 1968, we were told that the then government had hopes of solving the Jordan murder as well as the case of Jan Masaryk, who had either leapt or was pushed from a window to his death. In 1968 one paper reported that the questionable past acts of the police would be investigated, including Soviet responsibility for Masaryk's death. This allegation was immediately denounced by the Soviets as a provocation and apparently led to a demand from Moscow that the Czech security police, which included many Soviet agents, be held immune from public scrutiny.

NOVOTNÝ DETHRONED

As disenchantment with Novotný grew—even some dogmatists could not put up with the sterility and inflexibility of his rule—opposition within the party picked up strength. In the summer of 1967 the opposition, led chiefly by writers, journalists, and artists, were encouraged by the tests they had been making of Novotný's vulnerability. As mentioned earlier, the majority were party members and took communism for granted as an acceptable way of life. Their grievance was not that communism was inimical to literature and the arts—quite the contrary, since just as the Russian intelligentsia had flourished in the early days of the Revolution, their Czech counterparts luxuriated in the subsidies the state provided them to launch new art forms which expressed themselves in the efflorescence of the film industry and in experimental theater effects combining both stage acting and motion pictures.

The embassy was fortunate in having two extraordinarily competent public affairs officers, Robert Warner, and then Andrew Falkiewicz, who later followed me to Moscow. They spoke fluent Czech and were popular with the artists, whom they helped put in touch with visiting American correspondents. The more the Czech cultural elite became aware of their international recognition, the more determined they became to set their own lifestyle and make foreign contacts without fear of intimidation. People of stature who were accessible to visitors from abroad included Dr. Sorm, head of the Academy of Science and a well-known chemist; Forman, the famous film director; Svoboda, designer of stage sets and architect of Czech exhibits which won international prizes; and Ornest, a leading European stage director; as well as a host of writers, such as the playrights Havel and Kohout, and the noted writer Ludvik Vaculik. Several lively personalities also surfaced, including the Central Committee's psychiatrist and Prague's leading heart surgeon who, with his wife and son, ran a Beatle-type night show in a downtown cellar.

Otherwise, the times were grim and uninspiring. Talk about economic reform had failed to raise living standards. Public morale received a boost from the example of Israel as a victorious small power in the June Six-Day

War, but promptly suffered a setback with Czechoslovakia's breaking of relations with Israel which was accompanied by denunciation of Zionism expressed in terms obviously aimed at the Jewish cultural leaders at home. Nevertheless the spark of rejuvenation was being fanned by protests.

The definitive break between the regime and the intelligentsia began with the opening of the Czech Writers Congress in Prague on June 27, 1967. The subsequent events which led to Novotný's ouster seven months later are recorded in masterly detail in Gordon Skilling's *Czechoslovakia's Interrupted Revolution.* [1]

Our contacts kept us generally informed of discussions within the Writers Congress, where it was clear that a mortal struggle was impending. Far from being confined to literature, the debate questioned the whole range of government policy. Czechoslovak support of the Arabs in the Six-Day War was denounced. A delegate read a letter condemning censorship which Solzhenitsyn had addressed to an earlier Soviet writers meeting (the Soviets were to bring this up as a black mark against the Czechs after the August 20, 1968, invasion). Bitter attacks were launched against party controls, and nostalgic references were made to Czechoslovakia's traditional ties with the West. The most eloquent and devastating onslaught against the regime's failures in social and cultural policy was delivered by Ludvik Vaculik, one of the several dissenters who survived to sponsor the famous Charter '77 which was circulated in early 1977 to call attention to violations of human rights. It is interesting that

---

[1]H. Gordon Skilling, *Czechoslovakia's Interrupted Revolution* (Princeton, N.J.: Princeton University Press, 1976).

the Writers Congress concentrated on abuses which at the same time could be charged against the Soviet Union, a fact duly noted by the Moscow leaders. The development of a more distinctly social program came later under Dubček when Novotný had been cast aside.

It is curious that American public interest in Czechoslovakia, as compared with that bestowed on Poland in 1956, was not very great. One reason was that local opposition had not yet set the Czech public on fire. Vaculik, previously identified as a leading spokesman at the Writers Congress, declined to talk with Bernard Gwertzman, then of the *Washington Star,* explaining that he sought a Czech rather than an American readership. Another reason was that despite his unpopularity, Novotný seemed fairly well entrenched. The Thirteenth Party Congress a year earlier had strengthened his authority and he clearly enjoyed the continued favor of Brezhnev because Czechoslovakia had refused to recognize West Germany, as the Rumanian leader Ceaucescu had done.

Disasters cascaded on Novotný during November and December 1967. A seemingly harmless midnight student demonstration in Prague was beaten up, provoking mass meetings and a national student strike against "socialist illegality." With the country now fully aroused, the Central Committee and its Presidium, or Politburo, held a series of ad hoc meetings. The grievances against Novotný were of different kinds and sources, and converged on the objective of ousting him from the post of first secretary. As a Slovak leader, Dubček denounced Novotný's operating methods and called for Czech–Slovak equality. Smrkovsky, who had not yet been heard from but was later to play a critical role as a spokesman for the working class, made a strong attack, all the more remarkable since he was thought to be Novotný's friend and a supporter of the Soviet Union.

Reports vary about the part played by the Soviet Union in the crisis. Novotný broke off a Central Committee meeting to attend a celebration of the fiftieth anniversary of the Soviet Union in Moscow on November 7, 1967. It is said that he failed to see Brezhnev privately, perhaps because he reportedly had protested to the Soviet leader by telephone the latter's ouster of Khrushchev in 1964. On December 7, Brezhnev, supposedly at Novotný's invitation, paid a one-day visit to Prague, during which he talked with individual members of the Presidium but did not attend a full meeting. Whether he realized that Novotný was finished, or felt that the outcome would in any case be favorable to Soviet interests, he avoided publicly taking sides, allegedly remarking: "It is your affair."

Novotný's end was marked by suppressed drama. At one point we were told on good authority that the vote on his ouster stood at a five to five tie in a December Presidium meeting. There was evidence, later confirmed as unmistakable, that some figures in the party administration, a certain Miroslav Mamula and a Major General Sejna (who later defected to the United States with his mistress, his son, and a file of secret documents), were planning "military steps to influence the Central Committee," or to use force to prevent Novotný's ouster.

In his New Year's broadcast to the nation, Novotný tried to redeem himself by conceding the need for Slovak equality, for "greater democracy in socialism," and for a more liberal cultural policy. Counting on the fact that no Slovak had ever held the post of national party leader, he may have hoped to be renominated from the floor of the

Central Committee, but sentiment against him had hardened. At an expanded Presidium meeting early in January, Kolder, a Soviet sympathizer, proposed Party Secretary Strougal be elected to replace Novotný as first secretary. Strougal (who later became prime minister) refused, and in turn nominated Cernik of the Planning Commission, who also declined. Novotný suggested Prime Minister Lenart, a Slovak who likewise refused. Possibly anticipating that there would be other refusals, Novotný proposed Dubček, who accepted. The Presidium placed this recommendation before the Central Committee which adopted it, on January 3 and announced the change on January 5.

Chapter IX

Reform in High Gear

Dubček—First Impressions

PUBLIC information on Dubček before his accession to top party leadership was scarce, and even after the event he was a hard man to get a handle on. The biographies written about him are unconvincing. It was generally known that he had resided with his family in the Soviet Union until the age of seventeen. He had been an active Communist in Czechoslovakia before the 1948 coup, and he later returned to the Soviet Union to attend a Soviet party higher training school. This experience apparently produced no spectacular effects either on Dubček or on the Soviets. In Slovakia he had the reputation of being honest and a good party organizer.

As far as we are aware, the only acknowledged meeting Dubček ever had with a non-Communist Westerner was at a noonday reception given for the diplomatic corps on October 28, 1968, to celebrate the fiftieth anniversary of the Czechoslovak state. Those of us who attended the reception had only the briefest opportunity to offer our congratulations, which Dubcek received with dignified sincerity.

Incidentally, our Soviet colleague did not attend the ceremony which, of course, occurred after the Soviet invasion of Czechoslovakia and after Dubček's reinstatement as first secretary. Later that evening, the Soviet ambassador was to suffer a somewhat unpleasant experience on his way to the opera house to attend a gala performance of *Libyushe* by Smetana, an opera which is identified with the cause of Czechoslovak independence. The Soviet ambassador was foolish enough to fly his flag on his car, thus provoking several hundred students who were lined up on the pavements to block his passage amid catcalls and some jostling of his automobile. He never reached the theater, but his wife, who had come earlier, had a chance to express her outrage to a gathering of diplomats and Czech officials in the lobby. It was a tense evening, and had the Soviet ambassador suffered injury it is possible that the second Soviet intervention, in April 1969, which finally resulted in Dubček's dismissal, might have occurred earlier.

We tried to get a line on Dubček from several sources. Among the best were some of the East European ambassadors, in particular the Yugoslav and the Rumanian, who arranged the official visits of their respective heads of state in 1968 just before the Soviet invasion. These colleagues, while well disposed to Dubček, described him as shrewd, stubborn, and cautious, somewhat naive and lacking in glamorous inspiration. Our Czech acquaintances supported Dubček with affectionate admiration. We had the impression, however, that they were pressing him in so many different directions as to make it hard for him to formulate coherent policies.

This is exactly what Dubček was charged with during his early days as first secretary. His situation is nevertheless understandable. He was a minority representative, the first Slovak to be national party leader. Although Novotný was no longer first secretary, he temporarily remained on the Presidium and the government was filled with his appointees. Dubček, except for his support of Slovak nationalism, had not identified himself with specific domestic issues, although he had cautiously taken the side of the moderate reformers in such matters as freedom of expression and changes in the economy.

Dubček had no experience in foreign affairs but this did not prove a to be disability. As we shall see, his main problems were with management of the party and with relations between Czechoslovakia and its Warsaw Pact allies. The West benefited from the change through a certain normalization of contacts. The removal of a particularly obnoxious deputy foreign minister made things easier, but we gained little from the change in foreign ministers from David, to Professor Jiri Hajek. David was stupid and inflexible, but after he had made his hard-line pitch, he tried to be genial. His successor, Hajek, consistently and deliberately insulted the United States, possibly in order to combat any idea that we were supporting or conniving with the new government. While he was far from being one of my favorite statesmen, I give him credit for his outspoken advocacy of liberal dissent which led to his expulsion from the party and, since he had chosen to remain in Czechoslovakia, to his later opposition to the Husak regime.

In short, Dubček did not want to seem to have a foreign policy, and perhaps wisely so. To attain other ends, he wished to make it appear that Czechoslovakia remained dedicated to the Soviet line. The Soviets later charged that despite repeated warnings, representatives of his administration had undermined Warsaw Pact security by flirting with West Germany. This accusation was largely a pretext to justify the Soviet invasion ex post facto, since Dubček had neither the determination nor the capacity to carry out such action at the time. The very farthest he was willing to go in offering rapprochement with the West was to suggest that Novotný's rigid foreign policy be modified to "provide wider choices." He sincerely believed his loyalty was taken for granted by the Soviets who would thus condone some of the changes in Czechoslovakia which they might find distasteful. He apparently proceeded on the fatal assumption: "I know how to handle the Russians."

Reform activity took off at a fast pace at the beginning of February 1968. In a speech before the Agricultural Cooperative Congress, Dubček set a tone of "you have a friend in socialism" which met with a cordial and constructive public response. He discussed past grievances intelligently and proposed remedies for improving the farming system, offering promise that greater democracy was proper and feasible within the party. A flood of open debate broke out in the media, and in local party meetings, which led gradually to the formation of a Dubček "action program."

The range of ideas brought forth was spectacular and significant. Many of them could be held "excommunicable," since in the Soviet Union they would have been sure to incur condemnation, and even expulsion from the party, for their sponsors. With the aim of combatting arbitrary party action, the proposals aimed at enhancing the integrity and authority of government institutions, such as the legislative and the judiciary which were constitutionally committed to protecting individual rights.

A comparison between the Polish and Czech reform programs as they evolved respectively in 1956 and 1968 is instructive. The Polish, although equally vigorous in defending individual rights, was narrower and more nationalistic. The Czech pattern, on the other hand, seemed broader in social and humanistic scope. The reason may be that the Czechs had a better ordered life to revert to, having been less disturbed by the ravages of war and German occupation than the Poles. The Czech input was also more academically oriented, involving the active participation of such figures as Dr. Sorm, president of the Academy of Sciences; Professor Goldstuecker, vice-rector of Prague University; and Dr. Kriegel, a well-known physician and Spanish War veteran. At one time even the present party general secretary Dr. Husak could qualify as a progressive intellectual; he generally supported Dubček throughout 1968 and helped then to shape a new Czech–Slovak relationship, a domestic problem Poland did not have.

Besides Dubček and the personalities mentioned above, new leaders representing a broad spectrum of interests emerged. One of the more spectacular personalities was Smrkovsky, the one-time leader of the Communist partisans who had freed Prague from the Germans in early May 1945. When I first met him at a diplomatic reception he told me about a visit he had received on this occasion from several American officers who had made their way to Prague by jeep from U.S. Army headquarters in Pilsen. Fighting was still going on in the area and the Americans said they were authorized to offer the Czechs full military support. Admitting to me that he was determined to preempt victory for the Communists, Smrkovsky said he had declined intervention by our forces but indicated he would be happy to receive arms, ammunition, and trucks. Assistance proved unnecessary since the Germans retreated north and the U.S. was mandated by agreement with the Soviet High Command not to move east of the line from Pilsen to Budweis.

Smrkovsky, together with his wartime commander General Svoboda, later got into trouble during the Stalinist purges of the early 1950s. Incidentally, Svoboda, who eventually became president of Czechoslovakia, was rescued from a menial job on a farm by Khrushchev who, on a visit to Prague, casually inquired about his wartime Czech comrade. When rehabilitated, Smrkovsky was given the post of minister of forests and waterways. Later, as president of the National Assembly, he stood out as a loyal and eloquent supporter of Dubček and merits respect as a courageous, appealing, and tragic figure. In such contacts as we had with him he was friendly and sympathetic to the United States.

The activists, as I shall call them since they were far from being passive liberals, clearly gained the upper hand in March, and on March 22 Novotný resigned from the presidency. Although Novotný was to offer a stout defense of his policies at the April meeting of the Central Committee, the persons marked to succeed him came from the progressive ranks. Among them the parliamentary wing was the most authoritative and consisted of Dubček, Smrkovsky, Kriegel, and Cisar, a champion of the students, as well as Husak insofar as he opposed Novotný. The media professionals were, of course, the most articulate, besides being the least ready to consider any kind of retreat. Some can now be identified since they are no longer extant in Czechoslovakia: Milan

Weiner, a brilliant radio commentator who died in the summer of 1968; Liehm, a movie critic, and Pelikan, head of the state television, both of whom emigrated; and Jiri Hochman, editor of the student paper *Reporter,* violently anti-American at the time, who also left. The state motion picture industry was strongly progressive and anti-Russian; some of the best directors emigrated, while others later made their peace with Husak.

On March 28 I gave a luncheon for five or six of the most influential nonofficial reform leaders, including Weiner and Liehm. Relations between the United States and Czechoslovak governments continued to be bad because of the Vietnamese war, economic disputes and also because there seemed to be tacit agreement between us that such a state of inactive hostility would immunize the Czechs against any taint of Soviet suspicion of collusion with American imperialism. The State Department, while still angry with Czech material support of Hanoi, was keenly interested in the hopeful signs of change, although it was fearful that the Soviets would soon intervene to reverse the favorable trend. We in the embassy thought that direct contact with the party reformists would be the best way to circumvent the Stalinist Foreign Office; we were certain that our interest would be reported to the top leadership and possibly open lines of communication.

Our luncheon guests, who stayed all afternoon, welcomed the opportunity to inform us fully and frankly about the Dubček action program to be discussed the following week by the Central Committee. They made no mention of U.S.–Czech differences. While obviously trying to avoid discussion of the Soviets, they focused their bitterness against Novotný and his remaining Stalinist supporters. We told them of our government's sympathetic interest in their aims but asked if they really believed the Soviets could tolerate for long the new departures in policy. Our guests saw no reason why the Soviets should be upset, since the Czechs were good Communists and loyal allies. The Soviet reaction, they claimed, had not been outwardly hostile. (Our present knowledge indicates that this estimate was based either on ignorance or self-deception, because the very day after Novotný's resignation from the presidency, March 22, the Czechs were put on the carpet at a meeting in Dresden of all the Warsaw Pact countries, except Rumania. According to post-invasion accounts, the Soviets had stated at this meeting that they would not permit Czechoslovakia to fall out of the socialist camp, even at the cost of a Third World War.)

At their luncheon with us our friends referred to the right of Communist national parties to plot their own road to socialism. They said optimistically that, after all, 1968 was not 1956 when the Soviets had paid so heavy a price by using force in Hungary.

On April 10 the Central Committee adopted Dubček's action program, which was subtitled "The Czechoslovak Road to Socialism." Consisting of a long statement of principles intended for later implementation by specific decisions and laws, it was the first attempt to give cohesion to the various reform trends within the party. Particular note will be taken of its features which produced the domestic and international crises of July and August 1968.

From the very start the program could not help but give affront to the Soviet Union. Particularly offensive from the Soviet point of view was the insinuation that the party's claim to play a "leading role" as the instrument of the dictatorship of the proletariat could in actual fact lead to a monopolistic concentration of power. Leaning heavily on the assertion of human rights and freedom of expression, the document propounded such unorthodox ideas as the use of opinion polls and research to assist policy making; it also advocated suppression of censorship, holding government press conferences, and free travel abroad. The program was notably short on economic specifics and generally vague in supporting a foreign policy dedicated to "alliance and cooperation with the Soviet Union in defending Communism against aggression by world imperialism."

The April Plenum also approved changes in the top party posts. Novotný was dropped from the Presidium and the Secretariat. Dubček and Cernik, the latter considered a centrist, remained on the Presidium, and Smrkovsky and Kriegel were added as active progressives. Corresponding shifts on the government side resulted in the choice of Cernik to be prime minister and Smrkovsky to be president of the National Assembly. On March 30, 1968, the latter body elected General Svoboda the new president. I attended his inauguration and I recall remarking to my Iraqi colleague on our walk to the palace that the photographers seemed to be paying special attention to a group of students cheering their reformist heroes. My colleague wisely surmised that the secret police were doubtless updating their photo files for future use.

EVERYBODY WANTS TO JOIN

With their capture of the government, the reform forces found themselves heading a national crusade which pushed them beyond the framework of the Action Program. The advances made during the next few weeks before the Soviet invasion would have brought credit to other societies than one simply trying to moderate a hardened Communist dictatorship. In the course of this interval official censorship was abolished except over strictly military affairs. Jamming of foreign broadcasts was lifted and travel abroad was to be permitted, depending chiefly on the availability of foreign exchange. Besides the easing of legal restraints, a wave of liberalism swept through the party-dominated organizations and associations which ordered everyday life.

At the same time there arose a spontaneous popular desire to participate politically in some way in the current reawakening. This proved somewhat embarrassing since it ran counter to Communist theology which holds that the party shall be the ruling elite who may welcome the people's support but not their active interference. The passive Popular Front which embraced such moribund groups as the Socialist and People's parties had previously met the needs of the Communist leaders, who now became somewhat disturbed by suggestions that the Social Democrats be revived, presumably to lend their backing. The notion made little headway because of the basic hostility between the two ideologies which could be expressed in some such refrain as "how sour the name of social democracy sounds in a believer's ear." Some progress, however, was made with the establishment (and toleration, for a brief period) of an association called

[173]

KAN, or the "club of nonparty committed," which attracted people who supported Dubček but were reluctant to join a political party.

Another question which touched a sensitive nerve was the rehabilitation of, and the payment of restitution to, party and nonparty victims of the illegal acts of the Gottwald and Novotný regimes. Quite a few former political prisoners had been rehabilitated and compensated by sympathetic judges, but concern arose over an attempt to bring these ex-outcasts together in a group, called K231 after a pertinent paragraph of the penal code. One of its leaders was General Vaclav Poleček, who had been imprisoned because of his pre-1948 assignment as Czechoslovak liaison officer to General Eisenhower's Allied command. The work of rehabilitation was sabotaged by Novotnýites still in the secret police, who likewise turned aside demands that possible Soviet collusion in the death of Jan Masaryk be investigated. After the Soviet invasion, General Poleček, a fearless friend of the British and ourselves, emigrated to the United States where he died in 1975.

The Central Committee Plenum of May 1968 undertook the task of reforming the party organization itself, and for this purpose accelerated plans for the meeting of the party's upcoming fourteenth congress. The events set in train by these preparations could well have triggered the Soviet decision to invade. Of outstanding importance was the fact that the congress would elect a new Central Committee. Electioneering for delegates, therefore, began immediately after the Plenum and carried debate of the issues down to the lowest local levels. The progressives went so far as to put forth a democratic program which the Soviets could have justly regarded as possibly the most dangerous challenge to their system since the proposals which the Hungarian revolutionaries advanced in their final days to institute multiparty rule.

According to this "model," which was intended to provide a setting for revised party statutes, membership would allow voluntary withdrawal; voting would be secret at every stage; terms of office would be limited to permit rotation and to discourage monopoly of power; minority views would be protected; the party, instead of stressing social origin, would become an elite of politically committed progressives. Even more painful to the party regulars was the embodiment of these concepts in a declaration entitled "2000 Words" which was published in the literary magazine *Literarnini Listy* on June 27, 1968.

Drafted by the same Ludvik Vaculik who, as mentioned, was later credited with writing "Charter '77," the declaration was intended to reinvigorate political life by calling on the people to act on their own initiative and by their own decisions. While recognizing that reform must proceed under the Communist banner, and that "illegal and coarse methods must be avoided," it suggested that action be stimulated by the appointment of special citizens' committees for the protection of press freedom and the selection of managers and works councils. Although there was oblique reference to the validity of Czechoslovakia's current alliances, mention was made of the "threat of intervention by foreign [read Soviet] forces." The declaration ended with an appeal for support of the government by the use of arms (read Czech) if necessary.

The statement eventually collected thousands of signatures from such diverse groups as scientists, journalists, workers, and farmers, but became the subject of immediate controversy and occasioned discussion and dispute among Czechs attending our Fourth of July reception. Even Smrkovsky denounced it as "politically romantic," but in a talk which Senator Pell and I had with him on July 6 he jokingly said he could have subscribed to "one thousand nine hundred sixty words" in the original text.

Before embarking on the sorry story of how the progressives met retribution at Soviet hands, it is worthwhile to pause a moment and consider what kind of men these were who tried to impart a compatible element of humanism to orthodox communism. Honest, courageous, and perhaps somewhat naive and inexperienced, they nevertheless represented the most enlightened group of leaders produced by a Communist ruling party. While circumstances prevented personal friendship, we entertained a feeling of mutual sympathy with them. When a student group protesting Vietnam tore down the flag from our embassy, they were ordered to return it the next day with apologies. On July 4 a Czech general laid a wreath on the monument to American troops stationed in Cheb in 1945, a gesture which, Smrkovsky remarked to Senator Mansfield and myself in the course of our call on August 10, "was a long overdue recognition of the United States as a valiant comrade."

AN EFFORT TO DO BUSINESS

While Dubček gathered his resources during his first few weeks in office, action remained in relative suspense before picking up in February to play itself out at a breathless pace. Opportunity will be taken to mention two projects which our government reactivated to take advantage of a possible improvement in relations. In effect they represented the sum total of constructive effort which offered some prospect of success. One failed for understandable reasons, whereas the other, which is still pending, has been frustrated by mistakes more chargeable to us than to the Czechs. The first was our endeavor to promote sales of our commercial aircraft, and the second concerned a settlement of our claims for Czech nationalization of American property.

Despite obsolete Soviet equipment, the Czechoslovak national airline, CSA, managed to operate a fairly good service. In the course of negotiations between PanAm and CSA for a Prague–New York run, which was finally established in 1969, it became clear that the Czechs were reluctant to meet their requirements for a long-range plane by the purchase of the Soviet IL-62. They knew this dual-purpose passenger-military plane to be inefficient and uneconomical to operate for passenger service. (The fleets of IL-62s which one sees standing idle at Soviet airports·constitute a strategic transport reserve; as such, they cost far less to maintain than our specialized military air transport system.)

In any event, the Czechs encouraged Western manufacturers to interest themselves in bidding, and besides the Boeing 707 and DC-8, the British VC-10 came under consideration. CSA made it clear that while they preferred an American plane, other factors had to be weighed, such as credit terms, availability of spare parts, and, finally, whether CSA as a state airline would find it politically feasible to buy a non-Soviet product. A break for our side occurred in 1968 when PanAm decided to stock its fleet only with Boeings and to offer its Douglas DC-8s for sale secondhand at reasonable prices. Among other available possibilities, I pushed this opening personally with the Exim Bank and with the secretary of the Treasury, working out the outline of a deal whereby CSA would be able to benefit from the exceptionally favorable credit and interest terms applicable to American aircraft sales. In the summer of 1968, however, a Czech civil aviation delegation was invited to Moscow and returned with the expected news that they had committed themselves to purchase the IL-62.

The claims matter was more complex. On October 28, 1945, when Benes was president, the government had nationalized substantial American holdings, and the Communists completed the process. At one time our claims were estimated to amount to some $300 million but the total of the valid cases was later reduced to $77 million by the U.S. Federal International Claims Commission. In the meantime we held, and are still holding, in various banks 18,400 kilograms of monetary gold which the Nazis had looted from the Czechs and which had fallen into our custody with our occupation of Germany. While we have always recognized Czechoslovakia's absolute right to the gold, we have been withholding its return pending a settlement of our nationalization claims. The British and French, who also had overrun lesser amounts of looted gold, promptly turned it back to the Czechs, with the unfortunate result that they were able to collect only a minimal percentage on their nationalization claims.

A complication arose from the fact that just after the 1948 Communist coup in Czechoslovakia, we had forbidden the export from the United States of a modern steel mill which the Czechs had ordered from us and on which they had already paid $17 million. We were later able to sell the mill in the Argentine for $9 million, which we used to settle outright the small nationalization claims of our citizens which did not exceed $1000.

In the ensuing negotiations the U.S. side must have been encumbered by embarrassment or some other inexplicable inhibition, because we demanded only $12 million in total settlement, with the Czechs already credited with the $9 million we had received from the sale of the steel mill to the Argentine government. A statement of principles along these lines was initialed between the two parties in December 1961. At this point the Czechs made a monumental blunder by starting to quibble about procedures involved in the return of the gold, which at that time was valued at roughly $21 million.

The problem remained a major irritant in relations, with the Czechs exploiting to the full their grievance that the U.S. was withholding gold taken from them by the Nazis. In 1968 I participated in drafting a simplified plan which, as a gesture of support for the newly installed Dubček regime, offered easier terms of payment through deferred installments. An appointment had been made for the Czechoslovak ambassador to call at the State Department to receive our proposal on August 21, 1968, the very day his country was invaded by the Soviets; with more important questions on the minds of both parties, no meeting took place.

The history of the claims question has been somewhat tragic, since it means that many of the smaller claimants have died off. Presumably the large U.S. companies with claims of hundreds of thousands of dollars have been partially able to amortize their losses by tax deductions. The current rise in the price of gold, which brought the value of 18,400 kilograms up to about $88,736,000 as of late 1977, has opened new prospects for settlement. Incidentally, when my Czech colleague in Moscow, who is now foreign minister in Prague, used to complain about our intransigence, I pointed to the potential profit his country had already reaped from the delay.

THE SOVIETS SHOW THEIR TEETH

The summoning of Dubček to attend a meeting in Dresden on March 22, 1968, seems to have been the first explicit sign of Soviet determination to deal with this recalcitrant Communist. Under questioning by the Czech press, Dubček acknowledged that "the comrades" had expressed concern about antisocialist forces, but that he had been able to reassure them. This was the line that Dubček was henceforth to take publicly, and even privately with his trusted colleagues. In fact it is still difficult to know exactly what the Soviets kept telling the Czechs; some of the clearest indications are contained in the plausible accounts published in the Soviet press immediately after the invasion. Mystery still veils a one-day visit by Dubček to Moscow in early May which was followed a few days later by a Czech delegation, one of whose members later reported that the Soviets had strongly complained that there had been "no improvement since Dresden."

In the meantime, while the progressives seemed to be having it mostly their way in Czechoslovakia, the conservative opposition went back into action with obvious Soviet support. On June 19 a national rally was held in Prague of some ten thousand members of the People's Militia, the successors to the armed workers who took to the streets in 1948 to bring the Communists to power.

Although Dubček sought to appease them in a welcoming speech, they ended up by passing a resolution which, in pledging allegiance to the Czech–Soviet alliance, stated in part: "We do not agree with, and divorce ourselves from the irresponsible actions of some journalists who try to breach our friendship by spreading distortions from the bourgeois press."[1] As Schwartz reports in *Prague's 200 Days*, the text of the resolution was delivered to the Soviet Embassy and reprinted the next day in *Pravda*, setting off responsive messages from Soviet workers in plants throughout the country declaring their solidarity with the Czech People's Militia.

This was the period when Dubček, without offering specific explanation, tried to curb popular criticism of the Soviets. I attended an evening rally on the Old Town Square of the Prague party faction when he and Smrkovsky pled for patience in bringing reform. Both speakers were greeted by catcalls and random shouts of disagreement. Such seemed to be the popular mood of exhilaration which inspired the "2000 Words" and other acts of confrontation with the Soviets which the leadership seemed powerless to restrain.

Apart from the undisclosed warnings from their allies, the Czechs had other cause for worry, including rumors of troop movements in Poland and East Germany. An announcement soon followed that the Warsaw Pact countries would hold maneuvers, first described as staff exercises, in Czechoslovakia from June 20–30. Our attachés in Czechoslovakia and the adjacent countries had no difficulty in verifying the presence of the various

---

[1]Cited in Harry Schwartz, *Prague's 200 Days* (New York: Praeger, 1969), p. 166.

forces and, while they did not report the numbers as alarming, they were obviously a potential threat to the Czechs. In fact, Soviet troops remained for a longer time and even passed the date of July 13 which was set for their withdrawal. On July 15 General Prchlik, the Central Committee's military expert, held a press conference suggesting reorganization of the Warsaw Pact to give its individual members greater autonomy with less reliance on Soviet command. Soviet *Pravda* worked itself into a fury over the interview, as well as over a report of an American arms cache on the German border allegedly intended to support revolution in Czechoslovakia. The U.S. government denied the report and delivered a strong protest in Moscow.

The Soviets used their military pressures to force a political crisis in July which the Czechs withstood with courage and considerable skill. Early in the month the Soviet and other Warsaw Pact parties addressed letters to the Czechoslovak Central Committee which expressed grave concern about current developments and which proposed a joint meeting in Warsaw. The Czechs suggested bilateral discussions instead, but before this proposal could be acted on the other bloc parties met in Warsaw without Czech participation. On July 15 the Warsaw group addressed to the Czechs a harsh letter which in brief denounced the "forces of reaction" taking cover behind the new political organizations and clubs, the "2000 Words" manifesto, and the press and television. They called for a struggle against counterrevolution in which the "fraternal parties" could be counted upon for assistance.

The Czech party Presidium replied promptly and denied the charges, which it said were based on one-sided information. It granted there had been "negative and extremist aspects," which, however, could in no way be called counterrevolutionary and which were being corrected. The Presidium declared its loyalty to the Pact alliance, as confirmed by the staff maneuvers on Czech soil. A Central Committee Plenum shortly thereafter ratified the Presidium's response and published a speech by Dubček which quickly produced country-wide demonstrations of solidarity and support. A tense week ensued until plans were announced on July for direct meetings with the Soviets.

WESTERN REACTIONS

Throughout most of the crisis of 1968 action took place essentially between the Czechs and the Soviets, with the latter fully supported by East Germany and Poland. Having decided to play out the game directly with the Soviets —with an occasional welcome assist from Yugoslavia and Rumania—the Czechs deliberately foreswore any request for Western intervention or any kind of help which might prove embarrassing. Western reactions nevertheless did exert a certain incidental influence up until the time of direct Soviet–Czech discussions.

Prior to departing on home leave in early April, I asked my designated Foreign Office contact what subjects I might usefully stress in Washington. His reply was substantially "get us our gold back and leave us alone"; the Czechs in Washington were similarly reticent. In the United States I naturally found a great deal of sympathy and some concern with what was happening in Czechoslovakia. This feeling was conveyed in a formal statement on May 1 by the State Department spokesman who at the same time disavowed any U.S. intention to interfere. The

[183]

British expressed no disagreement when we told them in Washington "we are keeping quiet and not tinkering with the situation in any way." I was invited to meet with the Joint Chiefs of Staff who expressed anger with the continued supply of AK-47 automatic rifles by the Czechs to the Vietnamese. As to the Soviet maneuvers on the Czech borders, they were regarded both as a means of exerting pressure and a form of cover and deception masking future intentions. Administration resentment over Czech involvement in Vietnam definitely cooled our ardor to offer assistance.

President Johnson asked to see me. He was upset by the support the Czechs were giving the North Vietnamese. I thought there was little we could do to prevent these shipments which were made under Soviet pressure. He recognized that the current threats to Czechoslovakia's integrity threatened European peace. In reply to his questions, I told him we had received no signal for help from the Czechs and that the best way to support them would be to continue our active interest and keep watch on the Soviets. I returned to Prague after a stay of about three weeks.

As tension mounted in the succeeding weeks, our Paris embassy reported that De Gaulle remained calm and unworried while advising that "the Communists be left to settle the issues themselves." He may have been unaware that his prime minister, Debré, and his ambassador in Moscow, Wormser, seemed to disagree with him and had told us that armed conflict was inevitable, Debré adding that there was nothing we could do about it. Our own embassy in Moscow also took a dark view, pointing out that the Soviets were heavily committed, and that the only hope lay in concessions from the Czechs.

In Prague our progressive contacts displayed surprising confidence, saying that settlements could be reached with the Soviets once direct talks had begun. At the Polish National Day reception on July 22, the Polish ambassador told me that bilateral conversations had been agreed in principle and that the Czechs had won their point that they be held on Czech soil "for prestige and security reasons." Accordingly, our embassy was not unduly alarmed at this time.

Another factor helping the Czechs was the concern of several foreign parties that the attack on Hungary would be repeated. Longo of Italy and Waldeck-Rochet of France flew to Moscow reportedly to warn the Soviets against military action. Both the Yugoslav and Rumanian parties were known to be sympathetic to Czechoslovakia. A French appeal for a European Communist meeting on Czechoslovakia proved distasteful to both the Soviets and the Czechs, and helped force bilateral discussions.

ACCORDS OR ULTIMATA?

Against a dramatic background spiced by secrecy, the respective Politburos of the Czechoslovak and Soviet Communist parties (the Soviets, however, leaving two members in Moscow to manage the store) met from July 29 to August 1 at Čierna in Czechoslovakia, a town which was adjacent to the Ukrainian border. Not even our usually knowledgeable Czech party contacts, who understandably were below the Politburo level, could get information about what was said or happened at the meetings. The same was true with respect to the large and alert group of foreign correspondents who descended on Čierna and Prague to cover the event.

Despite the bitterness the Czechs must have felt over

the treatment they received, Communist discipline prevails even to this day to inhibit any authentic revelation of the proceedings. An outline, which is inconsistent in some details, nevertheless does emerge from certain published partisan accounts, such as the August 22 postinvasion article in Soviet *Pravda,* and finally, of course, Smrkovsky's "Testimony," contained in an interview with him taped shortly before his death in January 1974. Furthermore, a few color stories were bound to get out.

Brezhnev put on a shattering act by reading for two hours from a file, doubtless provided him by his local agents, and by asking how each of the listed acts, incidents, and statements tolerated by the Czech regime could be reconciled with communism. Dubček was greatly shaken and reportedly broke down in tears. According to Smrkovsky, the Soviets made six specific demands: (1) the removal of Kriegel from leadership of the National Front and (2) Cisar from the party Secretaryship; (3) a ban on the Social Democrats; (4) dissolution of KAN (the club of supposedly politically nonengaged) and (5) K231 (the club of former political prisoners); and (6) controls on the media, specifically meaning a cessation of anti-Soviet and antisocialist attacks in the press and radio. At one point the talks were broken off because Soviet Politburo member Shelest accused the Czechs of distributing separatist leaflets in the Ukraine. The Czechs walked out and only returned after a Soviet apology. In a private conversation Dubček and Brezhnev decided that the two delegations should meet in Bratislava on August 3 with other Warsaw Pact member countries.

A dispute later broke out about the commitments assumed by the Czechs at Čierna. In its August 22 editorial,

Pravda, as well as the East German press, asserted they had promised to take urgent concrete measures to "defend" socialist achievements and to halt political activity threatening the Communist party's monopoly of power in Czechoslovakia. On returning from Čierna, Dubček declared in a radio broadcast, "I can state frankly that you can be completely satisfied with the results, and our sovereignty was not threatened." Smrkovsky, in his "Testimony," says, "There were no agreements; we said that this was decided, or that this will be decided, and how it will be decided." It is reported that Bilak, a confirmed Dubček opponent, later stated in November 1968 that Brezhnev had declared at the last meeting in Čierna: "Comrades, we are not signing any agreement; we rely on your Communist word; we expect you to act and behave as Communists. If you deceive us once more, we shall consider it a crime and a betrayal and will act accordingly. Never again would we sit with you at the same table."

The Čierna communiqué did little more than announce the meeting to be held in Bratislava on August 3. This conclave, which lasted only a single day, appeared to be largely ceremonial but among the usual clichés there seems to have been inserted by design certain pregnant phrases such as an appeal to "pattern society on the guiding role of the working class" for the purpose of "strengthening fraternal mutual aid and solidarity" (words used later to justify Soviet "aid" against internal "threats"). Prime Minister Cernik declared publicly, however, that at Bratislava "not a word was said about our affairs." On the day the conference ended it was announced that the last Soviet forces had departed from Czechoslovakia.

The quiet optimism of the Czech leaders seemed too tame, however, for some of our activist friends, especially those among the media who were jubilant over the results, and in fact claimed a signal victory over the Soviets. The same view seems to have been reflected in the Western press and was soon carried to the point where the assistant press chief in the Foreign Office remarked to me just three days before the invasion that the American correspondents in Prague were doing his country a great disservice. On the other hand, the leaders themselves bear considerable responsibility, if some of the personal comments made by Smrkovsky are to be taken at their face value. During a call I made upon him with Senator Mansfield on August 10, he said, "In our last week's talks with our allies we felt it necessary to push the wheel forward a bit." He recalled that Czechoslovakia opposed conservatism in socialism and, as Dubček had stated, it felt socialism should show a human face. The new Czech regime's program had survived with its objectives untouched and now "had a little more freedom of movement." Smrkovsky ended by saying that Soviet Prime Minister Kosygin "had mentioned to a friend he was well aware that the U.S. in no way intervened in Czechoslovakia's dispute with its neighbors."

Several incidents occurred after Čierna/Bratislava, none of them in my opinion important enough in itself to precipitate the Soviet invasion, but the total effect of which may well have determined its date. It is my belief that military action was decided in principle in Čierna and that its imminent necessity was accepted after the Soviets had taken a reading of the prevalent mood in Prague as represented by Smrkovsky. Reverting to the example I cited earlier of Count Dzierzynski's practice of breaking down the Soviet Cheka's victims to confess their crimes in tears before having them shot, it may be noted that whereas Dubček was given to crying jags, he never acknowledged guilt but was convinced he was acting at all times as a true Communist, a most dangerous stand—which in Soviet eyes doubtless marked him for eventual liquidation.

I am leading up to the date of August 16 when I became all but persuaded that the Soviets were on the point of using force. Following a brief lull after Čierna/ Bratislava the Soviets and Czechs resumed sniping at each other in the press. A Prague literary magazine analyzed the "sources of error of Soviet policy in and vis-à-vis Czechoslovakia." Divisions in the Czechoslovak solid political front began to occur, doubtless inspired by Soviet agitation. Nasty disputes broke out about the alleged pro-Soviet attitude of *Rude Pravo*'s editor, Svestka, and of the People's Militia. Tension grew from other incidental happenings. Tito, who arrived on August 9, was given a tumultuous welcome but showed caution in declining to conclude a treaty which, he said, was unnecessary in view of the two countries' friendship. Ulbricht paid a visit to Karlový Vary and was credited with sending an unfavorable report to the Soviets. Soviet *Pravda* published critical articles on August 14 and 16 expressing doubt about the Czech leaders' ability to control the press. Ceaucescu arrived on August 15 and signed a Czechoslovak–Rumanian treaty of friendship. Dubček held a secret frontier meeting with Kadar on August 17 and there is good reason to believe that the Hungarian leader passed on a warning of the extreme measures to be taken by the Soviets if the Bratislava agreements were not fulfilled.

On the evening of August 16 I attended a farewell reception at the palace for Ceaucescu and vividly recall being struck by the tension-charged atmosphere of the gathering. My Mexican colleague, a former chief of protocol with brains and one of the best informed Westerners, was talking with a member of the party Secretariat who said that the Soviets were renewing demands for permanently stationing troops in Czechoslovakia, claiming this was envisaged in the Bratislava declaration. He also said, "The city is filling up with Soviet agents." The Mexican and I met up with the Soviet ambassador Chervonenko, who had not been visible for some months. He was somber and remarked that Dubček seemed to be "losing control." When we asked him about the Czechoslovak Party Congress, he said it might not meet in September because "the workers were undecided." He mentioned that there had been trouble with the party statutes (which were published the next day). Chervonenko thought the situation "might straighten out in about two months."

My Mexican friend and I believed we had real cause for worry, as I reported to Washington that evening. However, we observed nothing untoward at the airport the next morning (August 17) where the diplomatic corps had been summoned to see Ceaucescu off on his journey.

Husak later accused Dubček of failing to inform the Presidium of his talk with Kadar and the letter dated August 17 sent by the Soviet Politburo constituting a final warning that the Prague leaders had failed to carry out the Čierna and Bratislava agreements. In replying to this charge, Dubček said he had received the letter on

August 19 and had read it to the Presidium on August 20, after the invasion had already started.

Over the weekend of August 17 the embassy was occupied with the arrival of some one thousand Americans with families coming to attend a World Geographic Congress. At the reception given by Prime Minister Cernik on Monday August 19, I unfortunately refrained from asking him directly whether his country was about to be invaded, but I did get from him his opinion that he saw no reason to believe the congress would be affected by world events.

Chapter X

The Soviets Strike in the Dark

A PHONE CALL

AT about 11:30 in the evening of Tuesday, August 20, the duty officer at the U.S. Chancery received a telephone call from an unnamed U.S. citizen in Bratislava reporting that "the city is full of Russian tanks." Thereupon the call was cut off. I alerted our political officers to listen to the local radio and went across to the house of our counselor, John Baker. We drove together in my car down to the chancery, about a mile and a half away in the city. Already we heard the sound of the planes bringing in the Soviet troops and their equipment (which included weapons carriers and small tanks). At about 1:50 A.M. the announcement came over Prague radio that the country was being invaded by the "Soviet Union and its allies." We spent the rest of the night listening to the radio, reporting to Washington, and getting in touch with our citizens to warn them to stay indoors.

Daybreak revealed that we were being guarded and watched by a small Polish tank outside the chancery. It was the only "allied" vehicle I saw besides a Hungarian personnel carrier, and practically all the other non-Soviet

Warsaw Pact war equipment was withdrawn from the city within forty-eight hours. Civilian traffic began to pick up from 6:00 in the morning and many buses were running but soon became jammed up at the bridges across the river. Motor traffic was directed by the Czech police; a few Soviet soldiers were to be seen on foot but most of them kept to their vehicles and tanks, which were parked on sidewalks and side streets. Since as yet there was little or no shooting, crowds appeared on the scene and showed their shock and anger in harangues with the invading troops, who remained silent or tried to be friendly.

Foreigners who were not present have denigrated the military efficiency of the operation. This was certainly not the view of the Western service attachés on the spot, who gave it highest marks for the quality of the equipment shown and for its use. One former NATO supreme commander told me that the West could probably never be able to achieve such a high degree of coordination among allies. The feeling was that the Soviets might have been able to penetrate deeply into Bavaria with the ground forces deployed, but, of course, they would then have found themselves in a different kind of war.

As cited by H. Gordon Skilling, the numbers involved were as follows: Soviet forces, 170,000 (70,000 from East Germany, 100,000 from the USSR); Polish, 40,000; East German, 12,000 (or one division); Hungarian, 10,000; Bulgarian, 5,000; total, 225,000–230,000.[1] Conversations with Soviet soldiers disclosed that they had been in a state of readiness for ten days before action.

---

[1]H. Gordon Skilling, *Czechoslovakia's Interrupted Revolution* (Princeton, N.J.: Princeton University Press, 1976), p. 713.

Their discipline was exemplary, but the Soviets soon let it be known that there had been summary executions of two soldiers who molested civilians.

Our first duty was to evacuate the some thousand U.S. citizens who were calm but were becoming restive. Mrs. Shirley Temple Black, with laudable enterprise, hired all the taxis around the hotel and within hours led a small convoy to the Bavarian frontier. The David Wolpert company, which was doing a film on the battle of Remagen Bridge against a Czech setting, took care of themselves, leaving behind a half-dozen old Patton tanks which were later shown in photographs in the Soviet press as evidence of U.S. military intervention. The Czech Foreign Office claimed it could not help evacuate the remaining U.S. citizens, and the situation looked desperate until our economic officer got in touch with a friend in the ministry of transport and casually hired a train which took the rest of the civilians to Vienna. We pooled resources with the other Western embassies with the result each of us got complaints from our own citizens and glowing thanks from the citizens of the other countries we had helped.

As August 21 wore on, outbreaks of violence became inevitable. As happened in Budapest in 1956, crowds made for the central radio station downtown about noon. Firing started, provoked, it seems, by youths throwing Molotov cocktails under Soviet tanks. In the early afternoon shooting also broke out on Wenceslaus Square. The civilian death toll for the day was estimated at about eighteen. A day or so later my wife went downtown in the afternoon and witnessed an event which gave a measure of the people's mood. A solitary diminutive Czech climbed the uplifted arm of a huge construction crane, cheered on his way from below. When he reached the perilous summit he broke out a Czechoslovak flag, driving the crowd into transports of patriotic feeling. On the square my wife also met a sinister and extremely influential Polish journalist of our earlier acquaintance. She asked him if he was not ashamed of what his country had done. When he demurred, she asked him if he was not just a little bit ashamed, to which he replied that the invasion was indeed regrettable, but necessary. He mentioned incidentally that no Prague hotel would give him lodging and that he was staying at his embassy.

When darkness came the Soviets shot off some heavy antiaircraft shells and tracer bullets in the air. This became a nightly practice, and the falling shrapnel encouraged the population to keep their heads down and stay off the streets. The Soviets later steadfastly denied that they had ever imposed a curfew. On one occasion they had the bad judgment to shoot a couple of antiaircraft bullets through the top story of the Swiss Embassy located across from the Hradčany Palace. Hell knowing no fury like a violated neutral, my Swiss colleague sent a blistering protest which earned him an apologetic visit from the top Soviet general and an official expression of regret from the Soviet ambassador in Bern.

The Soviet authorities handled all Americans with kid gloves, and in fact ignored a provocation from one of our attachés in uniform who spat in the face of a Soviet major —which could easily have led to our man's being shot on the spot. Our local grievances were relatively minor, such as the theft of apples by a Soviet colonel wandering on the hilltop behind our chancery. (To put a stop to trespassing, I had the American flag flown from the garden house at the top of the hill where it could be seen from most parts of the city. Some of my successors thought so highly of the practice that they reinstituted flying the flag there on a permanent basis, a gesture which I find somewhat vainglorious in view of the fact that we have been able to do so little for the Czechs since 1948.)

A much more serious incident, where disaster would have been chargeable to the Soviets, was a fire which broke out in our chancery on August 25. The incinerator in which we had been burning files may have gotten overheated, but, whatever the cause, the rafters, which were perhaps some 150 years old, broke out in flames. The situation was very grave since the fire rapidly took hold, threatening not only our compound with its some half-dozen apartments, but also that part of the Old City between the river and the Citadel. We called the Prague Fire Department which told us they had seen the flames but could not venture out "because of the Soviet curfew."

We were left to fight the fire ourselves, with a half-dozen extinguishers and a leaky hose which soon burst. Fortunately, we received invaluable help from an unusual quarter. Because of conditions outside, the six or seven American correspondents in town usually spent the night on sofas and chairs in my large outer office. With our resident staff and six marine guards, the correspondents formed a bucket brigade which enabled us to get the fire under control, but for a good hour or so it was touch and go.

In the week which preceded the eventual reinstatement of a Czech government, the Foreign Office was of no use at all, pleading on the telephone that they themselves were captives. As incidents mounted, including the arrest of the Argentine ambassador and his dog, the diplomatic corps prevailed upon its understandably timid dean, a Finn, to protest to the Soviet ambassador, Chervonenko. He was too busy to receive us but made his counselor available. I sent our counselor, John Baker, to represent us, and I understand he made himself more than adequately offensive.

The last recorded occasion when Washington took up the Czechoslovak question with the Soviets was on July 22, 1968. At that time Secretary Rusk called in Ambassador Dobrynin to protest Soviet press charges that the U.S. had stored arms in Germany for use by Czech revolutionaries. The secretary said that the U.S. government was closely watching Soviet pressures on Czechoslovakia, a U.N. member which had a right to manage its own affairs. The next meeting on the subject was Dobrynin's call on President Johnson at 8:15 P.M. Washington time on August 20 (almost exactly at the time the invasion began) to deliver a paper with the unexpected news that "forces in Czechoslovakia were acting against the existing social order" and that in response to a request for assistance from the Czechoslovak government, the USSR and its allies were sending troops to that country.

Because we were acting on a strategy based on the concept that the Czechs discouraged Western intervention, and because the Western countries considered such a policy the least likely to provoke Soviet resort to force, there were no plans at hand to deal with the Soviet attack. The first thought was to limit the military repercussions, and this was what NATO was instructed to do in an early message which called for vigilance but not for a general alert.

Public debate switched to the U.N. Security Council which had been convened on August 21 by the Western delegations. The Czech representative, Jan Muzik, who was cut off from his government, attended the meeting but confined himself to citing radio announcements from Prague and to cautious use of information published in the Western press. For several days the U.S. delegate, Undersecretary of State George Ball, and the Soviet delegate, Malik, engaged in bitter debate along expected lines, and on August 24 the Czechoslovak foreign minister, Jiri Hajek, arrived to deliver a strong statement written for him in Prague. This was Hajek's last appearance as foreign minister, because as a result of the talks started in Moscow the next day between the Soviets and the Dubček regime, the Czechoslovak item was removed from the U.N. agenda.

The Czechoslovak Government Acts

As far as I am aware there is no record of a public acknowledgement by any Czechoslovak citizen that he had foreknowledge of the invasion. This observation applies particularly to Dubček and Smrkovsky. The latter made the point most emphatically in the following citation from his 1975 "Testimony":

> I can say that until half an hour before midnight on the night of August 20 I never heard either directly from anyone on the Soviet side or from the socialist countries, or through another person, that they were determined to enter our country and occupy it with their army. If I had heard anything of this kind, even at second hand, I would certainly have had to deal with it concretely; it would have had to be discussed at the Party Presidium; I simply could not pass it over. I never heard anything of this kind

and as far as I was a participant in several conversations with the Soviet leaders, such words were never uttered.

At a meeting held on the evening of August 20 the Czech Presidium was discussing a "report on the current political situation" and arrangements for the Fourteenth Party Congress, scheduled for September 9, when Prime Minister Cernik broke in with the news that Soviet troops had crossed the border. It is plausibly reported that Dubček, breaking down in tears, exclaimed: "It is a tragedy, I did not expect this to happen, I had no suspicion, not even the slightest hint that we would be attacked. I have devoted my whole life to cooperation with the Soviet Union and they have done this to me, it is my personal tragedy." The Presidium pulled itself together and drafted a proclamation calling upon the people not to resist the invading forces but to remain at their posts.

There are several versions of what happened immediately thereafter but there is no doubt that treachery was perpetrated, at least on an intermediate level, to support the Soviet cause. According to one account, Karel Hoffman, who was in charge of radio and telegraph communications, tried to delay the broadcast of the proclamation, pending the drafting of a substitute statement by Soviet collaborators within the regime. The story, as I heard it from an authentic source who is still in Prague as of this writing, is that the radio personnel loyal to Dubček locked Hoffman and his accomplices out of the studios and threw away the keys. In any event, the official proclamation which was drafted shortly after midnight was not broadcast until 1:50 A.M. on August 21.

In the early hours of August 21 Cernik was the first to be arrested in his office by Soviet security police, who then arrested Dubček, Smrkovsky, and Kriegel in the party headquarters. The Rumanian ambassador later told me that about 4:00 A.M. on August 21 he was called by telephone by Ceaucescu who instructed him to see Dubček and report on what was going on. My colleague found the party building then surrounded by Soviet troops.

Apparently Dubček was first flown to a Soviet base in Poland, whereas Cernik, Smrkovsky, Kriegel, and Cisar were taken to a town in Slovakia. The fact that Bilak, Indra, and Kolder, leaders of the pro-Soviet opposition, were not arrested led to the supposition that they had been chosen to consult the Soviet Embassy regarding the formation of a new government and in particular one which would have legalized the occupation by invitation. All of those mentioned have steadfastly denied conspiring with the invaders. In any event, the popular mood ruled out the possibility of acceptance of a puppet government.

Action from this point passed to President Svoboda and to the members of the rump government left behind in Prague. Without waiting for September 9, the date previously set for the Fourteenth Party Congress, Dubček's supporters convened the congress on August 22 in an emergency meeting. The initiative was taken by the Prague Party Committee, a Dubček stronghold, which called the some one thousand Czech delegates already selected to meet secretly in the industrial suburb of Vysocaný. The sessions were emotional and very confused. The Congress declared its continued allegiance to Svoboda, Smrkovsky, Dubček, and Cernik. It demanded the release of the imprisoned leaders and addressed an appeal for help to the Communist parties of the world to

restore Czechoslovak sovereignty. It called for a one-
hour protest strike at noon on August 23, declaring that
there should be no disorder however, and that the foreign troops simply be ostracized and ignored.

The burden of maintaining a semblance of authority in
fact fell upon the shoulders of President Svoboda, who
dealt with the Soviets locally. After consulting with the
national leaders in Prague he finally decided his best
course would be to negotiate directly with the top authorities in Moscow. On Saturday, August 24, he left
with a mixed delegation picked by himself which included the Slovak leader Husak, Defense Minister General Dzur, and three conservative representatives.

On arrival in Moscow Svoboda was received with full
honors due a head of state. Circumstances thus brought
about the presence in the Soviet capital of a fully representative Czechoslovak group consisting of the president,
his heterogeneous delegation, and the captive leaders
from Prague whom Svoboda ordered be immediately
brought before him. My unnamed informant reported
that Svoboda was deeply shocked by the physical and
psychological state of his abducted countrymen. He told
a weeping Dubček "Brace up, man," and commanded
that the group be properly fed and cared for before the
talks could be started.

Svoboda's conduct won understandable acceptance.
He had been attached to the Soviet army during the war
and he was prepared to give the side he served on the
same full allegiance when it came out on top politically
in Czechoslovakia in 1948. He seems also to have been
influenced by his daughter who was married to the
Czechoslovak ambassador to the U.N. and who was out-
spokenly anti-Western.

During the four days of negotiation in Moscow, the drama of an "underground in the open," as it was called by one writer, was being enacted in Prague. On Saturday, August 24, the day Svoboda left for Moscow, the one-hour general strike took place as decreed, preceded for ten minutes by the blare of sirens. Church bells were also rung (in defiance of one of the first bans the Communists usually impose after taking over a country). Thereafter there was silence and no movement in the streets except by Russian patrols. Contemporary press reports described the local scene in passionate detail, but one or two vivid memories stand out.

By day the downtown streets were crowded with young people carrying placards with the names of the collaborators or the license numbers of unmarked secret police cars. Walls were covered everywhere by anti-Russian graffiti, despite a threat that offenders would be shot on sight. The order was not enforced, but just to be safe, lookouts were posted to warn of approaching militiamen. The main radio stations were, of course, under occupation control, but a network of smaller clandestine transmitters had sprung into action after the invasion began. The operation apparently was a by-product of the military alert system installed during the Warsaw Pact summer maneuvers; Soviet efforts to jam it were frustrated by workers who sidetracked a train carrying the necessary equipment.

With the Czech forces locked in barracks by their government's order, the argument against the use of violence was compelling for the Czechs, while the Soviets for their part wisely decided to rely on patience and discipline to deal with the emotions of patriotism and indignation which inspired every Czech organization and association, including the Czech–Soviet Friendship Society. The steadfastness of their people at home may have given support to the Czech negotiators in Moscow, and may have helped produce the kind of compromise which relaxed tensions by temporarily diffusing them.

As happened at Čierna and Bratislava, the agreements reached in Moscow were never revealed in full, and thus became subject to different interpretations giving the stronger party the benefit of any doubt. At the beginning of the discussion in Moscow Svoboda won his point that Czechoslovakia should be represented by the still incumbent government despite the arrest of some of its members. The Czechs also came out well in passages in the communiqué which called for a relationship of equality and independence; which accepted Dubček's Action Program in principle; and which omitted mention of a "counterrevolutionary situation" or an appeal for help as justifications for the dispatch of troops. The "decisions" of Čierna and Bratislava were confirmed, and normalization was stated to be the common goal. Czechoslovakia was withdrawn from the U.N. agenda and both parties pledged themselves to strengthen the defenses of the socialist commonwealth and the Warsaw Pact.

The terms of the Czechoslovak surrender were incorporated in a "secret" protocol which was never published but was frequently referred to in subsequent negotiations. The protocol was said to contain eighteen stipulations, including the following: invalidation of the emergency Fourteenth Party Congress; convocation of a Central Committee Plenum to consider "questions of normalization" such as personnel changes, control of the media, and banning of antisocialist organizations such as the "political clubs" and the Social Democratic party;

steps against officials who left the country; and strengthening of the Interior Ministry. A treaty was to be concluded for the withdrawal of forces in stages as soon as the threat to socialism in Czechoslovakia had passed.

At the end of the meeting in Moscow, Ulbricht, Gomulka, Kadar, and Zhivkov were produced and the Czechoslovak delegation was invited to have a glass of cognac with them. This the Czechs refused to do. Just before departing for the airport, Dubček learned that Dr. Kriegel was being detained by the Soviets, apparently with the intention of putting him on trial. Dubček said that he would not leave for home unless Kriegel was put on the plane, where he was duly delivered. As a follow-up, Vassili Kuznetzov, the tough but competent first deputy minister in the Soviet Foreign Office with whom I was later to deal in Moscow, was sent to Prague to oversee ongoing negotiations. He was to remain there until the end of November.

PRELUDE TO THE END

Thus began the tragic end chapter of the Dubček venture. My good friend and colleague Sir William Barker, the British ambassador, left to take a professorship at Liverpool University, correctly predicting that the Czech struggle was over. Some of us who stayed a bit longer felt obliged to hope that the seemingly inevitable could be forestalled.

The leaders faced the forlorn task of explaining and seeking acceptance of the Moscow decisions on their return. In his radio address President Svoboda blandly declared that the outcome was neither a triumph nor a capitulation but was a practical solution. Smrkovsky agonized: "History will sometime judge whether we did well or whether we committed treason. I do not know. I acted on my own decision. But I hesitated a long time." Dubček, in a long, nontelevised radio speech which I recall was punctuated by sighs and groans, made it appear that the Moscow agreement was a condition for the survivability of the Action Program which he acknowledged would be slowed down.

The first popular mood was one of bitter shock but the public adapted itself philosophically to the Moscow results as they revealed themselves in their execution. By arrangement with the Soviet military command the graffiti disappeared in a single night. The emergency Fourteenth Party Congress was simply forgotten but an enlarged Central Committee Plenum, which met August 31 to September 1, included some fifty liberals, that is to say, members chosen by the secret congress. The Plenum reorganized the government along ambiguous lines, conforming to the new way of political life. Four conservatives including Kolder were dropped from the Presidium, as was Kriegel, a progressive leader. Four progressives were eliminated from the Secretariat, including Cisar. The top people in the new Presidium were Dubček, Smrkovsky, and Cernik; the two conservatives, Bilak and Piller; as well as Husak, the Slovak party chief who was winning influence as a local chauvinist and was soon to become the spoiler of the coalition.

The new government acted in a correspondingly paradoxical fashion. It clamped down on two ultraliberal periodicals, restricted some minor liberties such as free travel abroad, yet at the same time had the nerve to protest to the Soviets their distribution of a propaganda paper which was denounced as interference in Czechoslovakia's internal affairs. Although the liberal journalists, much to their annoyance, were told to behave, there was a freer press than in any other bloc country at that time, and there were no mass arrests. Skilling cites the following results of a popularity poll taken in mid-September among 1882 respondents: Dubček, 96.1 percent; Svoboda, 95.6; Smrkovsky, 73.3; Cernik, 72.6; Cisar, 37.6; Husak, 23.6; Sik, 15.7.[2]

The government successfully weathered several minor crises, especially the previously mentioned anti-Soviet demonstration at the Opera House on October 28 and a three-day student strike in early November. Such disorders were handled efficiently and with understanding by the local police. The occupation troops remained in barracks outside the cities and the Soviets were obviously disinclined to risk a second show of naked force in advance of the date of the Moscow World Communist Conference set for the following year.

Early in December we cabled the State Department that the regime might have a fighting chance. At the same time we noted that power was shifting to the cautious conservatives who, however, were still dominated by Prime Minister Cernik, and the Slovak wing led by Husak and Strougal.

In the next weeks it became very evident the Soviets were turning on political pressure and that factionalism was beginning to tear the united front apart. Husak had tightened his grip on Slovakia as the result of a new federal reorganization law. On the grounds that the president and prime minister were Czechs, he demanded that a Slovak be given Smrkovsky's post as president of the

---

[2]Skilling, *Czechoslovakia's Interrupted Revolution*, p.809.

National Assembly. As a compromise a moderate Slovak replaced Smrkovsky, who became chairman of the People's House in the Assembly. The continued popular backing of the regime was dramatically illustrated by the turnout of over a million people for a three-hour funeral procession in honor of the Prague student, Jan Palach, who burned himself to death on January 19 in protest against the Soviet occupation.

Despite their popularity, Dubček and Smrkovsky were in fact marked as mortally wounded politicians because of their failure to prevent the invasion. The Soviets moved in their men at intermediate levels in the ministries and complained bitterly about the government's duplicity, citing the example of the publication by the Czech Academy of Sciences of a "Black Book" recording the treacherous acts of numerous Czech collaborators. When I paid my farewell call on Prime Minister Cernik early in March 1969, he deplored his "fate in holding office at this point in [his] country's history."

On March 28 the Czech hockey team beat the Soviets, providing an occasion for a few nights of celebration in downtown Prague. For the most part the demonstrators were orderly and simply milled around the streets, but a few rowdy gangs, provoked or unprovoked, broke up the Soviet tourist and airline offices on the central square. Moscow seized the opening it had doubtless been waiting for and dispatched to Prague a delegation headed by Deputy Foreign Minister Semenov, supported by the persuasive presence of Defense Minister Marshal Grechko. On April 18, the day I presented my credentials as U.S. ambassador in Moscow, it was announced that Husak had replaced Dubček as first secretary of the Czechoslovak Communist party.

SOME CONCLUDING COMPARISONS

I have touched upon three challenges to Soviet ideology and rule—in Poland, Hungary, and Czechoslovakia. These experiences, I believe, show that the Soviet Union will go to any length—from granting concessions to the extremity of war—to maintain its hold on the countries within its European empire. Premier Kosygin, in a meeting with Senators Gore and Pell in Moscow in November 1968, solemnly declared that the action of the Warsaw Pact nations in Czechoslovakia had kept the peace because it had forestalled the loss of their socialist (and to them sacred) stake in that country and had prevented an unacceptable shift in the European balance of power.

Under more normal conditions the Soviets maintain their grip on the satellites by less violent means. These comprise a broad array of pressures exerted through interparty relationships, control over local personnel appointments, Soviet domination of the secret police command in each country, the complete dependence of the satellites upon membership in the Soviet economic system—and, should all of these fail, the possible use of force as a last resort, as applied in Hungary and Czechoslovakia. Concessions to unrest in the satellites are not the preferred method, but are not entirely excluded. Cases in point include the Soviet dumping of Gomulka in late 1970 in order to forestall a workers' rebellion in Poland and, most recently, Soviet tolerance of Kadar's deviations in Hungary.

In all of this, membership in the Warsaw military pact plays a curiously incidental role. On the one hand, a members is forbidden to leave the pact as Hungary tried to do. On the other hand, Rumania was able to stand aloof from its allies' pressures on Czechoslovakia, claiming that they represented unwarranted interference in internal affairs. The risks of Rumania's truancy were apparently judged acceptable because of its hard-line domestic policies and because Rumania shared no common border with a Western country.

It is undeniable that life in each of the satellites is easier now than it was at its Stalinist worst, and is generally less harsh than it is in the Soviet Union today. The distinct fact, however, is that Soviet control remains essentially undiminished. It is not clear how the still-free Euro-Communists assess this condition. Although they may hope to be given more latitude upon attaining power, it is certain that they would be subjected to the standard pressures once they had received Soviet aid, the first step toward the acceptance of Communist discipline.

Dubček and his reformers may have thought they could break the mold by subtle means. Some of the reasons for their failure stand out from the account I have given of the way they attained power, and their brief use of it. While they were spectacularly successful in building up popular support, they were unable to control it as a force, as wise and strong leaders should have done. It is also hard to believe that as skilled politicians who had fought their way to the top, they erred solely through simple naïveté; Dubček and Smrkovsky may have sincerely thought that the purity of their motives justified their being less than frank with the public, and indeed with their intimate associates, in withholding information about the dangers of the course they were pursuing.

Similarly, in dealing with the Soviets the Czech leaders counted too heavily on the hope that the mere offering of effusive declarations of allegiance to communism and loyalty to the Soviet alliance (which the Nagy government in Hungary had notably repudiated) would hold them safe against the perils of probing new limits of Soviet tolerance in such matters as party discipline and privacy. In Soviet eyes, preservation of these essentials took precedence over seeking popularity through appeals to humanistic and democratic sentiment.

Finally, the Czechs, like most of the rest of Europe, were beguiled by the conviction, fostered by incipient moves toward East–West détente, that the Soviets would not repeat their military aggression of 1956. When they did strike, the Soviets took the edge off their use of force by playing with skill, patience, and luck a political game which restored the Czech deviationist government to a purgatory of nominal authority before casting it into the foreordained outer darkness of rejection. In fact, the Czechoslovak venture won the Soviets spurious credit for moderation, sophistication, and even some nominal respect for legality. Apart from the shocks produced among the foreign Communist parties (which were largely papered over in the Moscow World Communist Congress in May-June 1969, but are still of some later consequence), the one-time heroes of the Dubček movement dropped from sight more rapidly and with less ceremony than their vanquished Hungarian counterparts.

Within a year after the invasion the partly rehabilitated Soviets were on the prowl for bigger game, in particular an exploration of the possible benefits to be obtained through an improvement in relations with the U.S.

THE AMERICAN ROLE

The United States government has often been reproached, especially by some of its own citizens, for having done so little for the Czech reformers. Perhaps the setting can now be reconstructed more objectively. The Czech Communists had been hostile to us since taking power in 1948, and some of this bitterness in the form of grievances on both sides carried over to the Dubček leadership. At best these leaders were indifferent to American interest. Our attitude toward them was completely honorable; our private and public media was wholly sympathetic. Radio Free Europe, whose mission is to disseminate to a particular country uncensored news about that country, and to advertise to the satellite area any advance achieved by a particular reformist group, was especially effective; it scrupulously refrained, however, from offering political advice.

A few days after the invasion which began on the night of August 20, a package of film landed from an American observation satellite showing in detail the final massive concentration of Soviet armor (identified by the painted white stripe later to be familiar in Prague) which had been building up on the Czechoslovak–Polish frontier for the last few days. My intelligence acquaintances claim that the state of activity at advance airfields showed the Soviet forces poised for action; my sources now say that they would have sounded the alarm had the films been received before the event. It is disturbing that despite all the political and scientific safeguards developed by our modern society, the Soviets were successfully able to carry out a massive surprise attack.

As to what the United States government might have done, it must be remembered that the Vietnamese War undermined both our moral leadership and our prestige. In 1968 we were still trying to persuade the Soviets to influence the North Vietnamese to bring about peace. Furthermore, partly because of election-year politics, the administration was pushing for a U.S.–Soviet arms control understanding.

Certain advance knowledge that the Soviets were about to attack Czechoslovakia would, of course, have given us a freer hand to mobilize world opinion against them and possibly to restrain them by threats to withhold favors and impose restrictions. In the end event, as will be next explained, the political reverses which both we and the Soviets suffered respectively from Vietnam and Czechoslovakia were to bring about a kind of enforced rapprochement.

Chapter XI

Normalization—A
Studied Effort

THE "NEW NIXON" NEW LOOK

I WAS President Nixon's personal choice for the post of U.S. ambassador to the USSR in 1969. Presumably he chose me because of the acquaintance established between us during his visits to Poland in 1959 (he seems to have associated me with his triumphal reception in Warsaw), and to Czechoslovakia in 1967. I have been told that had the Democrats won the election, their most likely choice would have been the writer-economist John Kenneth Galbraith.

One can speculate how and to what degree the Democrats might have matched the Nixon record of dealing with the Soviets. Because I was his personal nominee I felt especially obligated to serve him loyally in the office and for the term to which he had appointed me. I was able to do this in good conscience because of the successes he achieved during his first administration in two areas of my previous involvement, namely, U.S. relations with the USSR and the Communist Chinese, where frustration and failure had hitherto prevailed. Unlike some other officials who served the president in similar fashion, I do not feel called upon to comment on the events which led to his downfall and the culmination of a vastly depressing human tragedy.

In the interregnum between the U.S. election and Nixon's inauguration, a curious episode occurred. Even though he was a lame-duck president, Johnson was eager to impose his ideas on future arms negotiations with the Soviets; his eagerness to start the talks as soon as possible was well known. His initiative leap-frogged the Czech crisis in renewed efforts by his administration to open discussions during the last weeks of 1968, which hopefully would have ended in a summit between Johnson and a Soviet leader. Indeed, an outline of the Johnson plan was circulated secretly to the NATO council in Paris for its information. Despite the fact that the U.S. approach to the Soviets offered them a modicum of rehabilitation after their invasion of Czechoslovakia, the Moscow government put it off for the very good reason that they had been notified informally but emphatically that the new administration refused to engage itself before taking office.

When I came on board in Washington after being confirmed by the Senate in early March 1969, the Nixon administration had already established contacts through the Soviet Embassy for the discussion of three subjects; preparations for arms talks, Vietnam, and the Middle East. It was decided that when I arrived in Moscow I should undertake a broader presentation in the form of a personal letter which I would convey to Prime Minister Kosygin from the new president. As a candidate, Nixon had denounced the invasion of Czechoslovakia as an "outrage against the conscience of the world," but in his campaign speeches he had also expressed a hope for better relations based on improved contacts and peaceful competition; he implied that a summit meeting might be held in due course.

At just about this time fairly heavy clashes broke out between Soviet and Chinese forces on the disputed Ussuri River border. The buildup was worrisome, it being reported that the Soviets were holding some thirty divisions in reserve, but just recently former presidential staff chief, H. R. Haldeman, has attempted to assign the events a new significance by claiming that the Soviets proposed we join them in a bombing strike against China.[1] These assertions have since been denied by former Secretary Rogers and former National Security Adviser Kissinger.

In mid-March 1969 the Chinese carried out a heavy raid on Damansky Island on the Soviet side of the river, killing several Soviet soldiers. In Moscow the Foreign Ministry briefed our embassy on the seriousness of the incident and asked our government's "understanding." I recall being shown in Washington a carefully drafted reply urging restraints by both sides. While the Soviets may have had contingency plans for a strike, we rightly judged that after their experience with Czechoslovakia, they would hesitate to "jump" China, a second socialist country, so soon before the World Communist Conference scheduled to be held in Moscow within a few months.

We returned to work on the letter which I was to present to Premier Kosygin shortly after my arrival and which was to be a considered effort to set forth in con-

---

[1]H. R. Haldeman, *The Ends of Power* (New York, The Times Books, 1978).

ciliatory language the outlines of a new overall approach to U.S.–Soviet relations. The president laid down certain broad objectives described in "conceptual" terms, doubtless supplied by Henry Kissinger, his new national security adviser. The propositions set forth in the letter, which was kept secret at the time, were later translated into principles intended to guide the conduct of détente.

In briefest summary, the president proposed that all available channels be explored to obviate risks of confrontation and conflict. As regards the Middle East, which was "fraught with danger," no outside power was to seek advantage at the expense of any other, and foreign military assistance should be restrained. The president pointed out that as commander-in-chief he was responsible for the safety of American troops and for the enforcement of commitments upholding South Vietnam's legitimate interests. The U.S. had shown moderation, which had to be exercised mutually. (I was to add orally that we recognized the sensitivity of the Soviet Union's position because of its relations with China, and all we asked of the Soviets was that they should influence Hanoi in the direction of peace.)

As regards Europe, the president said, we were conscious of the great suffering the USSR had endured and we understood its desire to ensure against future disaster. At the same time American opinion had been profoundly shocked by the events in Czechoslovakia. We were also disturbed by flare-ups in Berlin where we were committed to defend West Berlin's integrity. Ways of improving the situation should be examined.

The president hoped that as dangers receded, so would the level of arms. The U.S. would be guided solely by the principle of a "sufficiency" which would meet needs required by national safety and allied defense commitments. I was asked to say that we were not stalling on arms talks but were simply engaged in a review. (It was alleged within the new administration that this review was being delayed because President Johnson had withheld certain papers which he had planned to use in the aforementioned last-minute, postelection approach on arms limitations.)

I was also to tell Kosygin that we had no interest in seeing the USSR and China in conflict, nor in exploiting their differences. As for ourselves, we hoped in the long run to achieve a normalization of relations with the Chinese and we were disappointed by the [then] breakdown of our talks with them in Warsaw.

Finally, I was to tell Kosygin that the president had instructed his administration to avoid harsh words even though the Czech situation had left a residue of suspicion. "Hegemonal relationships over smaller powers [were] self-defeating." Without giving the Soviets advice, we had the feeling this applied to their situation as well. We had no wish to complicate relations with anybody and would applaud normalization wherever it occurred. We would safeguard U.S. interests with due regard to those of the Soviet Union. We desired to remain in constant touch with the Soviet government on a whole range of subjects in order to make our relations increasingly cooperative and constructive. The president's message to Premier Kosygin ended on this note.

Just before I left for Moscow in late March, Soviet Ambassador Dobrynin asked Kissinger and myself for lunch. I remember Kissinger's making the point to Dobrynin that the president wished him (Kissinger) to attend "all discussions with foreign officials." Kissinger was present at my farewell talk with the president when we went over the draft of the letter to Kosygin. I was told to treat our talk with great secrecy. Since Secretary of State Rogers was away, I naturally left a memorandum for him reporting on what I had been doing, a step which I understand caused great annoyance to the White House staff. Incidentally, on a visit to Washington about a year later, I was advised not to take a note pad into a meeting I was to have with the president. Unaware at the time that our conversation would probably be recorded, I overruled the objection on the grounds that the president presumably would wish me to take down whatever instructions he had to give.

As background to the Soviet attitudes which I met with on my arrival in Moscow, I was aware that the Soviet posture toward the 1968 presidential campaign had been one of disapproving detachment. The Soviet media had, of course, exploited with glee the deplorable state of the Union as described by each candidate in blaming the other's party for our country's woes. And, of course, the strong condemnation by both American parties of the Czechoslovak invasion had been quietly played down. During the spring and summer of 1968 the Soviets apparently arrived at the estimate that Nixon would get the Republican nomination and be the likely national winner.

After the election, some reservations had been expressed editorially about the "old Nixon's" anticommunism and his support of "positions of strength." Kissinger, his new security adviser, had been both challenged as a "nuclear enthusiast" and defended as a rationalist European politician. Nixon's campaign call in August for the substitution of negotiation for confrontation had been formally noted and praised. After the election results were known, sanction for the development of relations had been sealed in numerous citations from Lenin about the necessity of doing business with the U.S. When I arrived in early April a restraint on expression was obviously in effect and, as a gesture of goodwill, the Soviets offered us help in locating the wreckage of a U.S. military plane shot down at sea by the North Koreans.

I had no particular friends among Soviet officialdom. In my last two foreign assignments, in Poland and Czechoslovakia, our policy had mainly been at cross-purposes with that of the Soviets. I had met Foreign Minister Gromyko abroad on several occasions but found it difficult to have a coherent conversation with him since he seemed more interested in scoring small points than in sustained discussion. When decisions had to be reached, however, I usually found him straightforward and helpful.

My introductory call on President Podgorny (which I referred to in Chapter X) was set for April 18 and it is hard to believe it had been planned one week in advance to coincide with Dubček's dismissal as Czechoslovak party first secretary on the same day. That event put quite a strain on my talk with Podgorny. He failed to mention it in his opening remarks so that I was obliged to raise it and protest that the simultaneous presence in Prague of Defense Minister Marshal Grechko confirmed charges of flagrant Soviet interference in Czechoslovakia's domestic affairs. Podgorny replied that Soviet action had been imperative to prevent a third European war threatened by indications of West German interest in Czechoslovakia. I denied his insinuation and referred to the unprovoked Soviet attack on Czechoslovakia in August. Podgorny's complacency over the complete success of the surprise invasion reminded me of the rewards which Hitler won from his military venture into the Rhineland in 1936 which I had witnessed. Military countermeasures were, of course, even more unthinkable in 1968 than in 1936.

Even though the timing did not seem especially opportune, I went ahead under Washington instructions with a request to call upon Prime Minister Kosygin to present the president's letter. Since Brezhnev had not yet made himself accessible to Western officials, as later seemed to follow from his assumption of primacy, Kosygin was the highest authority open to us. It was Kosygin whom President Johnson met in Glassboro, New Jersey, in the summer of 1967 in our vain search for Soviet help to end the Vietnamese War and to arrive at some understanding on strategic arms. His earlier renown rested on a reputation for ruthless efficiency as the mayor of Leningrad during the Nazi 900-day siege.

I had met Kosygin previously at a trade fair in Poland and was later to witness a demonstration of his cool precision at the Nixon–Brezhnev summit in 1972. On that occasion I was with a large delegation which called upon him to negotiate some economic matters. Taken aback by seeing Kosygin attended only by a single assistant, the leader of our group asked him whether he "minded our bringing so many experts." Kosygin replied, "Not at all, if you need them."

Prior to my call on Kosygin on April 22, I had provided his office with an advance copy of the president's letter for translation. At our meeting Kosygin had with him the head of the American Department and a couple of other assistants, whereas I had on my side our minister-counselor, Emory C. Swank, and an embassy interpreter. Kosygin thanked me for the "important message" and my comments which he said he would "share with his colleagues Brezhnev and Podgorny."

On May 27 Foreign Minister Gromyko called me in to hand me the Soviet reply. I am not at liberty to discuss its contents in detail, but I can say that it was regarded by the State Department as "positive in tone." Although it restated standard Soviet positions in moderate and polite terms, I commented to the State Department that it offered little by way of cheer or concession.

An interesting feature was that the reply raised the later, much-publicized issue of "linkage." Apparently answering some earlier Kissinger remarks about the crucial importance of finding solutions for Vietnam and arms control, Kosygin's letter declared it would be inadvisable to make the solution of one problem depend upon the solution of another, since this procedure might postpone a general improvement of U.S.–Soviet relations or of the international situation as a whole, and could create a vicious circle.

The exchange was useful in that it enabled us to put our positions on the record while the Soviet response gave some impetus to further discussion.

IRRITATIONS AND INCIDENTS

THE Soviets doubtless wished to get their reply to President Nixon out of the way before the meeting of the International Conference of Communist Parties (the World Communist Conference) which was to take place in Moscow during June 5–17. They knew that anti-American and antiimperialist statements would be inevitable at the conference. In fact, they tthemselves promoted some of the attacks. Three weeks later, however, Foreign Minister Gromyko was to stress the need for better U.S.–Soviet relations in a speech he delivered on July 10 before the Supreme Soviet.

Having been postponed from 1968 to 1969 because of the invasion of Czechoslovakia, the World Conference was in many respects an embarrassing event for all concerned. The Soviets had originally proposed that neither Czechoslovakia nor their quarrel with China be discussed, but realizing that this was impossible, they took the initiative in denouncing China for the serious border incidents which had been taking place along the Ussuri River since the month of March. The Soviets defended themselves on Czechoslovakia by invoking the so-called Brezhnev Doctrine of "limited sovereignty" that justified outside Warsaw Pact military assistance to a member afflicted by domestic troubles which might threaten party rule in that particular country.

Soviet speeches were published in full, the others being carried in summaries. We also kept ourselves informed through the embassies of countries which had delegations, most of whom were not afraid to report to their ambassadors. We were never favored by a call from Gus Hall, the head American delegate.

While the stooge parties such as the Mongolian and Bulgarian helped them on China, the Soviets drew fire on both Czechoslovakia and China from the Italians, Austrians, and Spaniards, as well as from Rumania's President Ceaucescu, who challenged the right of a conference of this kind to draw up guidance binding on all Communist parties. Ceaucescu also suggested the liquidation of both NATO and the Warsaw Pact.

The result was that the basic document was a hodge-podge of antiimperialist resolutions, some of them contradictory in their assigned order of priority. The final act was signed without reservations by sixty-one delegations out of a total of seventy-five. The outcome was less than a total Soviet success, but it was nevertheless something of an accomplishment to make it possible for parties with so many divergent views to meet and discuss mutual problems.

The World Conference had little effect on U.S.–Soviet relations. Although the remainder of 1969 produced no significant breakthrough, useful clarifying discussions were opened up. During the summer talks were held on the Middle East to define principles for a settlement, but they hit snags on the questions of total Israeli withdrawal, the number of refugees Israel could accept, and curbs on arms supplies to the area. Inconclusive talks were also held on Vietnam. Some progress was made in the disposition of several minor bilateral problems, including an agreement which I signed in May 1969 for an exchange of sites for new office buildings in Moscow and Washington. (As of June 1977 no building activity had as yet begun because of Soviet haggling over construction terms.)

In his speech of July 10 before the Supreme Soviet, Foreign Minister Gromyko, while taking occasion to disparage the sorry state of U.S. society, declared that the USSR attached great importance to its relations with the U.S. despite profound class differences. He did not reply to a previously submitted U.S. proposal for an August opening date on arms talks, but merely said that the Soviets were ready for them to begin.

Thus for the indefinite future, bilateral relations set-

tled down to a pattern which could be called normal—
neither Cold War, nor what was later to be known as
détente. Factors which later produced goodwill on order
—by fiat—had not yet begun to operate. The Soviet
government seemed boxed in by pressures from China,
and its leadership emerged from the World Communist
Conference looking confused and bereft of ideas.

Inquiries made directly to Gromyko and "information
passers" around Moscow, primarily Soviet journalists
and scholars, revealed that he had nothing special in
mind as regards new initiatives, beyond calling for
concessions from the U.S. In his speech before the U.N.
General Assembly that September he got no farther than
generalities criticizing the U.S., among other things for
its plans to develop antiballistic missiles (ABMs) and
multiple independently targeted reentry vehicles
(MIRVs). Agreement was reached, however, to open
negotiations on SALT in Helsinki later in the year.

In the course of the summer, cordiality had been somewhat dampened by President Nixon's visit to Rumania
on his European tour. The gesture was certainly pure
Nixon and was not Kissinger's idea, and was ostensibly
meant to reward Ceaucescu's independence in receiving
Nixon as a private citizen in 1967. Soviet officials showed
studied unconcern in commenting on Nixon's trip.

Responsibility for disturbing mutual relations did not
lie with the Soviets alone. In protest against Soviet curbs
on Jewish emigration, the militant Jewish Defense
League (JDL) in the U.S. intensified its harassment of
Soviet officials, especially in New York. The incidents
were approaching a level of such deadly seriousness that
I wrote the White House asking for help. Hearing nothing, I turned to my colleague George Bush, who was

then our ambassador to the U.N. and who was also being embarrassed by the JDL attacks. Bush went directly to the president and was responsible for the creation of the special Executive Protective Service which now guards foreign officials in the U.S.

One of the incidents, involving shots fired into the Soviet U.N. Mission in New York, led to a bizarre occurrence. The attack took place on November 6, 1971, and because of its seriousness Secretary of State Rogers had called in Ambassador Dobrynin to offer an apology, which was immediately publicized. Much to my annoyance, I was called down to the Foreign Ministry about midnight to receive a stiff protest from the first deputy minister. I offered my own apology and sympathy and pointed out that our secretary of state had made a public apology and that this was the response which really mattered. The minister, however, sharpened his protest, which prompted me to mention attacks which had been mounted against our embassy in the past, with official Soviet tolerance or connivance. I saw him look at his watch and heard the rumble of tanks in the distance. I then realized that the tanks were on their way to Red Square for the November 7 parade on the following morning, and would soon block off all traffic. In his eagerness to get me out of the building, the minister abruptly ended our meeting.

The JDL attacks were most regrettable and could have produced dire results if a fatality had occurred. The Moscow embassy suffered reprisals which often took the form of damage done to the cars of Jewish members of our staff. The New York authorities played down the activities of the JDL, but undoubtedly they affected our relations with the Soviets for a long time. It appears that none of the attacks was punished by a jail sentence, although some penalties were imposed on contempt charges and for disregard of injunctions prohibiting further violence.

I describe the above affair to illustrate the general conditions under which American officials work in Moscow. For weeks and months relations can be carried on smoothly at the local level, only to be suddenly interrupted by an unexpected and sometimes serious incident. Whenever our government expels a Soviet official from the United States for espionage, we know we will forfeit a member of our own sta against whom the Soviets make false or specious charges. Although more rarely than in the past, the Soviets occasionally try to recruit our citizens for espionage by entrapping them in embarrassing situations.

Efforts by Soviet nationals to seek asylum in our embassy, which we are instructed to deny except under stringent conditions, frequently caused me embarrassment. We told them that we were forbidden to take them in and that since the Soviet police had to know where they were, they would be better off to leave as soon as possible. We were faced with a particularly poignant case when about fifteen Volga Germans with their families sought refuge in the embassy on the ground that their religious sect was being persecuted. We informed the Foreign Office of their presence and asked that leniency be shown them because of the children and old people among them. We kept the group for a couple of days and, after receiving some assurances regarding their treatment, we put them on a police bus at the door. We asked them to inform us of their safe return home but, of course, heard nothing further.

The embassy staff were all handpicked volunteers, most of them with Russian language training. The rewards were mostly personal: an attachment to Russian culture and the Russian language; a liking for the people despite their perversities and despite the Soviet regime's cavalier disinterest in foreigners except for gainful exploitation; as well as vivid memories of the Russian landscape and the harsh but invigorating climate. State Department recognition was often slow and uneven because Russian specialists were hard to place and frequently languished in secondary jobs or in research offices before being sent back for another tour. Their modest profile was illustrated on one occasion when, as secretary of state, Kissinger was on the point of asking the head of the department's Soviet division to leave a meeting because he did not know him.

In the Soviet Union, length of duty was generally limited to two years because of ever-present pressures. These included indifferent housing, physical surveillance, and constant bugging of conversations by various types of concealed devices. Without revealing any secrets, it can be said that the embassy and residence were surrounded by an electronic atmosphere of their own. The United States government has been investigating whether such emanations are health hazards.

Chapter XII

Soviet Affairs—
The Domestic Accent

INFORMAL CONTACTS EXPAND

THE year 1970 started out badly for U.S.–Soviet relations. We were blamed for failing to prevent the Israelies from carrying out bombing raids deep inside Egypt (which came within five miles of Cairo). Prince Sihanouk's ouster in Cambodia in April was followed by the joint incursion into that country by the South Vietnamese and ourselves. Anti-American propaganda attained an intensity not far below the level of Stalin's day. In spite of this, certain accommodations were reached.

Our formal contacts with the Foreign Ministry had settled back into a rather unproductive routine. Its habit of asking in advance the nature of the subject one proposed to discuss did not encourage the idea of dropping in for an informal exchange of views. When in a bad mood, the officials would open the talk with an argument or a complaint. In exasperation I told one of our Soviet contacts that I had gained a clearer and more rational understanding of Soviet foreign policy in my talks with Polish Foreign Minister Rapacki than I had been able to do in Moscow.

Faced with such frustration, it became tempting to give heed to overtures from other quarters. My predecessor, Ambassador Llewellyn Thompson, was extremely wary of doing this, believing it could cross wires with the Foreign Ministry and invite provocations. With the best of intentions, the Austrian ambassador tried to arrange a dialogue between me and a Moscow professor who was reported to have access to the top Soviet leadership. The message which the professor wished to convey was that the Politburo was giving high priority to a review of U.S. relations and ways to improve them. I passed back the suggestion that a good start could be made by stopping anti-American propaganda. Incidentally, another neutral colleague, the Swiss ambassador (now deceased) tried to incite American retaliation against the Soviet media campaign, which he considered to be "intolerable."

A legitimate way to enlarge our contacts was facilitated by the efforts of elements in the party to assert a greater interest in foreign affairs. While they did not directly challenge the Foreign Ministry, they used channels available to them to keep themselves better informed and play a more open role in this field. For this purpose they relied on the apparatus of the Secretariat of the Central Committee. The KGB, or secret police, is the best known arm but it is not so well known that the apparatus also operates a political information service abroad, which, in parallel with, but separately from, the regular foreign service, reports directly to the Secretariat in Moscow. The select few Soviet ambassadors in large posts like Washington and Paris who are members of the Central Committee, are clued into the service, and doubtless control its agents in their missions.

Such agents are frequently identified publicly as KGB

men which, strictly speaking, they are not, although (as indicated) they are responsible to the Central Committee apparatus of which the KGB is a suborganization operating with its own agents in practically every Soviet office abroad. The Central Committee's political agents can usually be spotted by their air of confidence and competence. I overheard one of them, who had returned from an embassy abroad, tell a colleague how happy he was to renounce diplomatic life and rejoin the Central Committee staff.

The growth on the Soviet side of a kind of subministry concerned with foreign affairs was helped by the setting up of periodical international meetings of scientists and politicians which were originally organized by the American industrialist Cyrus Eaton. They became known first as Pugwash and then Dartmouth Conferences after the places where they were held. Meetings between U.S. and Soviet representatives are held alternately in the U.S. and the USSR. Since all the Soviet representatives are in effect state officials, they speak with an authoritative voice, whereas the American delegates, distinguished though they may be in their respective fields, speak as private citizens. In practice, however, our representatives consulted with interested branches of the U.S. government and were eventually gathered into Kissinger's National Security Council network in Washington. When they came to Moscow they kept me fully informed and, although in their bilateral meetings they conscientiously observed restrictions on classified information, I have the impression that they were more forthcoming than their Soviet counterparts, who perhaps gained more from the exchange.

In the spring of 1969 U.S.–Soviet contacts were facilitated by the establishment of an officially sponsored Institute for the Study of American (and later, Canadian) Affairs in Moscow. It was, and still is, headed by Georgi Arbatov, a political publicist who had been on the staff of the Central Committee and claimed, as is apparently true, that he is a close Brezhnev friend. He is also known to have General Staff connections. He was assisted by about a dozen quite respectable Soviet economists and political scientists, including the foreign minister's son Anatoliy Gromyko. The Institute publishes a monthly magazine in Russian on American affairs entitled *USA,* and maintains a library in English and Russian with which the embassy exchanges official publications. Its members enjoyed prestige and authority and provided a refreshing change from the stilted pronouncements of the Foreign Ministry bureaucrats. Arbatov has frequently been very rough in dealing with the United States in his speeches and articles, but we found him a valuable intermediary in that he had the prestige and qualifications to engage in serious discussions which he doubtless reported up the line.

Communications between our embassy's junior officers and their counterparts in the Soviet ministries became increasingly easier, even leading to reciprocal hospitality. With the notable exception of Ambassador Llewellyn Thompson, who as a young secretary had stayed in Moscow with the Soviet government during the darkest days of the German attack in 1941, few of our ambassadors seem to have enjoyed this privilege. Charles Bohlen mentions in his book[1] that he and his wife had

---

[1]Charles E. Bohlen, *Witness to History* (New York: W. W. Norton & Co., 1973).

never been to a meal in a private Soviet household. The single experience we had produced unfortunate consequences for our hosts, two Soviet mathematicians and their wives, with whom we spent a lively social evening with wine and music. Our attempt to return their hospitality was met with a polite refusal and a message that they would not even be able to attend our July 4 reception.

Dissent was already a thriving industry in Moscow in 1969 but had not yet attained the international significance it assumed from 1973 onward. Its expression was largely the function of the intelligentsia; for instance, the mass of the Russians were much less sensitive to world events and had little sympathy for the Czechs and their ill-fated cause.

The dissillusionment of the intelligentsia with the slowness of change covered a broad range of grievances, among others: Solzhenitsyn's philosophical attacks upon bureaucratic communism and Stalinist abuses; the intellectuals' protest against censorship; the complaints of harassed religious leaders; the sociologist Medvedev brothers' advocacy of "Marxism with a human face" (as of late 1977 Roy Medvedev is still in the USSR, while Zoares writes from London); Amalryk's prophecy of Soviet collapse by the year 1984; and the Soviet H-bomb developer Andrei Zakharov's leadership of the campaign for "socialist legality" which he inherited from the exiled Soviet dissenters Sinyavsky, Pavel Litvinov, and Chalidze, some of whom had been arrested in 1968 for publicly protesting the Czech invasion.

Solzhenitsyn in particular posed a problem for all concerned. One of his former Russian editors told me that

Solzhenitsyn's first drafts contained masses of eloquent but undigested writing which had to be organized into a coherent whole. The original manuscript of his *One Day in the Life of Ivan Denisovich,* [2] which Khrushchev allowed to be published, was three times the length of the finished book and was overloaded with vulgarisms and obscure passages which had to be edited out.

Prior to the regime's decision to expel him in 1975, Solzhenitsyn was under constant harassment and at one time took refuge in the garage of Mtsilav Rostropovic, the distinguished cellist and conductor who now lives in the U.S. His friendship with Solzhenitsyn brought down upon him the wrath of Madame Furtseva, the minister of culture. I recall her telling Rostropovic at one of our receptions that, as "punishment," his trips abroad would be cancelled and that he would have to spend the rest of the year playing for Soviet audiences. His immediate reply was "Since when, Madame Minister, has it been a punishment for a Russian to play before a Russian audience?"

The late Madame Furtseva was a person of overpowering presence and occasional charm, but had her difficult moments. On one occasion she protested to me about an intended visit of two representatives from the Metropolitan Opera of New York who, she said, were coming to Moscow to pirate ideas and costume designs for a production of Mussorgsky's *Boris Godunov* which they were planning to present in New York. I advised her that if she felt that way, she should cancel their visas and I

---

[2] Alexander Solzhenitsyn, *One Day in the Life of Ivan Denisovich* (New York: Bantam Books, 1963).

would be happy to announce the reason for this action. The visit took place as planned and was a great success for both opera companies.

The Soviets have a generally exaggerated opinion of the excellence of their ballet which, with the exception of a few standard productions, is now mediocre by comparison with some of our own. In the whole domain of artistic achievement, the Soviets miss no opportunity to seek unmerited self-glorification, and I remember that in Washington they advertised as the "Russian Art Show" a visiting exhibit of modern French paintings which they had kept hidden away in their cellars for years.

During the 1960s and early 1970s the embassy maintained a stand-off relationship with the local dissenters, which seemed to suit both sides. Several attended our public receptions and we let it be known that we were sympathetic to their cause. We made good use of their unpublished writings which were circulated widely in uncensored transcript in a form known as "Samizdat" (self-published). In fact, then as now, many Soviet authors and academicians, including some in the U.S. Institute, have been writing "for the drawer," that is to say, private manuscripts containing a true version and interpretation of events. Apparently these writers thereby assuage their conscience, while hoping that their work someday may be of historical use.

DISSENT—AN INTERNATIONAL ISSUE

Although the embassy thought it best to avoid direct contacts with dissenters which might embarrass us and cause them serious trouble, the case was different for the foreign and particularly American correspondents. The latter kept a vigilant watch on their dissenter clients and saw to it that the whole world would be informed if any of them should suffer official mistreatment. By definition the dissident group included large numbers of Soviet Jews who were being denied exit visas and/or were being harassed because of their religious and communal activities. It occasionally seemed that the attention devoted by the foreign press to local dissent was disproportionate to its influence in the Soviet Union, but the campaign, so to speak, made its own market. Visitors from the U.S. Congress would sometimes proceed directly from the airport to look up a dissenter whose name they had been given and who might be either a Jewish intellectual denied a visa, a banned author, or a freely speaking Russian Baptist.

Foreign interest, as it became increasingly aroused, furnished individual dissenters a form of protection. Many made frequent use of the international telephone to communicate their woes. During the era of "high détente," the Soviet authorities hesitated to proceed against offenders or to cut off these calls, which they probably found useful in keeping themselves informed. There do seem to be limits, however, as I warned one congressman who told me he planned to help an especially active group of dissenters. Against my advice he went ahead, with the result that he was asked to leave the country. The embassy immediately protested but we were taken aback when the Foreign Ministry showed us the congressman's statement to the press that his expulsion would assure his victory at the next election. I understand that in line with the Carter administration's emphasis on human rights, officers in our embassy now compete in claiming the number of "house dissenters" each of them cultivates.

In recent months the human rights problem has proven to be one of the major "basic incompatibilities" between us and the Soviets which I mentioned at the beginning of this book. Historically it has played a continuously significant role in our relations, going back, for instance, to 1911 when the U.S. abrogated a commercial treaty with the tsarist government because of the anti-Jewish programs then being carried out in Russia. The dispute was resurrected with much the same results in 1973 when the U.S. Congress passed the so-called Jackson–Vanik amendment curbing credits to the USSR because of its restrictions on Jewish emigration. As we shall see, the Soviet government thereupon suspended the effectiveness date of the U.S.-Soviet commercial agreement concluded in October 1972.

Our reactions have been illogical in the sense that they have been more in the nature of an emotional protest than a carefully planned tactic to get the Soviets to change their ways. Up until now the latest steps we have taken have proved self-defeating, as illustrated by the statistic that Jewish emigration reached a total of about 36,000 in 1973 and has recently fallen to a current rate of between 1000 and 1200 per month. Arbitrary or not, our response is a present fact and must be measured in perspective as one of the operative conditions governing our foreign policy.

On one ground alone I find it difficult to fault the administration's attitude, and that is, it seems only just that the Soviets should take the heat of our charges of human rights violations in repayment for their worldwide and often successful efforts to accuse us of a whole catalogue of "imperialist crimes." With the defeat of the Nazi and Japanese regimes which were identified with mass killings in Europe and China, the Soviet Communists of today still have to live down the heritage left by their not-too-distant predecessors, as well as their own responsibility for that monstrous monument to inhumanity, the Berlin Wall.

Dissident activity is a source of considerable embarrassment to the regime internationally and could cause serious trouble domestically should dissension break out inside the party. Since dissent is essentially "antiparty" in nature, the traditional orthodox elements can be counted on to defend themselves stubbornly against threats of this kind. Moscow, Leningrad, and the Baltic area are the main centers of dissent; its influence is apparently weaker elsewhere because of its fragmented appeal and difficulties of communication.

The ethnic Russians, who historically have been the shapers and shakers of political movements, have not had much exposure to human rights. Many subconsciously recall that the overthrow of tyranny has often been accompanied by terror and renewed reaction. Reform, such as Khrushchev's correction of Stalinist abuses, is universally popular, but the exchange of assured stability for uncertain freedoms is another matter. There is evidence that among the inert majority of the population, there are some who regard the dissenters as genuinely mad and dangerous.

The real basis for the Soviet opposition to liberalism is, of course, the fear that concessions, such as a human rights campaign calls for, could lead to the replacement of the Communist party in any particular country by another regime inimical to Soviet defense interests; or, worse yet, such reforms might succeed somewhere within the Soviet domain and thereby undermine the fabric of totalitarian control. This has been the thread of motivation for the use of force against activist reformers in Hungary and Czechoslovakia. In part it accounts for Soviet suspicion of the Euro-Communists who seem to be tainted by a similar infection. Dogmatic though they may be, the Soviets feel that insistence on their definition of the party's form and mission outweighs the double price they consciously pay in alienating the free world and in reducing the popular appeal of foreign Communist parties which they aspire to lead.

With its own public, the regime relies on two lines of defense. It contends that its program for strengthening peace and ensuring full employment fulfills the people's basic right to enjoy international security abroad and social security at home. It rejects the American campaign as an artificially inspired Cold War maneuver designed to humiliate the Soviet nation. While public focus on human rights is bound to have some effect in the long run, it looks as if the Russians and the Chinese will be among the last to make concessions in this direction.

As the Russians See Themselves

According to some observers, national differences offer a higher potential for dissension within the Soviet Union than limited dissent of the kind we have been discussing; true or not, these differences cause considerable unhappiness.

The reason, however, is not necessarily the oppression of a minority by a majority. The reverse can be true since the ethnic Russian majority was among those who were terrorized by the Georgian tyrant Stalin. To a lesser degree the Russians were also victimized by the Armenians, who did well for themselves when Anastas Mikoyan was first prime minister and then president. (He now lives in honorable and prosperous retirement.) As a result of these experiences it may be a long time before a minority leader again attains the top party position. Despite the many reservations held about the Russians, the populace seems to feel easier when one of them, or maybe a Russianized Ukrainian like Brezhnev, holds the post of party general secretary.

One of the peoples most hospitable to foreigners are the Georgians, whose pride is tempered only by a certain awe of their own notoriety. On my visit to the capital, Tiblisi, in 1970, our escort was a ranking local official who was a great admirer of Stalin. He became very friendly with my wife and myself, and in a spirit of honest inquiry, asked me how Stalin was regarded in the United States. I replied that he was held in high esteem as a wartime leader and ally in our common struggle against fascism, but that Americans had the feeling that he treated the Russians harshly. Our friend responded that this was not so, and that Stalin was a fair man who executed just as many Georgians as Russians.

The Georgians honored our request to visit Gori, Stalin's birthplace. At first they hesitated, apparently fearing that we might make fun of this sacred shrine. The installation is indeed impressive, starting with the concrete canopy built over the hut where Stalin was born, with the whole complex being dominated by a huge Stalin statue. The statue reminded me of the Moscow story about the plan of some of the poet Pushkin's modern admirers to erect a monument to him. To be on the safe side, they put up a statue of Stalin reading from a volume of Pushkin. The same motif very much pervades the large museum in Gori, where the only evidence I was able to find of Lenin was a picture of him shaking hands with Stalin. On our way through the museum I discerned a group photograph of Stalin talking with some of the participants in the 1945 conference at Potsdam, which included myself at the rear as one of the notetakers on our delegation. Our escort was visibly impressed.

The Georgians naturally resent the process of de-Stalinization but have had their revenge in their operation of a vast black market, mostly at Russian expense. They take advantage of cheap airfares to load the Aeroflot planes with choice produce, including live chickens, which they sell for huge prices on the small number of free markets permitted in Moscow. By one way or another they accumulate large sums which they bring to the capital to spend. My Canadian colleague was stopped by a Georgian who offered to buy the embassy Lincoln for 8000 rubles which he exhibited in a large roll of bills. Because of Canadian government regulations, the ambassador regretfully had to turn down the deal, which would have netted his embassy the equivalent of some $8500.

The other trans-Caucasian ethnic republics—Armenia and Azerbaijan—also have a strong sense of identity because of their separate histories and past association with cultures different from the Russian, including those of the Moslem Turks and Persians. A strong nationalist spirit inspires the Armenians who, like the Jews, have had to resort to extraordinary measures to survive. The Armenians let it be known that they are the only nation in modern times which voluntarily joined the Russian empire. (Their motive at that time was to protect themselves against massacre by the Turks and Persians.) The Armenian is one of the oldest Christian churches (as such, it is represented in Jerusalem), and is a world church with its center nominally established in Armenia. It receives contributions from the Armenian churches throughout the world, some of which are immensely wealthy. Thus the church brings money and prestige to the Soviet Union. Since it operates in the Soviet Union as a national church, it has avoided confrontation with the Soviet regime.

The trans-Caucasian republics are outposts whose turbulent local politics are reflected in occasional party purges. The Ukrainians who founded old Russia, and the Russians in Siberia east of the Urals who pretend to represent the new, also have a strong sense of independence and harbor a distinct resentment against the ruling Russians in Moscow. The chief reason is the arrogant attitude of the leaders from Moscow and Leningrad, who regard other peoples as provincials, if not racially inferior. While the ethnic minorities are permitted free study and use of their own languages, it is quite clear that knowledge of Russian is necessary for advancement in national politics and large state enterprises. On my trip to Georgia I witnessed a mild form of local retaliation. Since I was making an official visit as U.S. ambassador, I was quite properly accompanied by a representative of the Soviet Foreign Ministry in Moscow. Upon my arrival, my Georgian host turned to the Soviet escort officer and asked him in Russian whether he spoke Georgian. The reply being negative, my host remarked, "That is too bad because we shall be speaking nothing but Georgian, translated into English through an interpreter." For all practical purposes the man from Moscow was frozen out of all our talks.

The Russians are accustomed to ruling and, as I have remarked before, have on the whole probably done it better than any other group could. Their formal lever of power is the constitutional authority of the central government, but control of the local governments and parties is, of course, also important for Moscow. The Russian-dominated Politburo arranges, through its apparatus, that at least one or more of the leaders of the local parties is a "Moscow man," and is recognized as such. At the same time, the Soviet government is fairly generous in allowing for substantial development subsidies to the various republics; at least I heard few local complaints on this score. Since the Soviet Union is essentially an underpopulated country, such a policy is wise and necessary to promote industrial diversification and efficient labor utilization. Despite inducements of better pay and living accommodations which are offered workers sent under contract to the more inhospitable parts of the country, many of them ask to return to their native cities. Problems of isolation and lack of social amenities have not yet been solved, although the government claims it is working hard to find remedies.

As the ruling majority, the Russians bear chief responsibility for their nation's deficiencies as well as its glorious achievements. The peoples of the Soviet Union are second to none in their bravery, patriotism, artistic sensitivity, and reserves of brain power. Unfortunately, they also display some unappealing traits. They are strongly racist in their hostility to blacks and Asians. I recall that on a river excursion which we made near Moscow, an old crone came up to us to tell us of her distress that her daughter was consorting with a black from Lumumba University. As a sympathetic audience gathered about, she turned to my young son and said, "He is white; let me touch him, because white is beautiful." In addition to the black students at Lumumba, where racial violence occurs periodically, the African diplomats themselves were not too happy with thier status in Moscow and at various times sought a kind of social asylum in our embassy which, on Saturday afternoons during the winter, offered movie shows with refreshments.

The Soviets have also treated harshly some of their less wanted minorities, such as the Volga Germans and the Buriats. When we visited Siberia a representative of this tribe told us that they were being systematically starved out; they were considered a threat to the Soviet Union because a large group of Buriats lived in Mongolia, just across the border.

To my mind, Poland and Russia have been the most strongly anti-Semitic nations in Europe. There is a sixteenth-century fresco in a church in Jaroslavl, near Moscow, depicting the Last Judgment. Gathered on the right hand of the Father is a group of Russians in white raiment ascending into heaven. On the left is a sorry bunch descending into hell, explicitly designated as "Hebrews," "Arabs," and "Germans."

Whereas Poland has been helping the few remaining Jews to leave voluntarily, Russian opposition in principle to emigration is one of the reasons why so many Jews cannot depart. There are about three million Jews in the Soviet Union, and since an unknown but probably substantial number have assimilated themselves, it is hard to say how many would leave if free to do so. The religious and communal Jews are the ones who are the most harassed since they are considered exclusive and unassimilable. The Jewish problem exacts a certain price from the Soviet Union. It imposes a heavy charge on its relations with the West, and particularly with the United

States. On the other hand, a relaxation on emigration destined for Israel would cost the Soviets much credit with the Arabs.

Mention of exclusivity prompts the observation that this is a quality which the Russians, and now the Soviets, possess in abundance. It is an interesting fact that there have been relatively few defections in recent years. Large groups have visited the United States, and, although the majority is composed of the faithful Soviet elite, they have included some individuals of independent thought and not a few engineers and scientists who could have improved their position by remaining abroad. As in the case of some of the artists from Leningrad's Kirov Ballet, they could probably have left without endangering their relatives, but they have not.

Views about life abroad expressed in friendly conversation with Soviet citizens who have served in Western countries or returned from visits there are illuminating. They frequently claim to be put off by the kind of unordered type of existence they met with, its fierce competitiveness and lack of social and even physical security. It is interesting that they particularly resent that private property ownership usurps their right to roam freely about the countryside. Their acquiescence in the present system has curbed their spirit of adventure and they are quite obviously bound emotionally to their communities. The pains of withdrawal from the homeland which I have seen manifested in almost every recent refugee are sometimes dramatically distressing.

It is freely predicted that national differences and complaints will soon create major problems for the Soviet Union. I agree that this may be the case should strife within the party lead to its disintegration. The last census

of 1970 revealed that for the first time the Russian population was on the edge of losing its majority status to a
combined total of all the other peoples of the Soviet
Union, but the margin is not yet of great significance.
The small splinter ethnic minorities may find it harder to
hold their own but the non-Russian republics, because of
their resources, should benefit proportionately from any
kind of economic growth. It is certainly possible, however, that nationality problems may be among the
stresses and strains which would accompany forthcoming
change.

Chapter XIII

1970—A Year of Mixed Signals

AN INAUSPICIOUS BEGINNING

WHEN I arrived in Moscow in 1969, diplomatic activity regarding the Middle East was being carried on on several fronts. The specially appointed U.N. mediator, Gunnar Jarring, resided in Moscow since he also served as Swedish ambassador to the USSR. I was instructed to keep in touch with him and give him support, but he had little to do since he was only on call and his services were rarely enlisted.

In order to please the British and the French, quadripartite talks, which included the Soviets and ourselves, had been set up at the U.N. The Israelis held themselves aloof from these discussions because of France's hostile policy toward them. U.S.–Soviet bilateral talks, which started in July 1969 by the dispatch of a State Department delegation to Moscow, of which I was made a member, achieved some progress on secondary issues, such as consideration of demilitarized zones to implement a peace settlement and a special international regime for the straits which would prevent the Arabs from blocking Israeli access to the Gulf of Aqaba.

In a speech delivered on December 9, 1969, the U.S. secretary of state outlined certain proposals which became known as the "Rogers Plan." He suggested that a settlement "should not reflect the weight of conquest" (i.e., Israel should yield some occupied territory, including its seizure of all of Jerusalem); "special arrangements" should be made for the Gaza Strip and for international administration of the straits controlling the Gulf of Aqaba; homes should be found for refugees; and the United Arab Republic should "commit itself to peace," beginning with a resumption of diplomatic and economic relations. Israeli Prime Minister Meir a few days later criticized Rogers's speech for its "moralizing" character, stressing that the big powers could not impose peace. The Soviets replied indirectly on December 23 by turning down a more detailed U.S. proposal, suggesting that a joint U.S.–Soviet draft be given to the U.N. mediator Jarring to work out with the belligerent parties.

Because of an increasing number of Egyptian skirmishes across the Suez Canal, the Israelis began a series of "deep penetration bombing raids." Starting on January 13, 1970, the raids came within some miles of Cairo, prompting Soviet Prime Minister Kosygin to warn on January 31 that the Soviets would provide the United Arab Republic "with means to combat the raids." On February 12 the Israelis hit a scrap metal factory near Cairo, killing some seventy workers. The Soviets no longer hid the fact that they were furnishing the UAR with substantial military help in the form of surface-to-air missiles (SAMs) which later became the backbone of Egyptian air defense in the 1973 war. Soviet technicians accompanied the equipment, and the Israelis also claimed that Soviet pilots flew some of the Soviet MIG planes in the summer of 1970. I was instructed to make inquiry of the Soviet Foreign Ministry; its answer was evasive and did not fully deny the charges.

The Soviet buildup in Egypt worried the U.S. government considerably. On February 18, 1970, President Nixon stated, "Soviet preeminence in the Mediterranean would be a matter of grave concern." Some weeks later, Secretary Kissinger told the press that Soviet forces would have to be expelled before they could place themselves in a position to dominate the Middle East. On June 25 the U.S. proposed a cease fire along the canal, to be accompanied by a reopening of indirect negotiations between the parties under Jarring's auspices. The UAR accepted the proposal on July 26 and the Israelis on July 31, with the result that the cease fire entered into force on August 7.

In preparing for the cease fire the State Department informed me of our government's intention to police it unilaterally by U.S. observation flights over the canal. Foreseeing trouble, I suggested that this mission be given to the British, who had bases in the area and who wished to play some part in peacekeeping. This proposal was turned down, and sure enough we soon received protests about our alleged favoritism toward the Israelis. I recall being subjected to a sarcastic but amusing interview with Vladimir Vinogradov, the Soviet deputy foreign minister in charge of the Middle East. For my benefit he acted out the steps which U.S. pilots presumably took to "pull down the window blinds when they flew over Israeli territory." As the observation flights continued, we had to acknowledge publicly that there had been violations on both sides, but we made the point that the Arab infiltration of Soviet-supplied weapons close to the canal was the more serious.

About a month after the UAR–Israeli cease fire, a group of Fedayeen left-wing extremists, who favored immediate military action against Israel, started a revolt against the government of Jordan. Syria, which has generally favored strong anti-Israeli action, moved some forces into Jordan to help the Muslim Fedayeen. On September 30, 1970, Secretary Rogers called upon Syria to withdraw, and on September 24 the U.S. moved its Sixth Fleet to the eastern Mediterranean. On the same day the Syrians started to retire under Jordanian air attack and under Israeli threats to shoot down Syrian planes operating in Jordan. Nasser's death on September 28 and a coincidental statement by President Nixon that the U.S. intended to maintain a strong position in the Mediterranean cooled down Arab military activity.

When I returned to Washington on consultation in the summer of 1970, President Nixon asked me about the Middle East as viewed from Moscow. I replied that the Soviets were chiefly interested in keeping trouble brewing, without provoking a military confrontation which would produce another Arab defeat at Israeli hands. I remarked that both sides seemed to be locked into a state of "neither peace nor war." I stated my regret that we had not pushed harder for the Rogers Plan, and I thought the Israelis had made a serious mistake in carrying out deep bombing raids in Egypt, since their action invited the Soviets to interpose their own force in a way which could challenge Israeli superiority. The president did not discuss the Rogers Plan further but said that, quite aside from American domestic politics, it was essential to support Israel as the one sure bastion against the spread of communism in the Middle East.

Our government's firm stand during these troubled weeks of 1970 removed any doubt that we would continue to play a dominant role in the Middle East. Far from producing a negative effect on the Egyptians, it seems to have caused them to question the advisability of total dependence on the Soviets. After Nasser's death in September 1970 latent personal frictions came to the surface. Soviet suspicion of his successor, Sadat, was reflected in derogatory remarks made to us privately by influential Soviet commentators who warned that we would regret it if we were tempted to play his game. As we know, Sadat's disenchantment with the Soviets grew, and eventually, in June 1972, the Egyptians requested the departure of Soviet advisers from their country. Soon thereafter the Soviets expelled resident Egyptian students and trainees. On a cruise my wife and myself took on a Soviet ship in September 1972, we were able to observe the personal animus against the Soviets of a group of Egyptians who were being returned to their country via a stop at Alexandria.

Cambodia, the other serious crisis of 1970, created a greater commotion in the United States than it did within the Soviet Union, which one would have expected to be the more alarmed party. Prince Sihanouk, the Cambodian head of state, was visiting the Soviet Union in March 1970 when he was deposed in his own country, thereupon becoming a less welcome guest in Moscow, where he was referred to as "Mr. Sihanouk" in a published letter addressed to him by Soviet Premier Kosygin. When he left the Soviet Union to try his luck in Peking, where he felt he could pick up more support, the Soviets, according to our French sources, wished him well and somewhat coolly let him know that they would be ready to be of help if wanted.

Matters were brought to a head on April 30, 1970, when President Nixon announced on television that on that same night American and South Vietnamese troops were entering the "parrot's beak" area in Cambodia to clean out North Vietnamese–infiltrated forces which now threatened Saigon only "thirty miles away." It is unnecessary to describe the memorable reactions which broke out that summer in the United States and their enduring effects.

On May 4 Premier Kosygin gave a press conference in which, addressing himself to world opinion, he harshly denounced the American action and for the first time publicly criticized President Nixon. While saying that the attack would affect U.S.–Soviet relations, he made no mention of retaliatory steps, and indicated that the current talks on strategic arms would continue. In promising the North Vietnamese liberation forces "sympathy and support," he indicated that the Soviets, however, were prepared to recognize a "truly neutralist" Cambodian government, saying that the future of U.S.–Vietnamese talks in Paris was up to Hanoi.

From the consultations we pursued in Moscow, we had the impression that the Soviets were temporizing, and such seemed to be the case since they maintained their representation vis-à-vis the new, U.S.-supported Lon Nol government in Phnom Penh for the next three years. Officially the Soviets remained highly critical of the U.S., but certain authoritative commentators, doubtless with government sanction, tried to probe our intentions by leading us on with guarded statements that they understood our having to move in to fill a dangerous vacuum in Cambodia. They wondered whether our withdrawal of troops from Vietnam should not be tied to a reduction of Chinese influence in Southeast Asia. We had the feeling that while the Soviets wished to wear us down by attrition, they feared the possible consequences, in terms of U.S. reaction and Chinese advantage, of our elimination by total humiliation. Conforming to the perverse logic of the day, any glimmer of success was treated skeptically in the U.S. and was usually deplored, since it tended to prolong the American commitment to stay in Vietnam.

The year 1970 ended with a slight brush with the Soviets over Cuba. In early November a Soviet submarine tender anchored at Cienfuegos at about the time a Soviet naval group visited Havana. We made inquiries in Moscow which brought forth Soviet press denials that the Soviets intended to establish a base. In response to press questions in Washington, the State Department's spokesman stated on November 17, 1970, that the U.S. and the Soviets had a private understanding that the latter would not use Cuba as a nuclear base in return for American assurances that the U.S. would not invade nor intervene in Cuba. This statement was of the highest interest, inasmuch as the terms on which the 1962 missile crisis blockade was ended had never been made explicit. Hitherto, the U.S. had not acknowledged that such a deal had been concluded. An authoritative Soviet commentator confirmed to me that Kissinger had given the assurance personally to the Soviet Foreign Ministry.

WEST GERMAN SETTLEMENTS

While the Soviet Union was having its troubles with the U.S., and doubtless partly to offset them, it concentrated on making 1970 its "year of Europe." Its efforts were brought to fruition by negotiations centering chiefly on intensified contacts between the Soviets and the new West German government of Willy Brandt. In Moscow I gained interesting insights into the "hard facts" and decisions which became a matter of record.

From private communications I learned that Brandt's "Ost-Politik," or opening to the East, at first gravely disturbed the president's national security advisers. I was less concerned, since the Germans from Foreign Minister Scheel on down kept me informed when they visited Moscow. Paradoxically, the complex of agreements which resulted from the Federal Republic's eastern overtures became, as seen in retrospect, the foundation stone for the policy of détente which Kissinger and his associates later embraced so enthusiastically. Among Washington's worries in 1969 was the prospect that the Federal German Republic would conclude a treaty recognizing, on behalf of a future reunified Germany, Poland's western frontier on the Oder–Western Neisse, thus juridically settling the fate of some seven million Germans driven out of Silesia by Soviet and Polish forces. From my personal observation of Polish resettlement of the area, I thought it unrealistic to believe the frontier could be changed otherwise than by another war.

The Treaty of Moscow signed by Willy Brandt and by Soviet Premier Kosygin in Moscow on August 12, 1970 —exactly thirty-one years after the signature of the Soviet–Nazi nonaggression pact of 1939—provided for the

[253]

mutual renunciation of force and the recognition of existing boundaries in central Europe, including the boundary between the two Germanys, as well as Poland's western boundary on the Oder–Western Neisse Rivers. Both the Germanys were to regard the latter boundary "as inviolable now and in the future."

There were collateral understandings which had to be accepted as part of a total package. West German ratification of the Treaty of Moscow would depend on a satisfactory conclusion of four-power talks aimed at improving the Western position in Berlin; and a corresponding settlement had to be made between the Federal German Republic and Poland (which eventuated in the Treaty of Warsaw, signed in December 1970).

The resulting balance of advantage between East and West established by the new agreements was about even. On his return to Bonn in August 1970 Willy Brandt said that nothing had been lost that had not been gambled away long ago. Despite his write-off of past losses, especially the de facto cession of German territory to Poland, Brandt was able to safeguard his position on certain fundamental questions, and even to score some gains. It was apparent that Brezhnev desperately wanted to have some kind of East–West accommodation to present to the Twenty-fourth Soviet Communist Party Congress in the spring of 1971. The West Germans were aware of the strength of their bargaining position. Brandt's insistence that West German ratification be conditioned on a new agreement on Berlin permitted him to control the pace and course of the ongoing negotiations.

In the negotiations on Berlin in the summer of 1970 Brandt employed a two-pronged approach to safeguard the principle of German reunification. He represented

Germany as being in a transitional stage in which it functioned as "two states within a single nation." He held out the hope and prospect that Germany might be reunited peacefully, and through self-determination, by an eventual overall European settlement. Brandt contended that this position was compatible with the Moscow Treaty of August 1970, which only prohibited boundary change by the use of force.

Incidentally, at the end of the negotiations in Moscow in August 1970 the Soviets treated the West Germans to a veiled affront. On August 12, 1970, the night of the signature of the Moscow Treaty, the Soviets gave a large dinner party for the German delegation and then suggested that the Germans return Soviet hospitality at the German Embassy the following evening. This the Germans declined to do, since it was the ninth anniversary of the building of the Berlin Wall. Sometime later, when Chancellor Brandt paid a visit to Berlin, he was informed that Abrasimov, the Soviet ambassador to East Germany, my former colleague from Warsaw days, would be happy to receive him, an invitation which the chancellor ignored.

Soviet rewards from this set of negotiations were adequate. Brezhnev had a major East–West agreement to parade before the 1971 Twenty-fourth Soviet Party Congress. The settlement confirmed the Communist possession of the so-called central European heartland which the early British geopolitician Halford Mackinder postulated as requisite for ruling Europe and ruling the world. In reverse analogy, we were made to look as if we were bleeding ourselves to death in Southeast Asia by holding to Admiral Mahan's equally obsolete counter-prescription that the oversees projection of power was the key to world domination. In the eyes of the Soviets we were "colonialists," because, as Charles Bohlen used to say, their definition of colonialism implies that "you get there by sea"; Soviet annexation of the Baltic states and military intervention in Eastern Europe were, of course, exempted from such a stigma.

It is interesting that American influence in the end result was not diminished by the Moscow settlement, but in fact was enhanced through our leadership in the negotiations that obtained freer communication with West Berlin (even though the Soviets made it plain that elimination of the wall was nonnegotiable). It was also significant that for the better part of a decade the Moscow series of agreements concluded in 1970–1971 has served as a powerful pacifier in Europe. For the foreseeable future it seems unlikely that any of the parties will be interested in upsetting them.

Chapter XIV

The Pieces Begin to Fall in Place

TRADE AND "LINKAGE"

DURING the years 1969 and 1970 very little had occurred in bilateral relations to promote the president's "grand design" for settlements with the Soviets which was laid down in his letter I delivered to Premier Kosygin in April 1969, and which the Soviet premier had then commented on favorably.

A calmer manner of doing business brought some slight improvements during 1969 and 1970, but the very grave differences over the Middle East and Vietnam persisted, and were occasionally aggravated by incidents which stimulated virulent anti-American media attacks. The Soviet–German agreements were primarily European settlements, and in fact seemed to have encouraged the Soviets to believe that the Europeans could be persuaded to reduce America's role in their affairs. This seemed to be the purport of early Soviet plans for a European security conference from which the U.S. and Canada were to be excluded. At the end of 1970 it would have been hard to discern any event which could be expected to lead to the improved relationship which was forged in 1972. Three developments in 1971 promoted this latter result: a growing Soviet interest in acquiring U.S. technology; a basic agreement on SALT on May 20; and Nixon's July 15 announcement of his intention to visit Communist China.

In January 1971 a very important development occurred. I have mentioned Washington's misgivings about Chancellor Brandt's "Ost-Politik." A concern which loomed large at the end of 1970 was that the West Germans, as a result of their comprehensive agreements with the Soviets, "were beginning to get ahead of us." Washington was also conscious of the need to send positive signals to Moscow in advance of the Twenty-fourth Party Congress. In any event, Kissinger and Nixon believed a new U.S. initiative was called for. In January 1971 Kissinger passed a message through Ambassador Dobrynin that the U.S. was interested in serious negotiations on disarmament and Berlin.

The postponed Twenty-fourth Soviet Party Congress, which finally met in March-April 1971, treated Europe positively, China negatively, and the United States for the most part moderately "in the light of the state of existing relations." Brezhnev and Gromyko regretted that, by comparison with the "radical turn toward relaxation and peace on the continent," certain U.S. positions had hardened. They left the door open, however, by stating that Soviet policy toward the U.S. was based on the premise that improved relations were possible.

Shortly after the Soviet Party Congress, word was passed to the embassy, through the previously mentioned Arbatov channel, that Brezhnev desired an improvement for the particular purpose of acquiring U.S. equipment which would benefit Soviet industry. Evidence of some change came with the support given by the influential Soviet State Committee on Science and Technology to American bids for the sale of gear-cutting machinery and foundry equipment. Kosygin's son-in-law, German Gishiani, was especially active in intervening with us to expedite issuance of the necessary American export licenses which had been held up for several weeks.

The brief delay was explained to me when I visited Washington on consultation in May 1971. At that time a break in the impasse on strategic arms talks was a crucial point. The Soviets had held out for a freeze solely on antiballistic missiles, which would yield them the advantage of keeping their weapons already-deployed around Moscow, whereas the U.S. would be obliged to stop development of its antimissile program. On our side, we wished to impose limits on offensive weapons; the Soviets, on the other hand, wished such limitations to apply only to our use of the NATO forward-base system in Europe (FBS). On May 20 it was announced that a breakthrough had been achieved in a joint decision to concentrate on working out an agreement on antiballistic missiles, and also "to agree on certain measures with respect to the limitation of offensive strategic weapons."

With this much achieved, the U.S. government gave clearances for a considerable number of pending export licenses. Although no official statements were made, the significance of linkage was not lost on the Soviets.

In connection with trade expansion, the experiences of some American exporters who were entering the Soviet market for the first time were interesting. I recall the frustration of an American company president who told me that as a result of the Soviets' playing him off against his American competitors, his winning the contract would net him very little or no profit. Another American businessman said that had he been able to buy off his principal American competitor by paying him a million-dollar bribe, both of them would have been better off. Although this kind of practice is doubtless prohibited by our federal antitrust legislation, it seems to be successfully employed by the Japanese in their "single window" approach to overseas trade; this enables particular Japanese industries involved to support in turn only one of their member firms to compete for a specific foreign contract.

THE CHINA CONNECTION

The touchstone to the turn-around in our relations with the Soviets was the president's announcement on July 15, 1971, that he would visit China the following year. I had been questioned by Foreign Office officials and Soviet newsmen about our earlier relaxation of restrictions on trade and travel, dramatized by the expedition of an American Ping-Pong team to China. My reply had been that we favored normalizing relations with all countries, a process which we had hoped would proceed at a swifter pace with respect to the Soviet Union.

At the beginning of 1971 the U.S. government was reconciled to the certainty that in the fall the U.N. would finally vote Nationalist China out of the organization, and Communist China in. It was a master stroke of Nixon–Kissinger strategy to parlay our weak position in the U.N. into a vicarious but substantial diplomatic victory. By a vigorous but vain rear-guard campaign to try to prevent the Nationalists' expulsion, we cut our losses with the Chinese Nationalists. Their misfortune opened the way for the establishment of a form of relations which gave us direct access to the Communist Chinese, thus in turn furnishing us potential leverage in dealing with the Soviets.

The Soviets withheld official comment for ten days after Nixon's July 15 announcement of his intention to visit China, indicating that they were treating this development with thoughtfulness and care. Communist press comment elsewhere, however, ascribed anti-Soviet motives to the intended visit. Eventually, on July 25 *Pravda* came through with this simple message: Soviet policy toward both the U.S. and China was unchanged, but the Soviet Union would maintain a careful watch and would draw its own conclusions.

Washington adopted much the same attitude. Eventually the State Department issued general guidance to our delegation regarding the line to take at the U.N. General Assembly. This was to the effect that we had made no secret agreements, and our move toward Communist China was not aimed against anybody but was simply a step toward normalization. We had not abandoned our commitments to Nationalist China and still opposed its expulsion from the U.N. In order to show that we were not petitioners, we let it be known that Mao had told the late American correspondent Edgar Snow in December 1970 that Nixon or a representative of his would be welcome in China.

On July 28, 1971, I was summoned by Gromyko for a long talk on the state of our relations. Gromyko's fortunes had improved considerably since his days of service under Khrushchev. One of my predecessors told me that at a particularly boisterous celebration of the November 7 national holiday in the Kremlin, Khrushchev spotted his foreign minister and announced loudly: "Look at

Gromyko—he'd sit two hours on a cake of ice if I ordered him to." Despite his past discomfitures, Gromyko in 1971 had held the post of foreign minister longer than any of his European colleagues. His two assignments in the United States—as counselor and then ambassador—have made him a useful institution in the sense that even though we may dislike his policies, he makes their meaning unmistakably clear. As probably the best Soviet foreign minister we have had to deal with, his disenchantment with us is relieved by a doleful sense of humor.

Gromyko opened his talk with me by remarking sorrowfully that unlike Soviet policy, which was consistent, the United States had followed a "zigzag" course in dealing with the Soviet Union.

Gromyko said that Brezhnev felt there was a lack of clarity about U.S. intentions, especially toward the Soviet Union. Gromyko himself was puzzled, "as is the entire leadership," and he had been instructed to find answers if possible. He was not asking for them "in a day or a week," but hoped they would be forthcoming.

I told Gromyko that I knew Brezhnev's personal interest would be much appreciated in Washington. I said that our positions on the main points at issue were quite clear, but that I was not going to reargue them, since the important thing was to assure that his inquiry received a considered and informed reply which would take into account the proceedings of the Twenty-fourth Party Congress and "current" world events.

Although Gromyko was obviously fishing for information, the subject of China was not mentioned. For my part, I felt that this could be taken up in the next round of discussion after Washington had decided to communicate what conclusions it had drawn. A few days later I

[262]

delivered to Gromyko Washington's interim response, which stated that his inquiry was receiving attention at the highest levels of the U.S. government. Thus a path of discussion was confirmed which led inexorably, albeit through some murky episodes, to the May 1972 summit in Moscow.

It is timely and logical at this point to deal with the phenomenon which shaped the form and substance of our government's decisions, and that is the feud, in reality a "no contest," between Kissinger and the State Department. In David Frost's widely publicized television interview broadcast May 12, 1977, President Nixon reported that Kissinger had told him that when it came to important matters "I will not tell Rogers [Secretary of State William P. Rogers] because he'll leak." Nixon disputed this with Kissinger, blaming leaks on the "State Department bureaucracy." Nixon did acknowledge that "there could be only one person," namely "Henry," to handle certain major issues such as Vietnam, China, Russia, and the Middle East. According to Nixon, Rogers "did not resent Henry handling such things" but felt that Henry got too much credit. Rogers also made the point with Nixon that as secretary he should be kept informed to enable him to make public announcements and answer questions from Congress.

Nixon's story about Rogers permits me to relate that Kissinger repeated a similar allegation when he made his visit to Moscow in April 1972 before the summit. He had informed neither myself nor his deputy then working in Moscow on arrangements for the summit, but, just before leaving, he called me to his Soviet villa to give me a fill-in on his discussions. At the end, he explained that while the president had confidence in me, I was not to report to the State Dpartment about what he had told me, since the president could not rely on "Rogers not to leak." I told Kissinger I never had in mind telegraphing the State Department about what was obviously presidential business. Incidentally, we were then taking a stroll in the dark through the trees and bushes outside the villa when I heard the click of a rifle and yelled out to the guard that we were Americans (hopefully assuming that at least the guard had advance notice of Kissinger's visit).

The "feud" between Rogers and Kissinger, as the president himself called it in his David Frost interview, can be explained objectively. As I indicated earlier in the case of Eisenhower, no recent president or his staff has been fond of the State Department, regardless of who was secretary of state. Traditionally the State Department operates in a seemingly ponderous and unimaginative way. It is slowed down by a tedious clearance process designed to assure accuracy in matters of fact and a consensus in submitting recommendations. Kissinger had recruited a first-class national security staff, some of whom came from the State Department (and several of whom later defected and wrote unflattering books about Kissinger). The Nixon White House manifested its impatience with the State Department from the very start, and I remember on two occasions coming back from Kissinger's office to find the State Department working on long papers on subjects which Kissinger had already presented to the president in brief memoranda several days before.

As long as he had Elliot Richardson in the second spot of undersecretary, Rogers, who as Nixon acknowledged was his close personal friend, made out fairly well. Kissinger respected Richardson as a competent lawyer and an experienced Massachusetts politician who possessed added snob appeal as a certified Boston Brahmin. The two worked together very effectively and Richardson was able to defend and uphold the department's legitimate role. When Richardson left to become secretary of health, education and welfare and was succeeded by John Irwin, Kissinger had already begun to assume the mantle of indispensability and supremacy.

Kissinger qualifies as a historical figure on many counts. With a true sense of its meaning, he made history; he expounded and recorded his policies with rare lucidity and eloquence. He had some somber traits as well. His towering intellect would have brought him to the top without the need to deploy his gifts of intrigue and defamation, which he enjoyed doing. Exploiting the president's and his own aversion to bureaucracy, he built himself a private chancery and communications system. In important reserved areas he established a "back channel" of direct contact with foreign governments which circumvented the State Department and its representatives. Resort to this channel was understandable and indeed appropriate in many instances to reduce leaks of sensitive information. Kissinger used it as a weapon against his enemies to exclude them from his magic circle of power.

While Kissinger was highly respected by the Soviets, they identified in him some of the characteristics they most feared in the Germans. He was never petty in negotiations, but won his points with ruthlessness and skill. Taking his dealings with the Soviets in isolation, I find little to fault him for. He is known to have had a rather low opinion of his Soviet counterparts, with the exception of Ambassador Dobrynin whose authority derived from his membership in the Central Committee and long service in Washington. Kissinger was, of course, beholden to him as the transmission belt in the "back channel." A question mark in the Soviets' mind was the degree of influence Kissinger had on Nixon, whom they regarded as unpredictable but in whom they had a certain implicit trust because his political stake in détente matched that of Brezhnev.

Chapter XV

The Nixon Summit

THE LEAD-IN

THE process of U.S.–Soviet engagement was vigorously pushed in August 1971, and continued through the fall meeting of the U.N. General Assembly in New York. The U.S., the U.K., French, and Soviet negotiations in Berlin improving Western communication with that city were concluded speedily and successfully in August. As a follow-up to the May 20, 1971, breakthrough settling important questions of principle, a new impetus was given to the SALT discussions. A joint review was undertaken in Washington of secondary matters which might be ripe for early agreement. It was announced on October 12, 1971, that President Nixon had accepted an invitation to visit the Soviet Union the following spring.

The outbreak of the Indian–Pakistani war created a rift between the Soviets and ourselves later in 1971. The Soviets were bound to support the Indians under a treaty concluded in August 1971, whereas the U.S. favored Pakistan for balance of power reasons, and also to repay the Pakistanis for serving as an intermediary in arranging

Kissinger's secret trip to Peking in July which produced the invitation to President Nixon to visit China. In December 1971 elements of the U.S. Seventh Fleet were dispatched to the Bay of Bengal, while a Soviet squadron was sent north from the Indian Ocean. It is possible that but for the press leak of Nixon's instruction to his subordinates to "tilt toward Pakistan" the whole affair, which ended with a quick Indian victory, would have received less notice than it did. The situation in Moscow was calm, and I exchanged useful information with the Foreign Ministry about the new break-away state of Bangladesh, about which both of us knew very little. My Pakistani colleague told me he was treated considerately, and it was evident that the Soviets did not wish to cut themselves off from his country.

Moscow's intention to improve atmospherics was demonstrated in the warm reception the Soviets gave to a succession of important American visitors. They included a party of state governors (Governor Mandel of Maryland provoked the Soviets the most); a group of over a hundred American businessmen; a trade mission headed by Secretary of Commerce Stans; and an official delegation sent to open talks on measures to prevent incidents at sea between vessels of the U.S. and Soviet navies.

The Stans mission, which spent the last ten days of November 1971 in the Soviet Union, was the most interesting. In 1970 U.S.–Soviet trade amounted only to $179 million, consisting on our side of imports chiefly of Soviet chrome, furs, timber, and some industrial diamonds, which helped pay for Soviet imports of American industrial goods. Obstacles arose from both sides during the Cold War era: the U.S. withdrew most favored nation tariff treatment from the Soviets in 1950, and imposed export and credit embargos; the Soviets' state trading monopolies discouraged American business and allocated foreign exchange only for purchases to meet urgent needs.

This pattern contrasted with the huge outlays put out by the early Lenin regime for American heavy industrial equipment shortly after the Soviet Revolution. Perhaps in an effort to recreate the past, in April 1970 the Soviet government invited Henry Ford II to be its guest and tried to interest him in a primary contract for the construction of a new truck plant on the Kama River. Ford pointed out that he was not a major truck producer and seemed reluctant to involve his company in such a large venture in the Soviet Union. The approach showed that the Soviets had plenty of resources to devote to projects of this kind and that planning was going ahead on a large scale.

Important American businessmen who were quickly alerted to these new opportunities gave support to the ambitious program which Stans brought with him to Moscow. I was somewhat skeptical at first that the Soviets would permit our companies to make adequately profitable returns, but we soon found out that our ideas seemed to fit in with the thinking of a state-directed economy. In the Stans discussions, both sides agreed in principle that the U.S. would ease its restrictions on credits and exports and the Soviets would offer our businessmen freer access to Soviet markets. Further study of economic relations was pursued at the summit and in later meetings, eventually leading to the conclusion of two comprehensive economic and financial agreements in October 1972. As will be shown in due course, the failure of these agreements virtually brought the first phase of détente to an end.

A later commercial traveler to Moscow was Secretary of Agriculture Earl Butz. On April 11, 1972, he and I were invited to call on Brezhnev and thus were the first non-Communist Americans he had seen since he had received Glenn Seaborg, head of the Atomic Energy Commission, when Brezhnev himself was head of state. At our talk Brezhnev recalled meeting Vice-President Nixon at the famous "kitchen debate" in Moscow in August 1959. Taking a crack at Khrushchev, who Brezhnev intimated had started the altercation, he said that there had been "a lot of empty talk" and he "didn't feel so good about it." He asked us to pass a message to the president about the Soviet people's strong reaction to our bombing of North Vietnam; otherwise he expected that he and the president would find they had much in common at the approaching May summit. Secretary Butz brought with him some grain experts who succeeded in interesting the Soviets in buying feed grains and soy beans. Butz claimed that the pressures on him to reduce domestic surpluses were driving him to desperation; under the circumstances one can understand his enthusiasm for massive sales which led to the so-called Soviet grain steal of some two months later.

Three noteworthy events occurred before the opening of the U.S.–Soviet summit in May. Nixon's China visit, ending with the communiqué issued in Shanghai on February 27, 1972, passed off with minimal effect on U.S.–

Soviet relations. One passage, apparently inserted by the Chinese as a stab at the Soviets, declared that both the Chinese and the U.S. opposed efforts by any country to establish hegemony in Asia and the Pacific. My Soviet contacts asked me about the meaning of this statement, claiming that "hegemony" was not a Russian word. I replied that the expression spoke for itself as far as we were concerned, and that they should make inquiries of their Chinese friends. (Actually the word was first used in the letter I delivered to Kosygin in April 1969, and later in the first foreign policy report which Nixon submitted to Congress in January 1970.) Recalling the fuss the Chinese had made over the "two-China" concept in my talks with them in Warsaw, I was amused to see that they tied this question down once and for all by declaring in the Shanghai communiqué that they opposed the idea of one China, one Taiwan; or one China with two governments; or two Chinas and an independent Taiwan; or saying that the status of Taiwan remains to be determined.

On May 11, eleven days before the summit was to open, the U.S. bombed North Vietnam and mined the harbor of the port city of Haiphong. This was deemed a military necessity even though the majority view in Washington was that it would probably cause the Soviets to call off the summit. I am told that nervous uncertainty produced some rug-chewing in the White House cellar offices. In Moscow we continued to report that the last-minute preparations for the meeting were proceeding smoothly and that the Soviets were unlikely to yield the diplomatic heights to the Chinese by cancelling.

A WEEK OF STRENUOUS COOPERATION

When visited by the head of state he represents, an ambassador has no formal mission except to take hard knocks, but I was a member of the U.S. delegation and, upon leaving, the president autographed my copy of the summit agenda with a note congratulating me on taking part in a "great historical event." The Moscow meeting was the summit of Nixon's hopes and achievements. Time will separate the historical from the spectacular, but the meeting's most immediately visible features were its careful preparation and the candor and convincing logic of its public presentation.

Since it is elemental to Kissinger's concept of détente, an off-the-record press conference he gave on May 21 is worth noting briefly:

Although divided by profound ideological differences, the U.S. and the USSR were the only nuclear countries whose policies had a worldwide impact on each other almost everywhere. Peace required the two countries to exercise restraint in their policies and also to demonstrate "creativity" in putting their relationship on a more stable basis. The U.S. sought to redirect the momentum of the accumulated past with the aim of establishing a vested interest for both governments in a network of cooperation. Each party would thus be bound to the other by mutually profitable agreements.

Holding a U.S.–Soviet summit had been a primary administration objective since its time of taking office. Various confrontations and secondary crises, such as Vietnam, the Middle East, and Cuba, had stood in the way, but these problems had been sufficiently contained, if not solved, eventually to narrow the conditions for a summit meeting down to two: that the Berlin negotiations be successfully concluded and that the SALT discussions reach a stage offering prospects of agreement.

The meeting would not take the form of a summit about Vietnam; it would try to fit this problem into the general U.S.–Soviet relationship. The U.S. had not informed the USSR in advance of the May bombing of North Vietnam; this act had not been directed against the USSR. The summit would have taken place regardless of the new turn in U.S.–Chinese relations. U.S.–Soviet trade should concentrate on interchange between two huge economies rather than merely lift current restrictions. The president would bring to the "attention of those with whom he is speaking" the million or so petitions from American Jews urging freer emigration from the Soviet Union.

The summit proceedings generally followed Kissinger's outline. Another point he made in later press conferences was that because of the intensive preliminary preparations, neither side surprised the other by making proposals which had not first been explored together. This course of conduct contrasted with the practice of an earlier era when heads of government shot off propaganda messages to each other, as happened, for instance, in the exchanges between Eisenhower and the Soviet Bulganin–Khrushchev duo in the late 1950s. The correspondence became so meaningless that the State Department turned it over to a young officer who customarily dictated a reply in less than half an hour.

It was easy to see that Nixon and Brezhnev quickly established a close and personal rapport. Brezhnev did not meet Nixon on arrival—he was not required to since he was not then head of state—but received him before the state dinner that evening for a two-hour private conversation with no one else present but the Soviet interpreter. Incidentally, because Nixon and Kissinger apparently feared leaks from the U.S. delegation, they did not use the State Department's interpreter, an excellent one, but employed the services of Viktor Sukhodrev, Brezhnev's interpreter and assistant. Sukhodrev was skillful and had style, but unfortunately the U.S. side had to rely on the Soviet record of the top leaders' talks.

Brezhnev and Nixon deferred to each other at joint delegation meetings, which, however, were usually a waste of time since the Soviet leading team—Brezhnev, Prime Minister Kosygin, and President Podgorny—each felt it necessary to make a speech in that order on every subject under discussion. The Nixon–Kissinger group customarily dealt with Brezhnev and Secretary Rogers with Prime Minister Kosygin. Podgorny's occasional presence was intended to symbolize the Soviet political balance, but beyond irritating everybody he contributed little, and his dismissal in the summer of 1977 will hardly be mourned. My impression of Brezhnev, after seeing him in action in these and other meetings, was that he was rational, moderate, in acknowledged authority, but not very quick in debate.

For the better part of a week the U.S. delegation, of which I was a member, lived cheek by jowl with the Soviet Politburo. Obviously to demonstrate their solidarity, they turned out in full force for the signing of the various agreements, an event which occurred almost daily, and sometimes twice daily. Besides chatting with them in informal groups, we were distributed among Politburo members at two formal dinners. The Soviets were on their best behavior, with one exception, Piotr

Shelest. A veteran Ukrainian political leader, he was said to have agitated strongly for the attack on Czechoslovakia in 1968. Three days before the Nixon visit he had been dismissed from the Politburo, reportedly because he opposed a U.S.–Soviet agreement on SALT. We had not included him on our guest list for the dinner the president gave on May 26, but at the last minute we were requested to do so by the Foreign Office, and I seated him at table number four. He protested that he had been ranked too low, so I took him at my own table, which came after the head table and that of Secretary Rogers. Acting like the caricature of a Soviet political boss, he did not contribute to the gaiety of the evening.

As expected, we found the Politburo members a rough and self-confident group who were not afraid to talk freely. We turned to some of the "younger" members, mainly those under the age of sixty, to test them for flexibility of outlook. For our pains we found that prominent leaders such as Polyansky and Masurow, who then seemed to be on the way up, were among the more dogmatic, possibly for the very reason that doctrinal purity was a prerequisite for advancement. Ironically, Suslov, the Politburo's senior ideologue, was the most courtly. I had liked him since a visit Senator Scott and I had paid on him the year before. He had been supplied with a sheaf of notes by his Foreign Office assistant, from whom I expected the worst. Suslov took a look at the papers, dropped them in the scrap-basket, and then engaged us in a pleasant and informative talk.

At the summit, the delegation's administrative center was in the Hotel Rossiya, but the president's suite in the Kremlin was the real headquarters. Considering the work to be done, the delegation was not overlarge. What little infighting occurred was settled by Nixon's rule—let the strongest prevail—with the predictable result that honors went to Kissinger. As I had seen him perform in Warsaw in 1959, the president was impressive in his meetings with the Soviets—forceful, concise, and in control of the subject matter. When an impasse was reached with Brezhnev, Nixon would suggest turning political questions over to Kissinger and a Soviet designee. Foreign Minister Gromkyo and his deputy, Vassili Kuznetzov (recently elected vice-president of the Presidium of the Supreme Soviet) would usually act for the Soviets in this capacity.

In all meetings, whether in Washington or Moscow, where I have seen Nixon and Kissinger together, the latter invariably yielded, not only in manner but also with respect to having the final say. Some former White House insiders make the same point in recent writings, that Nixon was generally dominant in initiating and determining policy. Whether or not this was really the case, the public impact of the administration's decisions owed much to Kissinger's skill in interpretation and explanation.

Nixon made few public appearances outside the Kremlin; the authorities controlled the numbers as well as the enthusiasm of the crowds. Work rather than show was the keynote of the summit and both leaders, of course, profited from the parade of agreements signed, and the toasts exchanged, which were duly broadcast by television to Soviet and world audiences.

Although stimulated by publicity, the mass demonstration of concord represented a useful breakthrough. By easing visa and sponsorship problems, the agreements met the aspirations of large numbers of American and

Soviet scientists, scholars, and professional men who had been seeking contact. The range of subjects included environmental protection, health and medicine, space cooperation, agriculture, science and technology, and so forth. The exchanges found immediate favor with many Americans captivated by the Russian mystique and by thought of paid travel to the Soviet Union.

The programs have generally been of lasting value, although there has been some disillusionment on the American side caused by a capricious exercise of Soviet controls and their plundering of opportunities to obtain advanced technical information. An agreement to prevent incidents at sea between the two navies is of interest; while overdue, it fails to cover submarine activity which has produced some hair-raising skirmishes falling just short of collision.

THE ARMS AGREEMENTS

Whereas most of the agreements had been prepared in advance, the one on SALT, which was made the key to summit success, was hammered out in Moscow under intense pressure. The process of negotiating disarmament with the Soviets is worthy of comment in this connection. Without the added necessity of meeting a deadline, the task contains enough inherent difficulties of its own. It is almost unbelievable, but nevertheless true, that in recent years we have let the Soviets put us in the position where we negotiate with them on the basis of *our* estimate of their weapon strength. We believe these estimates to be fairly accurate, but as a general rule the Soviets refuse to confirm the information we have obtained through our own devices.

Furthermore, because of the involvement of so many

interested U.S. agencies and parties in disarmament—the Pentagon, the White House, the CIA, as well as the Congress—a great deal of effort is dissipated in negotiating with ourselves. Leaks ensue which help the Soviets; sometimes when we cannot agree among ourselves we put forward varied options on particular points. When the Soviets understand them, they naturally choose the most favorable. Only rarely do they feel compelled to put forward a viable initiative on their own. A dramatic and authoritative account of negotiating with the Russians on disarmament is provided in John Newhouse's book *Cold Dawn—A Story of SALT*.[1]

A review of the basic problems involved in the Moscow 1972 SALT agreement shows that we probably attained the best possible deal under less than ideal circumstances. Up until 1971 the Soviets concentrated on limiting or banning defensive antiballistic missiles (ABMs), since they were beginning to see that U.S. technology would soon give us superiority in this domain. (Even though these missiles could not guarantee the invulnerability of our attack missiles, we were pressing their development as a bargaining counter.) The U.S. at the same time was chiefly concerned with the Soviets' clearly indicated intention to catch up and surpass us in the number of intercontinental missiles (ICBMs) and submarine-launched missiles (SLBMs). In the previously mentioned joint communiqué of May 20, 1971, we were able to obtain agreement that SALT deal with limitations on both defensive and offensive weapons.

Intensive negotiations held alternately in Vienna and

---

[1]John Newhouse, *Cold Dawn—A Story of SALT* (New York: Holt, Rinehart & Winston, 1973).

Helsinki (the Soviets found Vienna too hot in summer) began to give shape to an understanding on the following lines. We each agreed to two ABM sites on a side, each containing no more than 100 missiles; there would be one near Moscow and one near Washington, plus another for each side for the protection of a designated land-based ICBM complex.

The U.S. rationale on offensive weapons (land-based ICBMs and SLBMs) was that we could provisionally permit a specified Soviet superiority in numbers since our development and deployment of missiles equipped with multiple independently targeted reentry vehicles (MIRVs) would continue to give us an imposing superiority in nuclear warheads. The concept made sense because, pending the development of a new system, we had no plans to build more missiles. We knew that the Soviets would go ahead with their construction anyway, and we therefore thought it better to impose on them a negotiated restraint which would maintain some kind of off-setting balance to their superiority in missile numbers.

The ABM agreement was embodied in a treaty (the only treaty to emerge from Moscow) which was of indefinite duration, subject to review every five years. (In the summer of 1974 it was revised to provide for only one ABM site on each side; the Soviets kept Moscow, and we opted for Grand Forks, North Dakota, but Congress has refused to appropriate any money for ABMs.) The agreements on ICBMs and SLBMs were much more complicated and were based on formulae worked out in Moscow in the last few hours before signature at 11:00 P.M. on May 26.

For those who are interested, here is the arithmetic involved in the last group of agreements. As of the time of signature the U.S. had a total of 1054 ICBMs, and the USSR had 1618 (our estimate) which it was capable of adding to at the rate of 250 a year. The U.S. had 656 SLBMs, and the USSR had between 680 and 700 which it was increasing at an annual rate of about 128. The USSR agreed to freeze ICBMs at the then-current level, but insisted on going ahead with new SLBM construction, one of the reasons given being that they required more submarines in order to operate efficiently from relatively more distant bases. At a current rate of eight new submarines per year, within five years they would reach a level between 80 and 90, as compared with a present U.S. total of 44 SLBM submarines, which would remain the same. The interim agreements signed at Moscow, with a duration of five years, provided that the U.S. "may have no more" than 710 SLBMs and 44 SLBM submarines; and the USSR "no more" than 950 SLBMs and 62 SLBM submarines. The U.S. gained a kind of compensation in the provision that, in order to obtain their quota of new SLBMs, the Soviets would have to destroy 210 old KBMs and 30 SLBMs.

Kissinger forcefully defended the SALT agreements in a press conference he gave in a hotel nightclub salon at 1:00 A.M. after the signing ceremony. His main points were: the freeze concerns only two categories of offensive weapons. It does not include warheads, in which we have about a three-to-one numerical lead, nor bombers, of which we have a larger number, nor forward-based weapon systems, such as those we may have on allied territory. Since we had no ongoing missile programs, he said, the question to ask was "not what is the situation that SALT perpetuates, but what is the one it prevents," in the light of potential Soviet construction. He emphasized that the freeze made a significant contribution to arresting the arms race.

A summit document of considerable interest was the statement of "basic principles of relations between the USA and the USSR." I recall that earlier secretaries of state, and Dulles in particular, had dismissed as meaningless such vague slogans as "general and complete disarmament," unilateral pledges of non-first-use of nuclear weapons, and above all, promises for their total abolition. Picking up some of the phraseology of the previously mentioned Nixon letter of April 1969 to Premier Kosygin, the Moscow statement endeavored to establish a code of conduct. It called upon both parties to moderate situations which might exacerbate relations; to avoid military confrontations and to exercise mutual restraint; to eschew efforts to obtain unilateral advantage at the other party's expense; and to prevent conflicts or situations from arising which would serve to increase international tensions. The document was not without value, since we later invoked it publicly to complain of Soviet support of the dispatch of Cuban troops to Angola.

Because the chief business of the conference was bilateral, less attention was devoted to international issues. The Middle East was left in abeyance; a frank discussion of opposing views on Indochina, however, may have given impetus to later direct U.S.–North Korean talks. Some progress was made on a matter of interest to the Europeans. It was agreed that preparations should go forward for a "Conference on Security and Cooperation in Europe," which later became the Helsinki Conference of 1974–1975. It was agreed that negotiations should be started on a "reciprocal reduction of armed forces and armaments" in Europe.

The Soviet leadership staged an impressive farewell reception on May 26 in the magnificent St. George's Hall in the Kremlin. It was a feast of reconciliation which included the patriarch, the chief rabbi, a sprinkling of Catholic and Protestant clergy, and one or two dissident writers. In a mood of merited exhilaration, the Nixon party took off that evening for Kiev on their way to Tehran.

Chapter XVI

Some Shattered Illusions
in Need of Repair

EARLY OPPOSITION TO THE SUMMIT
AGREEMENTS

T HE presidential party left the Soviet Union under
good omens. A further cause for elation was advance
secret intelligence communicated to them at the time of
their departure from Moscow that the Sadat government
was about to expel a considerable number of Soviet advisers in that country. The actual step did not take place
until the middle of July.

In the normal course of events, a dip was bound to
occur in the rising curve of U.S.–Soviet relations. The
downward trend started with the so-called grain steal. As
was later brought out in congressional hearings, our embassy had accurately reported throughout 1972 that
there would be a drastic shortfall in Soviet wheat production for that year because of severe drought. In the late
spring, the acting minister of foreign trade summoned
me on a Saturday to request visas for two Soviet officials
due to leave the next day for Washington. I would have
issued them anyway on an emergency basis, but I became
suspicious when the minister refused to tell me the pur-

pose of the visit. We soon found out that the two Soviets were grain experts, which seemed to gladden the hearts of interested parties in Washington. At the time, the mood in Washington was that if Soviet grain purchases were a mistake, it was the kind of mistake that Secretary of Agriculture Butz had been praying for when he called upon Brezhnev in April.

What happened was that an agreement was concluded in early July 1972 providing for the shipment of $750 million worth of feed grains over a three-year period. When the magnitude of the drought became apparent to the Soviet authorities, they switched their main purchases to wheat which was needed for the sustenance of their people. The transactions were carried out through open-market channels by Soviet buyers who worked quietly and separately with the leading American grain dealers in New York. The only U.S. government subsidy was that paid to the American shipper which enabled him to sell wheat for export at the same price he received at home.

The massive Soviet purchases soon had the effect of driving world market prices upward, eventually to the same level as that prevailing in the U.S. Because crops were poor elsewhere, large purchases were also made in the U.S., the only available supplier, by countries in Western Europe, Africa, and Asia, including Japan. These operations drove world prices beyond the domestic level, and, as soon as the two were equalized, the government subsidy should have ceased. Unfortunately, it was continued for about a week longer than was necessary, needlessly costing the government about $30 million. The fault was the failure of U.S. agencies, and in particular the Department of Agriculture, to anticipate the world shortage and to monitor and coordinate information concerning the sales made to the Soviets by local dealers. The Department of Agriculture explained by way of mitigation that American farmers would have protested had the subsidy been terminated earlier, and that the loss of $30 million was compensated by a reduction of storage costs resulting in quick sales to the Soviets. As to the cost to the American consumer, domestic prices would have risen in any event because of a world wheat shortage.

Although Nixon handily won the 1972 election, his critics tried to make the most of issues on which they thought he might be vulnerable. There were many other Americans who had honest doubts about the SALT agreements of May 26, 1972. First of all, there was the numerical superiority they conceded to the Soviets in ICBMs, in missile size, and above all in missile submarines and submarine missile launchers (SLBMs). To such doubters it was of secondary importance that we surpassed the Soviets in numbers of warheads, the majority of which consisted of MIRVs, or that we had no plans to build new submarines or SLBMs because of such superiority. In the submarine category, the agreement was obviously an arms limitation measure since it placed curbs on the numbers of weapons the Soviets would otherwise build.

Greater stress might have been put on more legitimate questions about our methods of negotiation. The development of our own antiballistic missile (ABM), the Safeguard, was a singular feat of engineering, but we soon realized it was unlikely to provide complete protection. In the knowledge, however, that we had already surpassed the Soviets on the way to possible technological perfection, we used our development of the weapon as a "bargaining chip" which we were prepared to sacrifice in order to obtain Soviet agreement to the simultaneous negotiation of restraints on offensive weapons such as heavy ICBMs and SLBMs, which the Soviets intended to produce in large numbers. It was an expensive bargaining chip since the development alone cost us some $2 billion, and in the end we never deployed the weapon, although under the ABM treaty we had the right to station 100 ABMs to protect our missile site at Great Forks, North Dakota. (The Soviets exercised their right to deploy the same number to guard the city of Moscow.)

Possibly, had we not been negotiating SALT under pressure in Moscow to make the summit a success, we might have devised a less expensive bargaining chip in the form of economic trade-offs or other pressures. With more time, we might also have obtained a more favorable ratio on offensive missile numbers. The inferiority we accepted especially rankled Senator Jackson, and the Senate went on record to urge and request "the President to seek a future treaty that *inter alia* would not limit the U.S. to levels of intercontinental strategic forces inferior to the limits provided for the USSR."

At any rate the Senate approved the SALT agreements, with the abovementioned understanding, whereas the U.S.–Soviet economic agreement concluded later in 1972 broke down under conditions causing bitter feelings on both sides. Negotiations started off with the dispatch of a mission headed by Secretary of Commerce Peterson to the Soviet Union in July 1972. I participated in a visit to Yalta where we were Brezhnev's guests, but beyond his exhorting us to "think big" and to invest huge sums in the joint exploitation of Siberian oil and natural gas, little else of consequence was achieved. We had an opportunity, however, to enjoy Brezhnev's rather spacious quarters which he uses to entertain the first secretaries of the satellite Communist parties who customarily pay him a visit each summer, presumably to receive their midyear instructions.

The economic agreement which was eventually concluded in October 1972 in Washington granted the Soviets most favored nation treatment as regards tariffs, and provided for a lifting of the discriminatory trade barriers which we had imposed during the Korean War. In return, our goods would receive equal treatment in the Soviet market and trade disputes would be settled by arbitration. At the Soviets' suggestion, the text expressed the expectation that as a result of the favorable conditions to be created, which would include long-term credits, U.S.–Soviet trade would at least triple in the next three years.

Our granting of most favored nation treatment was conditioned on Soviet settlement of their wartime Lend-Lease account with us. In the 1950s we had demanded $10 billion for the equipment which was left in the Soviet Union for civilian use after the war. In light of Soviet wartime sacrifices our conscience eventually prompted us to accept a far lower figure. In a separate instrument signed at the same time as the economic agreement, we accepted a total of $722 million, payable in installments through the year 2001.

The feeling in the State Department and in our embassy was that the U.S. had come out with a fairly good deal. The granting of most favored nation treatment did not bother us since Soviet manufactured products could not compete in our markets, and the Soviets wished the concession chiefly for prestige reasons. The prospective sales of U.S. industrial equipment and grain, repayable in U.S. dollars, were attractive. We had also tried to counter examples of past Soviet chicanery as best we could by demanding fair treatment for our exports, and the arbitration of commercial disputes. Finally, the Lend-Lease payment was far from insignificant and, I am told, gave us a slightly better return than we obtained from our settlement with the British.

The trade and Lend-Lease agreements were signed on October 18, 1972, in Washington. We were somewhat surprised in Moscow to note that on October 4, Senator Jackson, with the support of more than seventy senators, had introduced legislation which in effect would deny most favored nation treatment and U.S. government credits to nations which did not give their citizens the right and opportunity to emigrate. It would be natural to assume that under the circumstances the Soviets would have broken off the negotiations unless they had received assurances that the matter could be solved to their satisfaction. In effect this is what was actually attempted, through the medium of a curious kind of tripartite bargaining—Kissinger with the U.S. Congress and Kissinger with the Soviets.

At the May 1972 summit, Nixon and Kissinger had informed the Soviets that their prohibitive taxes on emigration[1] and the relatively small number of persons permitted to leave the Soviet Union, especially Jews and

---

[1]The Soviet justification was that since the socialist economy supported the costs of the emigrés' education, the Soviet Union expected reimbursement for the expensive training which, upon emigration, would benefit another country.

members of separated families, created a political problem in the U.S. which stood in the way of settling other issues. As the matter dragged on, the Soviets furnished Nixon and Kissinger, and later President Ford, with indications that the rate of emigration would increase and the punitive taxes would cease. The question came to a head with the entry into force on January 3, 1975, of the new U.S. Trade Act which embodied the so-called Jackson–Vanik amendment passed in the Senate by a vote of 88–0 and in the House by a vote of 319–80. The amendment placed a ban on the granting of most favored nation treatment and credits to countries which restricted emigration; in doubtful cases, it required the president to submit a waiver of exception that a particular country met the criteria of eligibility regarding freedom of emigration.

On October 18, 1974, exactly two years after the signature of the U.S.–Soviet trade agreement, Senator Jackson accepted Kissinger's view that Soviet assurances on emigration were sufficiently forthcoming to permit the president to execute a waiver of exemption entitling the Soviets to tariff and credit privileges. The Soviet news agency Tass then released the text of a secret letter from Gromyko to Kissinger dated October 26, 1974, rejecting as an unwarranted interference in Soviet domestic affairs the linkage between Soviet emigration policies and the fulfillment of the trade agreement. Kissinger maintained that the letter did not alter the Soviet assurances he had earlier received.

The moment of truth came on January 15, 1975, when Kissinger was constrained to announce that the Soviets had notified him they "would not put into force" the 1972 trade agreement. While Kissinger was accused of deceiving Congress regarding Soviet acceptance of the Jackson–Vanik amendment, it is possible that the Soviets really broke with us over the Stevenson amendment, which placed a limit of $300 million on Exim Bank loans to the Soviet Union and which they regarded as clearly discriminatory.

The causes of the break go back to the fall of 1972 when several influential senators and representatives, supported by American Jewish groups, protested that the trade agreement gave the Soviets everything they wanted—technology, industrial equipment, and huge credits—whereas the U.S. was receiving very little in matters of interest to its citizens, such as Soviet respect for human rights, freedom of communication, and liberal emigration. While this line of thought was highly motivated, it prompted immediate reactions which benefited no one. In 1972 Jewish emigration had risen to about 2000 per month, and reached almost 36,000 for the year 1973. The Netherlands Embassy in Moscow, which handled visas for Israel, was quite upset when the Jewish groups protested that this was too low a figure, since the Dutch felt that with quiet persuasion they could obtain an increase to a higher number of emigrants whom Israel could conveniently absorb. In 1974 and 1975 the rate fell to about 1000 per month.

As to American economic interests affected by the breakdown of the trade agreement, our loss of potential profits has been substantial but far from disastrous. In 1976 our trade surplus with the Soviet Union was $2.085 billion, made up chiefly of grain exports. A regrettable casualty of the breakdown of understanding was the Lend-Lease agreement which would have brought us revenue and would have disposed of a long-contentious issue.

I have overrun my alloted schedule. I retired from the Foreign Service on January 31, 1973, one week after leaving Moscow. I had not intended to deal with events after that date, but I felt it useful to bring the subject of economic relations up to the point where it has remained lodged for so long.

The momentum of the 1972 Moscow summit carried up to, and through, a second summit which met in Washington during June 18–25, 1973. Since I resided in Washington I observed the proceedings from the periphery. The conference produced little new of significance except the Agreement on the Prevention of Nuclear War. Negotiated with Kissinger's customary secrecy, it appeared to anger some of our NATO allies who felt that the two parties had made the question of preventing (or, by implication, starting) a nuclear war the exclusive concern of the U.S. and USSR. A happening of major importance was that Brezhnev apparently learned for the first time that his partner, Nixon, was in serious trouble at home. It seems that this realization was unmistakably conveyed to him during the visit he made to San Clemente just before leaving, when the American press concentrated their questioning on Watergate, rather than on the summit.

In the foregoing narrative account I have presented certain incidental conclusions. There are others of more general pertinence which also derive from my experiences. In the following pages I deal with them *seriatum,* avoiding, as best I can, offering advice, speculation, or prediction, which are among the chief hazards of reporting on Soviet affairs.

NIXON–BREZHNEV AXIS

There is little doubt that Brezhnev felt a close personal attachment to Nixon and was probably more at ease with him than with Communists like Tito and Ceaucescu or other leaders whom he could not come to accept as equals. The relationship was a paradoxical one. Basically Brezhnev respected power, which Nixon possessed during his first term; Brezhnev liked the channel of access which Nixon and Kissinger reserved for him in their exclusive method of transacting business. It obviated bothersome distractions: except for occasional outbursts over Soviet human rights violations, Congress generally approved détente; the troublesome State Department, which always seemed to know too much about Soviet affairs, was bypassed by Nixon and Kissinger.

Two examples of paradox come to mind. The Soviets recognized Nixon as a determined anticommunist foe but believed that, like Brezhnev, he was committed to détente for the rewards it could produce domestically and internationally. The Soviets also knew that Nixon was unpredictable and would not hesitate to use force, as he did in Cambodia in May 1970 and when he ordered the bombing of North Vietnam in May 1972 and again at Christmas of the same year. Consequently, the Soviets treated his warnings with great seriousness.

The personal relationship between Nixon and Brezhnev, which survived some tough talking, was demonstratively warm. Even after Brezhnev belatedly became alerted to Nixon's troubles over Watergate, he treated the president with high respect. It appears that Brezhnev's courtesy continued through the last trip to Moscow in the summer of 1974, which Nixon planned for the main purpose of boosting his failing prestige.

"Convergence" and Ideology

It has been the dream of quite a few political scientists that an ideological truce, or even peace, can be brought about either by an agreed stand-off or by an eventual convergence of the doctrines of communism and capitalism.

The Peace of Westphalia of 1648 offers an example of the first solution in the *modus vivendi* brought about between the German Catholic princes and the German Protestant princes who fought each other for thirty years. The Westphalian treaties established the principle of *cuius ragio euis religio,* meaning that the contracting parties obliged themselves to respect the right of each sovereign to impose his religion, Catholic or Protestant, on his subjects. The concept does not fit the Soviet Communist book which proclaims that "ideas [namely, theirs] travel without visas," and that ideological struggle and international class warfare must be carried forward to achieve Communist victory. This view, of course, refutes Kissinger's idea that accommodation can be reached by establishing "interdependence" through a network of agreements.

The proponents of "convergence" include the Soviet dissenter Sakharov, and the Yugoslav statesman Kardelj (possibly his country's second most influential leader) who believed that since socialism is the order of the day, it may be possible to arrange a painless compromise between communism on the one hand, and social democ-

[293]

racy and enlightened capitalism on the other. It is inconceivable, however, that the Soviets (and also the Chinese) would permit a reversal of the trend they call for, namely, a progression from capitalism, through socialism, to communism.

The ideology which the Soviets defend against change is that which they practice and feel they have the right to try to impose internationally. What is at stake for them, as the senior and most powerful Communist nation, is leadership of a world movement which has achieved phenomenal, although not total, success. Paradoxically, at home ideology is not a motivating force, but as one very high official describes it privately, is "dry bread." Soviet citizens rarely describe themselves as Communists. Rather, they identify themselves by rank in the government or party. The regime is taken for granted as the official bureaucratic establishment. Communism is thus no longer an inspiration, but a powerful sanction to enforce conformity.

It is not entirely Brezhnev's fault that the presides over a rather doltish regime. Testing periods such as the Czechoslovak crisis, the rise of vocal dissidence at home, and the confrontation with Euro-Communism, have failed to bring forth any new talent. Neither former President Podgorny nor Prime Minister Kosygin have been a real challenge to Brezhnev, who has prevailed as a common denominator of competence and caution. It is difficult to see what direction change will follow with the inevitable replacement of aging Politburo members, but a new general secretary is likely to face a strenuous testing period.

In the meantime Brezhnev can take a certain pride in his stewardship. He may rate low marks in the Mao school of "continuing revolution," but one only has to look at what has happened in China. Brezhnev heads an outwardly stable government with a fairly strong economy which, although it may only advance at a small percentage rate annually, seems to satisfy the relatively modest expectations of the people. The nation is respected for its power, if not necessarily for its worldwide popularity.

ARMS AND THE MEN IN THE KREMLIN

At the time of wriing, it appears that we shall be engaged for some months in negotiating, and obtaining congressional approval for, a SALT II arms agreement. As in the case of SALT I, the aim of the talks will be to curb an arms race, this time by "measures of restraint and reduction." At the present stage it is useless to cite figures which are certain to undergo constant change in the effort to find a balance between asymmetrical categories of strength. In SALT II the U.S. will try to reduce the high levels set for ICBMs at the 1974 Vladivostok meeting which, incidentally, the Soviets justified by their need to defend themselves against the Chinese. According to press reports, one of our great concerns will be to offset the growing vulnerability of our fixed land-based launchers to the effects of increasing Soviet accuracy and numbers. Reportedly, we will look to our cruise missiles as an auxiliary weapon. The Soviets are insisting on limitations on the missile, which we are reportedly matching with demands limiting the deployment of their Backfire bomber. The introduction of these new and exotic systems raises questions of verification and inspection likely to cause great difficulties in treaty drafting and obtaining Senate approval. The interests of our European allies, especially their access to cruise missiles, will have to be taken into greater account than in SALT I which was a U.S.–Soviet deal. If the American plan is adopted, SALT II will establish guidelines for SALT III, which will start immediately so that there will be a continuous round of negotiations.

The Soviet buildup since SALT I in all departments of military strength has been most disturbing, since its purpose, or focus, is not clear. In a study I wrote over a year ago for the Georgetown University Center for Strategic and International Studies, I remarked that the Soviets seemed bent on forestalling surprise situations which they were powerless to influence. A repetition of our 1958 Lebanon adventure, or other independent U.S. action in the Mediterranean, probably could not now occur without a Soviet reaction. In the 1973 Yom Kippur War, the Soviets suggested joint intervention to prevent Israeli destruction of the Egyptian Third Army. As is well known, we rejected the proposal and concentrated on arranging a cease fire.

The Soviets probably have as much difficulty as we do in defining military "equivalence." For them the "perception of military power" is probably paramount. They may, of course, make a go at unmistakable superiority, but for the time being they seem to be concentrating on reaching and maintaining relative force and arms levels by which they will be "perceived" as being entitled to a role of unchallenged arbiter in world events—that is to say, to have the right to be consulted, share in decision-making, and perhaps to prevail. A particularly worrisome Soviet move would be the buildup of a strong reserve of mobile forces capable of being transported to war theaters throughout the world by air or sea. So far the Soviets have been content to experiment, in itself a risky undertaking, with the dispatch of proxy Communist forces, such as Cubans, to remote trouble spots.

A possibility dramatized for me by what I saw in Czechoslovakia in 1968 would be a successful Soviet surprise attack against Western Europe by conventional forces; such an event would force us to a choice of whether or not to submit to "nuclear blackmail," that is to say, to respond by nuclear weapons which, including even those of a tactical nature, would invoke the risk of retaliation against our cities. In view of the fact that present Soviet interest seems best served by peace in Europe, this would appear to be an unlikely Soviet move, but potential danger persists in the Western nations' inability so far to negotiate a reduction of the vast Communist tank and field armies in the satellites and East Germany.

As of general interest, note may be taken of Soviet strategic theories and dogma regarding the waging of war. These subjects are being debated intelligently and openly by Western experts, but the reaction of the Soviet high command has been disclosed neither in open statements nor in private discussion. It is understandable that the Soviet leaders would not want officially to subscribe to concepts of mutual deterrence through "mutual assured destruction" (MAD). To acknowledge these concepts would lead to questions that the superiority of communism could in some way be deterred from ultimate victory. Furthermore, the Soviets would probably not like the Chinese to get the idea at this time that Soviet reaction might be precluded by initial Chinese aggression. There is an American school of thought which believes that we pay too much attention to measures to deter war, whereas the Soviets concentrate on the whole range of weapons and steps necessary to win a war should it break out.

IN THE WAKE OF MUTUAL DISENCHANTMENT

Arms control and trade are likely to remain root questions in U.S.–Soviet relations for a long time.

It is impossible to foretell whether arms negotiations will be the most significant or the most futile of efforts. There is no guarantee that limitations will prevent war. It is more certain that every available weapon, including those chosen for limitation, will be used in the event of war. It is hard to believe that a "flexible" limited nuclear response to victories won in conventional warfare would be long tolerated by a nuclear-equipped adversary.

Congress chose to regard Soviet bans on emigration as an abnormality which precluded a normalization of economic relations, an added advantage we could dispense with in view of our natural trade balance. The breakdown of the trade agreement caused more bitterness than any other event since the Moscow summit, because the Soviets felt they were being subjected to discrimination after signing the 1972 accords in good faith. They regarded this as another example of U.S. "zigzag" diplomacy, and resented our interest in emigration as interference in their domestic affairs. It is now recognized in some American political circles that the steps which led to the suspension of the 1972 agreements were a mistake, since they cut down our exports and at the same time induced the Soviet Union to curtail emigration further. If rectification were attempted, one of the most difficult problems would be to establish how high the rate of emigration would have to rise before Congress would reverse itself by lifting its restrictions on credits.

The decisions and agreements of the 1972 and 1973 summit meetings contributed to a more orderly management of our dealings with the Soviets. Unfortunately they were vitiated by a series of mishaps: they became associated with an unpopular president who lost the power to see them through; some, like SALT and trade, suffered from lack of congressional consultation and from charges that they were sprung on the public by stealth and surprise; finally, it was taken too much for granted that the convergence of interests achieved at the summits would overcome our long-standing mistrust of the Soviet record on human rights.

There are periods when we come to regard the Soviet Union as our number one military and political problem (even the Marshall Plan was in part a response to a Soviet threat). The first assumption is still true, but there seems to be less reason now to make the Soviet Union the focus of our policy. We are beginning to reap credit from our withdrawal from Vietnam whereas the Soviets, once the champions of national liberation, are being subjected to humiliation by a country like Egypt seeking to free itself from Russian contamination. Placing U.S.–Soviet relations in their proper perspective, we should find it more congenial to cultivate our circle of allies and friends whom we neglected for the theatrics of superpower politics.

Bibliography

Bohlen, Charles E. *Witness to History.* New York: W. W. Norton & Co., 1973.

Deane, John R. *The Strange Alliance.* New York: The Viking Press, 1947.

Edmonds, Robin. *Soviet Foreign Policy, 1962–1973.* New York: Oxford University Press, 1975.

Eisenhower, Dwight D. *Mandate for Change.* New York: Doubleday, 1963.

———. *Waging Peace.* New York: Doubleday, 1965.

Gilbert, Martin. *Russian History Atlas.* New York: Macmillan, 1972.

Hiscocks, Richard. *Poland: Bridge for the Abyss?* New York: Oxford University Press, 1963.

Hlasko, Marek. *The Eighth Day of the Week.* New York: E. P. Dutton, 1958.

Khrushchev, Nikita S. *Khrushchev Remembers.* Boston: Little, Brown & Co., 1971.

Kulski, Wladyslaw W. *The Soviet Union in World Affairs: A Documented Analysis, 1964–1972.* Syracuse, N.Y.: Syracuse University Press, 1973.

BIBLIOGRAPHY

Legvold, Robert. "The Nature of Soviet Power." *Foreign Affairs,* October 1977.

Lewis, Flora. *A Case History of Hope.* New York: Doubleday, 1958.

London, Kurt C., ed. *The Soviet Impact on World Politics.* New York: Hawthorn, 1974.

Newhouse, John. *Cold Dawn: A Story of SALT.* New York: Holt, Rinehart & Winston, 1973.

Schwartz, Harry. *Prague's 200 Days.* New York: Praeger, 1969.

Shawcross, William. *Dubcek.* New York: Simon & Schuster, 1971.

Shirer, William L. *The Rise and Fall of the Third Reich.* New York: Simon & Schuster, 1960.

Skilling, H. Gordon. *Czechoslovakia's Interrupted Revolution.* Princeton, N.J.: Princeton University Press, 1976.

Sonnenfeldt, Helmut. "Russia, America and Detente." *Foreign Affairs,* January 1978.

Soviet Economy in a New Perspective. Joint Economic Committee, U.S. Congress. Washington, D.C.: U.S. Government Printing Office, October 14, 1976.

Ulam, Adam B. *The Rivals: America and Russia Since World War II.* New York: The Viking Press, 1972.

Vali, Ferenc. *Rift and Revolt in Hungary.* Cambridge, Mass.: Harvard University Press, 1961.

Wolfe, Thomas W. *Soviet Power & Europe, 1945–1970.* Baltimore: The Johns Hopkins Press, 1970.

Yergin, Daniel. *Shattered Peace.* Boston: Houghton-Mifflin, 1977.

Young, Kenneth T. *Negotiating with the Chinese Communists.* New York: McGraw-Hill Book Company, 1968.

Index

INDEX

INDEX

INDEX

Index

INDEX

Index

[315]

INDEX

[316]